CURRENT RESEARCH
IN EGYPTOLOGY 2003

CURRENT RESEARCH IN EGYPTOLOGY 2003

Proceedings of the Fourth Annual Symposium

which took place at the

Institute of Archaeology, University College London
18–19 January 2003

edited by

Kathryn Piquette and Serena Love

Oxbow Books

Published by
Oxbow Books, Park End Place, Oxford OX1 1HN

ISBN 1 84217 133 X

This book is available direct from
Oxbow Books, Park End Place, Oxford OX1 1HN
(Phone: 01865–241249; Fax: 01865–794449)

and

The David Brown Book Company
PO Box 511, Oakville, CT 06779, USA
(Phone: 860–945–9329; Fax: 860–945–9468)

or from our web site

www.oxbowbooks.com

Printed in Great Britain by
Antony Rowe, Chippenham

Contents

Preface vii

Symposium Papers Not Included in This Volume ix

Symposium Introductory Address *(Professor Harry Smith)* xi

A Previously Unpublished Contract of Sale from Memphis *(Maria Cannata)* 1

Behind the Corn-mummies *(Maria Costanza Centrone)* 11

The Lisbon Mummy Project: The employment of non-destructive methods in
  mummy studies *(Álvaro Figueiredo)* 29

Plying the Nile: Not all plain sailing *(Angus Graham)* 41

The Spitting Goddess and the Stony Eye: Divinity and flint in Pharaonic Egypt
  (Carolyn A. Graves-Brown) 57

From the Cradle to the Grave: Anthropoid busts and ancestor cults at Deir el-Medina
  (Nicola Harrington) 71

Iaau and the Question of the Origin of Evil According to Ancient Egyptian Sources
  (Mpay Kemboly) 89

Flower Arranging in Ancient Egypt? A new approach to archaeobotanical remains
  (Sally McAleely) 105

A Kushite Temple in a Western Oasis? *(Hironao Onishi)* 121

Bifacial Technology, Socioeconomic Competition, and Early Farming and Herding
  in the Fayum *(Noriyuki Shirai)* 135

Royal Funerary Cults During the Old Kingdom *(Yayoi Shirai)* 149

Abusir South at the End of the Old Kingdom *(Petra Vlčková)* 163

The Festival Calendar at Deir el-Medina *(Heidi Wikgren)* 179

Preface

The fourth annual Current Research in Egyptology Symposium (CRE 2003) was held on 18–19 January 2003 at the Institute of Archaeology (IoA), University College London (UCL), and brought together graduate students of Egyptology from a number of institutions. Building on the vision of CRE's founders – of fostering communication and exchange of ideas among students of Egyptology in the British Isles – we extended the invitation to present papers to students from abroad. A welcome addition to the symposium was the sizable contingent of international students. It is hoped that this broader international dimension may be sustained over future years. In total, 26 papers were presented, 13 of which are published in this volume and others published as listed (see p. viii). These papers illustrate a range of subject areas, approaches and methods; an underlying theme, though, is apparent: a greater degree of reflexivity and a wider engagement with interdisciplinary research.

In addition to the presentation of papers, the final event of the symposium was a roundtable discussion, which Dr. David Wengrow (formerly of Christ's College, Oxford, and now at the IoA, UCL) kindly agreed to chair. The main topic for discussion was the future of Egyptology, with related issues including the relationship between academics and the general public, field methods, and the role of the graduate community in shaping the future of the discipline. The future aims of CRE were also discussed and a general consensus reached on particular issues.

With regard to the relationship between academics and the public, several delegates, who were members of ancient Egypt societies, felt that Egyptology as a discipline was not accessible enough to the general public. Some delegates expressed feelings of exclusion at CRE itself and advocated increased interaction between junior and senior academics, and these with ancient Egypt societies. In considering how to overcome the academic/non-academic divide, it was pointed out that for many people popular books and television programmes are often the first point of contact with ancient Egypt, and the interest stimulated by these sources has led to the tremendous growth of societies within the UK. Other delegates shared their viewpoint as academics, objecting to frequent misrepresentations of ancient Egypt in the media. Experiences ranged from specialists who feel "hounded and harassed" by television researchers, only to be misrepresented in the final programme, while others related more positive experiences with the media and insisted that it was imperative to ensure that the media and the general public receive accurate information.

Another issue raised was how the study of ancient Egypt is defined as a discipline and the value of the traditional divisions between Egyptologists and Egyptian archaeologists. Some practitioners felt that their research and methods did not fit into either sub-discipline. Some researchers who work on Egyptian material, such as osteological or botanical remains, felt that their work was perceived as less valid within Egyptological circles because of their lack of specialist training as Egyptologists. These issues fed into a discussion of the need for increased integration between Egyptology and other regionally focused disciplines, as well as with archaeology in general. For example, it was observed that Egyptology has tended to isolate itself from African studies, and, albeit to a lesser degree, from the study of the Eastern Mediterranean and the Ancient Near East, although this has improved over the last few years, for example the Encounters with Ancient Egypt conference held at UCL in December 2000 (and the subsequent eight-part series published in 2003 by UCL Press).

Fieldwork methods were also discussed with reference to establishing standardised techniques for Egyptian archaeology. Since the early days of Egyptology, many different countries have been working in Egypt, each with different aims and methods. With post-colonial concerns in mind, the question was raised as to who should set such standards. With regard to the practical implications of standardisation, many argued that excavation conditions vary widely throughout Egypt, and different kinds of excavation conditions required different techniques. Nevertheless, the overriding concern was that colonial attitudes must be avoided, and any dialogue on these topics must include the views of the Egyptians themselves. In the same vein, it was noted that there appeared to be a lack of Egyptian delegates in attendance. The CRE Committee responded to this point, noting that two Egyptian students had submitted paper abstracts but ultimately were unable to attend due to a lack of funding. The Committee expressed its hope that future committees will be able to set up a travel bursary, or similar form of funding, to assist graduate students from Egypt in meeting the financial cost of attending and presenting their research at CRE.

After a lively discussion and debate which provided much food for thought for everyone, the roundtable was concluded with final thoughts on the future of CRE. There was agreement by the majority of those present that CRE should maintain its status as a forum for the presentation of current research by international graduate students, defined as those who had not yet obtained a permanent post. Further, by a majority vote it was also agreed that CRE should establish a standing committee with the aim of encouraging and facilitating increased interaction and collaboration between students studying Egypt's past. [Since the time of writing, the CRE Standing Committee has set up a web site, http://www.currentresearchegypt.fsworld.co.uk, where information about upcoming CRE symposia and related information can be accessed.]

The symposium, which was well-attended by more than 100 delegates, could not have taken place without extensive help, both practical and financial. We would like to thank the speakers who gave papers and those who participated as session discussants. We would also like to extend a special thanks to Prof. Harry Smith (emeritus UCL) who inspired us with his opening address, and has consented to its publication here, and Prof. John Tait (UCL) whose insightful and forward-looking comments provided a fitting conclusion to the symposium. Thanks go to our fellow conference organisers, Joanne Rowland and G. J. Tassie. We are also indebted to the willing and helpful cohort of student volunteers, including Yvette Balbaligo, James Brigden, Jenny Butler, Robert Wallace, and others who ensured the smooth running of registration, coffee breaks and projection equipment. Our gratitude also goes to the staff of the IoA, including the Director Prof. Peter Ucko, Barbara Brown, Jo Dullaghan, Katie Farrant, Susan Brackstone, Paul Kirby, and Ash Rennie for his valuable help with the web site. Thanks are also due to the Friends of the Petrie Museum of Egyptian Archaeology for their hospitality, as well as Christopher Coleman of the Bloomsbury Academy, and the Institute of Archaeology for their sponsorship. We owe a particular debt of gratitude to Aloisia de Trafford and Andrew Gardner. Thanks also go to Julie Eklund, Steve Townend, and Xander Veldhuijzen for their advice and assistance. Finally, we would like to thank those who kindly agreed to referee the papers for this volume, for their invaluable comments and for the promptness with which they responded, and to David Brown and Val Lamb of Oxbow Books for making the publication of the proceedings of this symposium possible.

Since the London meeting, the University of Durham hosted a successful fifth CRE in January 2004. The sixth symposium is scheduled to take place at the University of Cambridge in January 2005.

Kathryn Piquette and Serena Love

September 2004

Symposium Papers Not Included in This Volume
(alphabetical by author)

A Possible Case of Elephantiasis in Ptolemaic Memphis
Charlotte Booth
Institute of Archaeology, UCL

Feminism, Gender Archaeology and Their Impact on Egyptology
Rachel Dann
University of Durham

Direction and Orientation Concepts and the Creation of Sacred Space in Ancient Egypt
Katherine Griffis-Greenberg
Institute of Archaeology, UCL

Bioarchaeology in the Dakhleh Oasis
Scott Haddow
Institute of Archaeology, UCL

Myos Hormos, the Red Sea Port: Its archaeology and some textile finds
Fiona Handley
Institute of Archaeology, UCL

Gerontology and Ancient Egypt
Rosalind Janssen
Birkbeck College

A Symbolic Landscape of Memphis?
Serena Love
Institute of Archaeology, UCL
Published as: Love, S. forthcoming. Stones, Ancestors and Pyramids: Investigating the pre-pyramid landscape of Memphis, in M. Verner and M. Bárta (eds.), *Old Kingdom Art and Archaeology*. Academy of Sciences of the Czech Republic, Prague.

Duality or Duplicity? Frameworks of approach to Ptolemaic ruler cult
Rachel Mairs
University of Cambridge

Tell Edfu: Aspects of a provincial town at the end of the 3rd millennium B.C.
Nadine Moeller
University of Cambridge

Published as: Moeller, N. 2003, Tell Edfu: Aspects of a provincial town at the end of the 3rd millennium BC, *Egyptian Archaeology: Bulletin of the Egypt Exploration Society* 23, 7–9.

Observing Egypt from Space: Applications of remote sensing and satellite imagery interpretation in Egypt

Sarah Parcak

University of Cambridge

Published as: Parcak, S. 2004, Satellite Remote Sensing Resources for Egyptologists, *Göttinger Mizellen* 198, 63–78.

Conceptualising the Body in Ancient Egypt

Kathryn Piquette

Institute of Archaeology, UCL

Published as: Piquette, K. E. 2004, Representing the Human Body on Late Predynastic and Early Dynastic Labels, in S. Hendrickx, R. F. Friedman, K. M. Ciałowicz and M. Chłodnicki (eds.), *Egypt at Its Origins: Studies in memory of Barbara Adams: Proceedings of the Conference on the Origin of the State: Predynastic and Early Dynastic Egypt, Krakow, 28th August – 1st September 2002*. Peeters Publishers, Leuven.

The Application of Mortuary Data to the Problem of Social Transformation in the Delta from the Terminal Predynastic to the Early Dynastic Period

Joanne Rowland

Institute of Archaeology, UCL

Published as: Rowland, J. M. 2004, The Application of Mortuary Data to the Problem of Social Transformation in the Delta from the Terminal Predynastic to the Early Dynastic Period, in S. Hendrickx, R. F. Friedman, K. M. Ciałowicz and M. Chłodnicki (eds.), *Egypt at Its Origins: Studies in memory of Barbara Adams: Proceedings of the Conference on the Origin of the State: Predynastic and Early Dynastic Egypt, Krakow, 28th August – 1st September 2002*. Peeters Publishers, Leuven.

Ancient Egyptian Hair and Sexuality

G. J. Tassie

Institute of Archaeology, UCL

Symposium Introductory Address

Professor Harry Smith

It is an honour and a real pleasure to welcome such a large body of Egyptological research students from so many academic institutions and of so many nationalities to the Institute of Archaeology at University College London to participate in your fourth annual symposium on Current Research in Egyptology. I should like particularly to thank those who have travelled from abroad to join us, and hope that they will find the symposium a stimulating and rewarding experience and will encourage their compatriots to attend in future years. That these annual meetings should have been founded, organised and maintained by research students on their own initiative is a most valuable and promising development in our studies, and one which fills a longstanding and important need. Learned studies and research should not be carried out in isolation, for, as the wide-ranging programme for this symposium amply illustrates, Egyptology now embraces so many humanistic, natural scientific and social scientific disciplines that it is of the essence for you to understand from early in your careers each other's aims, method and results. Only through such understanding can they become integrated into a constantly evolving picture of ancient Egyptian culture and its place in the development of human society.

The present venue is a happy choice on three counts. The earliest chair of Egyptology in Britain was founded in 1892 at University College by Amelia Edwards for Flinders Petrie, the first great scientific archaeologist of Egypt, whose amazing collection still forms a major treasure-house for Egyptological researchers. The Institute of Archaeology, under its far-sighted director, Professor Peter Ucko, is now engaged in innovative schemes of teaching and research in World Archaeology. Lastly, London is a longstanding and lively centre of extramural study and research in Egyptology, as is evidenced by the tremendous and enthusiastic support given to lecture programmes, symposia and museum tours, to the Bloomsbury Summer Academy held at this Institute and to the Friends of the Petrie Museum. This is important, because in the final analysis, it is intelligent and creative public interest that keeps our studies alive. Thus, both by its tradition and its inspirations, University College London is an appropriate focus for this excellent venture, and we hope that, now and in the future, you will enjoy and benefit from its facilities.

For several decades now there has been talk of a crisis in humanistic studies, not only for the intellectual reason that research in these disciplines does not lead, like that in the natural sciences, to quantifiable and testable results with commercial or other practical potential, but also (in Britain at least) because of various financial, political and social pressures. I do not propose to tread this particular primrose path to the bonfire today – but Egyptology does seem to have various current problems and a number of vital opportunities peculiar to itself, and I shall presume upon your patience to air these to you, as such an opportunity will almost certainly not recur.

Whereas learned interest in ancient Egypt goes back to the Renaissance, professional academic study is of barely a century's duration. Although a great number of scholars have been involved in handling a vast material, neither the literature of the subject nor the essential scholarly tools have been brought up to date. In contrast to other disciplines, the relevant publications of primary evidence may often go back as much as 150 years; although the

A Previously Unpublished Contract of Sale from Memphis

Maria Cannata

Introduction

The document discussed in this paper, P. Bodl. MS. Egypt. a. 41(P), is one of three private deeds written in the Demotic script, which I translated and edited as part of my MPhil thesis at Oxford University. Originally part of the Curzon collection of Egyptian antiquities, P. Bodl. MS. Egypt. a. 41(P) is a deed of cession, for a property located in the enclosure of the Anubis temple within the Saqqara necropolis. The deed of cession, or *sh-n-wy*, is one of two legal documents, the second being the *sh-db3-hd* (or document of money), that together formed an Egyptian contract of sale in the Ptolemaic Period. This paper analyses the different uses of these two types of deeds. A translation of P. Bodl. MS. Egypt. a. 41(P) is given together with an analysis of some of the legal formulae it uses. The evidence provided by legal documents such as P. Bodl. MS. Egypt. a. 41(P) is then compared with the data recovered by archaeological excavations in the Anubis temple.

P. Bodl. MS. Egypt. a. 41(P), currently held in the manuscript collection in the Bodleian Library at Oxford, originally belonged to the Hon. Robert Curzon, 14th Baron Zouche who possibly acquired it during his travels to Egypt and the Near East around 1833 (Dawson *et al.* 1995, 113). Although nothing is known of its exact place of acquisition, evidence within the document suggests the Memphite necropolis as its site of provenance (Figure 1). The contract recorded on Bodl. MS. Egypt. a. 41(P), in fact, specifies that the property concerned was located within the Anubieion, the Greek name by which the Anubis temple precinct in the Saqqara necropolis was identified.

The papyrus was purchased at Sotheby's by the British Egyptologist, Francis Llewellyn Griffith, on the 2nd of November 1922, when the Curzon collection of Egyptian antiquities was sold (Dawson *et al.* 1995, 113) and presented to the Bodleian Library on the 13th of the same month (Bodleian Library manuscripts handlist). The papyrus, whose overall dimensions as preserved are 98 cm in length by 19 cm in height, shows considerable signs of damage, especially in the lower half of the right-hand section. Indeed, a close examination of this area seems to indicate that the papyrus may have undergone repair, probably after its acquisition in the 18th century and before being framed, perhaps as a way of enhancing its aesthetic appeal and value.

Typological and legal analysis of the document

The document is a so-called *sh-n-wy* and concerns the transfer of ownership of a property located in the Saqqara necropolis. By chance, the corresponding *sh-db3-hd* is also preserved. The latter manuscript, P. BM 10075, was originally part of the Egyptian antiquities collection of the British diplomat, Henry Salt, later acquired by the British Museum. The document was published by Jelínková in a two-part article in 1957 and 1959.

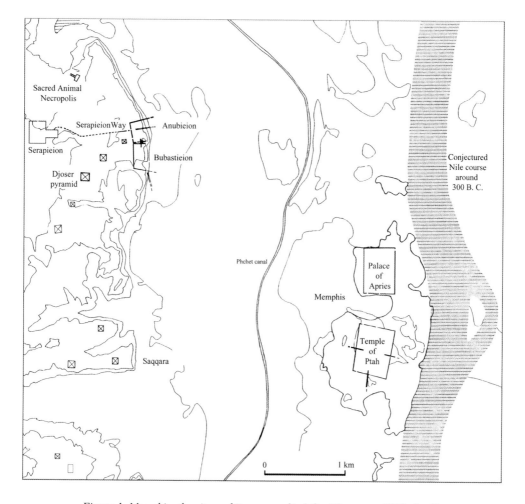

Figure 1. Memphis: the city and its necropolis (after Thompson 1988, fig. 2).

As mentioned, the *sẖ-ḏbȝ-ḥḏ* and *sẖ-n-wy* are the two legal documents that formed an Egyptian contract of sale in the Ptolemaic Period. Until the end of the Persian Period only one document was used for the sale and transfer of property ownership, while in the Ptolemaic Period two documents, it would seem, became necessary in order to complete the transaction, possibly as a result of a development of the country's notarial traditions. The *sẖ-ḏbȝ-ḥḏ* recorded the agreement between the two parties, while the *sẖ-n-wy* served to transfer the legal ownership to the new owner, testifying that the vendor renounced any claim on the property (Cruz-Uribe 1985, 45–46). Some scholars suggest that a *sẖ-ḏbȝ-ḥḏ*, without a *sẖ-n-wy*, would give only a right to use the property. However, according to Depauw (2000, 5, 7) a *sẖ-ḏbȝ-ḥḏ* simply represented written proof of an oral agreement reached between the parties. As such, a *sẖ-n-wy* was an optional document in which the alienator gave further confirmation that he or she renounced any claim on the property, rather than a necessary instrument in the transfer of ownership.

Further, both the *sh-db3-hd* and *sh-n-wy* could be used independently of a *real* sale in a range of legal operations. A *sh-db3-hd* could be drawn up, for example, as a guarantee on loans of money. Should the debtor fail to return the money to the lender, the latter would become the owner of the property pledged, while a *sh-n-wy* would be drawn up by the borrower renouncing any legal title on the said property (Depauw 2000, 5). A clear example of this use of the *sh-db3-hd* is found in P. Philadelphia XV (259 B.C.) in which party A states that she has borrowed a sum of money from party B: "You have 3 silver pieces … owing from us, in respect of the money which you have given us, and we will give it back by the year 26, last day of the second month of the winter season", and that, if the debt is not extinguished by the date stipulated, the agreement will be considered as a sale and the sum as the payment for the property: "If we do not give it back by year 26, last day of the second month of the winter season, then you have caused our hearts to agree to the silver as price for the house" (El-Amir 1959, 65–67, lines 1–2).

A *sh-db3-hd* could also be used to transfer ownership in place of a will, a usage which may represent a practice from the Pharaonic Period when a so-called *imy.t pr* was used as a transfer document for inheritance, generally to a person different from the testator's heir(s) (Johnson 1998, 1413, n. 91). The purpose of using these types of documents as wills may have been that of specifying the share in the inheritance of each of the heirs, as well as determining their responsibility with regards to the payment of the testator's burial costs (Pestman 1969, 63). An example of this is found in P. BM 10026 (265–264 B.C.) where, following the list of properties and titles transferred, the testator asserts: "You are to provide for my embalming, my entire mummification and burial, in accordance with what is customary for a person (of my status)" (Andrews 1990, 16–22, line 10). In this use of the *sh-db3-hd*, a cession document may not have been necessary since ownership would have passed to the beneficiary at the death of the vendor (Depauw 2000, 5; Pestman 1969, 62).

Finally, a *sh-n-wy* may also be drafted, independently of sales, with the purpose of acknowledging the rights of the beneficiary with the promise to respect them (Pestman *et al.* 1977b, 6). Such a document could be drawn up, for instance, following a trial by the party against whom judgement was given. An example of this is found in P. BM 10446 (230 B.C.) in which a priest from the necropolis of *Djeme* declares: "I have been in dispute with you before the judges … The judges have given judgement in your favour against me regarding them (*i.e.* the property). They belong to you" (Andrews 1990, 66, lines 2, 4).

Contents and legal formulae

The contract (comprising both documents) was written in year 18 of king Ptolemy XII Auletes (Neos Dionysos) in 64 B.C. and records the sale of a property by *Nht-nb=f*, together with his two brothers and a sister (party A), to their cousin, the woman *'Is.t-wry.t* (party B). The property was located in a settlement within the Anubieion (Figure 2). It included a house, some storehouses and a building probably used for the storage, and possibly the production, of textiles.

The format of the deed is consistent with other similar documents used during the Ptolemaic Period. The contract begins with the date (line numbers are indicated in brackets):

Maria Cannata

(1) Regnal year 18, fourth month of the inundation season, day two of (Pharaoh)¦ (Ptolemy)¦ the god who loves his father and who loves his sister, and the priests of the (Pharaohs)¦ who are registered at Alexandria.

There follows a statement by the vendor in which the contracting parties are identified both by patronymics and matronymics:

Has declared the merchant from the Anubieion which is under the authorities of Memphis, *Nḫṭ-nb=f* son of *Ḥr-nd-iṭ=f*, together with *Ḥr-m-ḥy* the elder, of the same profession, son of *Ḥr-nd-iṭ=f*, together with *Ḥr-m-ḥy* the younger, son of *Ḥr-nd-iṭ=f* together with the woman *T3-šr.t-ḥr-m-ḥy* (2) daughter of *Ḥr-nd-iṭ=f* being three persons, the younger brethren of *Nḫṭ-nb=f* aforesaid, being four persons with one voice, their mother being *Nḫṭ=w-s*, to (the) woman *'Is.t-wry.t* daughter of *P3-ty-nfr-tm*, called *3rs*, her mother being *T3y-r-r=w*.

The declaration continues with the specification of the property sold, including details of its size expressed using the *mḥ-nṭr*, or god's cubit (52.5 cm, formerly *mḥ-nswt* or king's cubit) (Vleeming 1985, 208–210):

(2) We are far from you (in respect) to your house, which is built, it being roofed, it being complete with door and window (and) which measures 18 god's-cubits from the south to the north, by six god's-cubits from the west to the east, together with your (3) cloth-place (and) your storehouses that are built at their entrance, which is to its north, and which are in the Anubieion on the southern side of the dromos of Anubis-who-is-upon-his-mountain, the great god, (and) which includes everything that came to us as a share in (the) name (of the) woman *Nḫṭ=w-s* daughter of *P3-ty-ij-m-ḥtp*, her mother being *'Is.t-wry.t*, our mother, the sister of your mother.

There follows a reference to the first part of the contract, the *sḫ-db3-ḥd*, which in this case is represented by P. BM 10075:

You have bought the house, the cloth-place (and) the aforesaid storehouses (4) from us, concerning which we have made for you a *sḫ-db3-ḥd* with *Ḥr-nd-iṭ=f* son of *P3-ty-wsir-ḥp*, our father, at the aforesaid date.

Then we find a list of the neighbouring properties, recorded in the order south, north, west and east, a sequence typically used in legal documents for the specification of properties:

Their neighbours:
South: the house of the woman *Ta-by* which was held by *Ḏ-ḥr* son of *Ḥr-p3-r⁽* (and) which is (now) held by the children of his offspring;
North: (the) dromos of Anubis-who-is-upon-his-mountain, the great god;
West: the house of *⁽nḫ-ḥp* which was held by (the) woman *Ta-mr-wr*, his daughter, (and) which is (now) held by the children of (5) her offspring;
East: the house of *Pa-iḥ.t* which is held by another man while the alley (of the house) is between them. Totalling (the neighbours).

There follows the clause of 'declaration of possession' and that of 'quitting claim' in which the vendor confirms that the ownership of the property now rests with the buyer, and that he no longer has any right to make a claim on the assets sold (Cruz-Uribe 1985, 55–56):

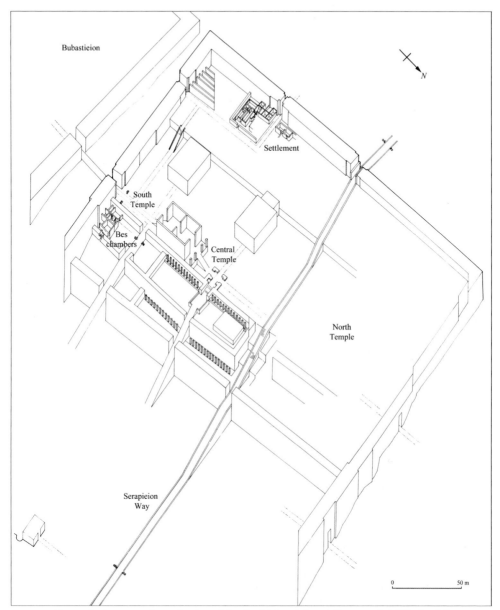

Figure 2. Axonometric projection of the Anubieion (after Jeffreys et al. 1988, fig. 62).

To you belong (the) house, your cloth-place (and) your storehouses, whose measurements of their boundaries are written above, in accordance with that which is written above from today onwards. We do not have any claim at all against you on account of them.

The following clause is one typically used in both *sẖ-ḏbꜣ-ḥḏ* and *sẖ-n-wy* deeds to confirm that the vendor will help the buyer clear the property from any claim which may arise in a legal dispute concerning its ownership (Pestman 1985, 201). This, it would appear, was one of the obligations the alienator had towards the new owner, even after the sale had been completed:

> (As for) the one who will come against you on account of them, we will cause him to be far from you by compulsion (and) without delay.

There follows a declaration by the father of party A who appears to have acted as guarantor, undertaking to fulfil the obligations of the deed should his offspring fail to comply:

> While the merchant, a man (6) from the said village, *Ḥr-nḏ-it̠=f* son of *P3-ty-wsir-ḥp*, his mother being *Ta-ij-m-ḥtp*, the father of the four persons aforesaid, declares: "execute all (the) aforesaid matters, my heart is satisfied with them. You have a legal claim on me to act for you in accordance with everything aforesaid. That which the four persons aforesaid, my children, will not do for you, I will do it for you within five days of the said month, by compulsion, without delay".

The document is also confirmed by all five members of the family together, who undertake to fulfil the obligations of the *sḫ-n-wy*:

> While the five persons say: "you have a legal claim against any one of us you want, totalling the five persons, to fulfil for you the obligation of the deed (7) aforesaid. Should you wish to make a legal claim against us, as the five persons, you will be (able to have a claim)";

as well as the obligations of the *sḫ-ḏb3-ḥḏ*:

> You have a claim on us (also) with respect to (the right of the) *sḫ-ḏb3-ḥḏ* which we made for you concerning them in regnal year 18, fourth month of the inundation season, day two of (Pharaoh)¦ (Ptolemy)¦ who lives forever, completing (the) two documents. You have a claim on us with respect to them and their obligation.

> Wrote *Pa-ḥrṭ* son of *Ḥr-s3-is.t* the younger.

Thus, the document ends with the signature of the notary *Pa-ḥrṭ*, a member of a family of scribes working in the Memphite area (Pestman *et al.* 1977a, 32).

As in all legal documents, we would expect to find a list of witnesses on the verso of the deed, although this is no longer visible in Bodl. MS. Egypt. a. 41(P) since the papyrus appears to have been stuck onto a backing material before being framed. However, an analysis of contracts for which both the *sḫ-ḏb3-ḥḏ* and the *sḫ-n-wy* have survived seems to suggest that the same individuals would have witnessed both deeds, hence, it may be possible that the people who signed the verso of P. BM 10075, in which such a list is partially preserved (Jelínková 1957, 54–55, pl. 5; 1959, 62), were also those who witnessed Bodl. MS. Egypt. a. 41(P).

The Anubieion

The complex of the Anubieion extended over three large terraces and included at least three temples covering about 250 sq m (Davies and Smith 1997, 114; Thompson 1988, 21, 33). The various levels were linked by a series of roads, the main one being the Serapieion Way which, from the wall on the east, led through the Anubieion and the west enclosure wall, into the desert and the Serapieion. Another stone-paved causeway led from the Bubastieion via a granite gate in the south enclosure wall, through the temple areas and a north gate, into the desert (Davies and Smith 1997, 114; Thompson 1988, 25).

Both archaeological and textual evidence suggest that the temples in the Saqqara necropolis had become integral parts of Memphis and important centres of activity from around the 4th century B.C. (Davies and Smith 1997, 120; Jeffreys *et al.* 1988, 77). Textual evidence suggests that the Anubieion was also an administrative centre and the location of a *grapheion,* a bureau where documents were registered (Thompson 1988, 26; Wilcken 1927, 620–621). Although its exact location within the enclosure is not known, textual sources suggest the *dromos* itself, or adjacent areas, as possible locations for such an office (Pestman 1981, 161).

Against the west wall on the uppermost terrace, excavations have unearthed evidence of settled habitation indicated by the presence of domestic utilities, as well as organic and animal remains (Smith and Jeffreys 1979, 21). The archaeology, however, appears indicative of communal rather than family life. This seems to be suggested, for example, by the plan of the architectural remains which includes a number of small chambers situated around long rooms that may have been used for communal dining, and by the absence of personal effects and other objects, such as spindles and bobbins, often associated with the activities of women (Smith and Jeffreys 1979, 21; Jeffreys *et al.* 1988, 39). The excavators suggest that the position of the settlement in relation to the temples, together with the limited evidence for the presence of women and children, may indicate that the area was used for housing temple personnel, which would, of course, account for the communal nature of the buildings (Jeffreys *et al.* 1988, 38). In addition, the discovery of a large number of votive figurines may indicate that the area, or part of it, also served as a hostel for pilgrims (Jeffreys *et al.* 1988, 38–39). Its presence is, indeed, also suggested by indirect textual evidence, such as a petition to the *strategos* Poseidonios, recorded on P. Louvre 2335 (157 B.C.), in which a certain Harmais mentions his sojourn in the Anubieion during a pilgrimage to the area (Bottigelli 1941, 25).

The presence of such a settlement within the temple complex is also attested by a small number of private legal documents such as Bodl. MS. Egypt. a. 41(P). However, contrary to the surviving archaeological evidence, textual sources seem to suggest the presence of more than just communal housing for priests or a hostel. The transactions recorded in these documents are, in fact, concerned with a number of private dwellings which have either been sold to another party or handed down through generations. Bodl. MS. Egypt. a. 41(P), for example, records that the house of ꜥnḫ-ḥp was held by his great-grandchildren. Furthermore, these documents seem to indicate that women also lived within the settlement, since they are often found as parties to the contracts, or are mentioned as holders of neighbouring houses. Although it may be argued that their mention as owners of properties in the Anubieion does not necessarily constitute proof of their inhabiting it, some sources appear to indicate that women may indeed have lived in the area. This is, for instance, the case in P. Leid. 378 (160 B.C.) which is an agreement concerning the preservation of a light-well between two contiguous houses, where a brother and his sister are recorded as occupying adjacent properties (Glanville 1939, 25–26; Revillout 1878, 113–120; Thompson 1988, 168). In addition, among the settlement's inhabitants mentioned in these deeds, several are merchants, as in the case of Bodl. MS. Egypt. a. 41(P) and P. BM 10075 (Jelínková 1957; 1959), although their presence within the Anubieion is probably not entirely surprising since some of them may also have held office as priests (pers. comm. David Jeffreys).

It seems quite possible that the apparent discrepancies between archaeological and textual evidence are due to accidents of preservation, since very little of the upper terrace survives as a result of later disturbance and modern occupation (Jeffreys *et al.* 1988, 2; Smith and Jeffreys 1978, 12). In fact, it is possible that the surviving structure served as priests' living quarters, or possibly a hostel, while the settlement proper may have disappeared altogether. In addition, although domestic implements, such as stone and wooden tools, basketry and bins, were also recovered, they are relatively few in number considering the long occupation of the site (*c.*400 years), and may indicate that occupation was not continuous (Jeffreys *et al.* 1988, 38–39). Finally, the apparent differences between the two types of evidence may also be due to the limited amount of textual evidence regarding properties within the Anubieion and to possible uncertainties about the translation and transcription of some texts which are available only in very old publications.

Conclusion

The study of Bodl. MS. Egypt. a. 41(P), in conjunction with other private deeds from the Anubieion, offers the opportunity for a comparative analysis of textual sources and archaeological remains (a full analysis of the material is currently in progress). The additional information provided by the textual sources allows for a re-evaluation of some conclusions drawn from the archaeology, thus exemplifying the need to combine both types of data, whenever available, in order to achieve a more complete and cohesive picture of the subject, since neither type of evidence alone can fully address the question.

Furthermore, the study of the hitherto unpublished Bodl. MS. Egypt. a. 41(P) has enabled the restoration of lacunae in P. BM 10075 (also damaged in places), a new edition of which is also in progress (Cannata forthcoming). Finally, the analysis of this document has proved valuable in bringing together the two parts of the original contract which, by chance, have both been preserved in two different English collections.

Oxford University

Acknowledgements

I would like to thank the organisers of the *Current Research in Egyptology 2003* for the opportunity to present my paper at the graduate symposium. I should also like to express my gratitude to my supervisor, Dr. M. Smith (Oxford University), for bringing to my attention the document presented in this paper and for his invaluable advice. I would also like to thank Dr. D. Jeffreys (UCL) for his useful comments on the archaeology of the Anubieion. My thanks are also due the staff at the Bodleian Library (Oxford) for their permission to study the document and the information they provided on the acquisition of the papyrus.

References

Andrews, C. A. R. 1990, *Catalogue of Demotic Papyri in the British Museum, 4: Ptolemaic legal texts from the Theban area.* British Museum Publications, London.

Bottigelli, P. 1941, Repertorio topografico dei templi e dei sacerdoti dell'Egitto tolemaico, *Aegyptus* 21, 21–49.

Cannata, M. forthcoming, Papyrus BM EA 10075 and Papyrus Bodleian MS. Egypt. a. 41(P): Two halves of a Ptolemaic contract of sale reunited. *Journal of Egyptian Archaeology.*

Cruz-Uribe, E. 1985, *Saite and Persian Demotic Cattle Documents: A study in legal forms and principles in ancient Egypt.* Scholars Press, California.

Davies, S. and Smith, H. S. 1997, Sacred Animal Temples at Saqqara, in S. Quirke (ed.), *The Temple in Ancient Egypt: New discoveries and recent research*, 112–131. British Museum Press, London.

Dawson, W. R., Uphill, E. P. and Bierbrier, M. L. 1995, *Who Was Who in Egyptology.* Egypt Exploration Society, London.

Depauw, M. 2000, *The Archive of Teos and Thabis from Early Ptolemaic Thebes.* Fondation Égyptologique Reine Élisabeth, Brepols Publishers, Brussels.

El-Amir, M. 1959, *A Family Archive from Thebes: Demotic papyri in the Philadelphia and Cairo Museums from the Ptolemaic Period.* General Organisation for Government Printing Offices, Cairo.

Glanville, S. R. K. 1939, *Catalogue of the Demotic Papyri in the British Museum, 1: A Theban archive of the reign of Ptolemy I, Soter.* British Museum Press, London.

Jeffreys, D. G., Smith, H. S. and Jessop Price, M. 1988, *The Anubieion at Saqqâra, 1: The settlement and the temple precinct.* Egypt Exploration Society, London.

Jelínková, E. A. E. 1957, Sale of Inherited Property in the First Century B.C. (P. Brit. Mus. 10075, ex Salt coll. No. 418), *Journal of Egyptian Archaeology* 43, 45–55.

Jelínková, E. A. E. 1959, Sale of Inherited Property in the First Century B.C. (P. Brit. Mus. 10075, ex Salt coll. No. 418), *Journal of Egyptian Archaeology* 45, 61–74.

Johnson, J. H. 1998, Women, Wealth and Work in Egyptian Society of the Ptolemaic Period, in W. Clarysse, A. Schoors, and H. Willems (eds.), *Egyptian Religion: The last thousand years: Studies dedicated to the memory of Jan Quaegebeur*, 1393–1421. Peeters, Leuven.

Pestman, P. W. 1969, The Law of Succession in Ancient Egypt, in J. Brugman, M. David, F. R. Kraus, P. W. Pestman and M. H. Van der Valk (eds.), *Essays on Oriental Laws of Succession*, 58–77. E. J. Brill, Leiden.

Pestman, P. W. 1981, *L'archivio di Amenothes figlio di Horos (P. Tor. Amenothes): Testi Demotici e greci relativi ad una famiglia di imbalsamatori del secondo sec. a. C.* Istituto editoriale Cisalpino – La Goliardica, Milan.

Pestman, P. W. 1985, Le Démotique comme langue juridique, in P. W. Pestman (ed.), *Textes et études de papyrologie greque, démotique et copte (P. L. Bat. 23)*, 198–203. E. J. Brill, Leiden.

Pestman, P. W., Quaegebeur, J. and Vos, R. L. 1977a, *Recueil de textes démotiques et bilingues, 1: Transcriptions.* E. J. Brill, Leiden.

Pestman, P. W., Quaegebeur, J. and Vos, R. L. 1977b, *Recueil de textes démotiques et bilingues, 2: Traductions.* E. J. Brill, Leiden.

Revillout, E. M. 1878, *Nouvelle Chrestomathie Démotique, Mission de 1878: Contracts de Berlin, Vienne, Leyde, etc.* Ernest Leroux, Paris.

Smith, H. S. and Jeffreys, D. G. 1978, The Anubieion, Temple-Town Survey: Preliminary report for 1976–77, *Journal of Egyptian Archaeology* 64, 10–21.

Smith, H. S. and Jeffreys, D. G. 1979, The Anubieion, North Saqqâra: Preliminary report, 1977–78, *Journal of Egyptian Archaeology* 65, 17–29.

Thompson, D. J. 1988, *Memphis Under the Ptolemies.* University Press, Princeton.

Maria Cannata

Vleeming, S. P. 1985, Demotic Measures of Length and Surface, Chiefly of the Ptolemaic Period, in P.
    W. Pestman (ed.), *Textes et études de papyrologie greque, démotique et copte (P. L. Bat. 23)*, 208–
    229. E. J. Brill, Leiden.
Wilcken, U. 1927, *Urkunden der Ptolemäerzeit (Ältere Funde): Erster Band (Papyri aus Unterägypten)*.
    Verlag von Walter de Gruyter and Co., Berlin and Leipzig.

Behind the Corn-mummies

Maria Costanza Centrone

Introduction

The aim of this paper is to provide a brief summary of my PhD research on corn-mummies and to consider their symbolic meaning. Corn-mummies are mummiform objects made from a mixture of earth, sand and corn – or grain – wrapped in linen bandages. They are commonly found in decorated and inscribed falcon-headed coffins. Various items placed on or around the mummies have led scholars to conclude that these figures are representations of Osiris, presumably manufactured for the annual 'mysteries' of Osiris. To date, I have documented more than 80 specimens located in museum and private collections around the world.

In the following, several examples of corn-mummies are presented with an examination of their various features. The symbolic meanings behind the corn-mummies will then be discussed. As a living entity whose existence followed a cyclical pattern of life and death, corn embodied the idea of renewal and resurrection for the ancient Egyptians. The planting of seeds and the emergence of new shoots from the earth offered an analogy for the triumph of life over death and was often symbolically equated with the rising up of Osiris' soul. Given that corn-mummies contain corn and bear Osirian characteristics, this research explores how corn-mummies may have related to Osiris and Egyptian notions of death and rebirth.

Excavation reports and museum records document corn-mummies exclusively from funerary contexts. Only five necropolises are known to have yielded these objects: Tehne el-Gebel, Wadi Qubbanet el-Qirud near Thebes, El-Sheikh Fadl, Meidum, and a cemetery near Tuna el-Gebel, the precise location of which has been lost. Unfortunately, for a large number of specimens, the precise archaeological context was not recorded, or the objects were obtained from the art market. Internet searches for corn-mummies have led to art market or auction web sites where supposedly-authentic corn-mummies are sold. However, queries to dealers concerning the provenance of the advertised specimens have gone unanswered. Therefore, when incorporating such unprovenanced specimens into this research, analysis has necessarily focussed on stylistic features in order to relate them to specimens for which the archaeological context is documented.

Definition and descriptions

Corn-mummies, variously referred to as 'grain Osiris figurines', '*Kornmumien*', '*Kornosirise*' and '*Osiris végétant*', are mummiform packages about 35–50 cm in length. The term 'corn' refers to the grain used in these figures, which was either emmer wheat (*Triticum dicoccum*) or barley (*Hordeum vulgare*) (Wasylikova and Jankun 1997). These mummiform packages of earth, sand and corn were wrapped in linen and occasionally covered by a linen shroud secured with strips of linen. The wrappings appear to have been soaked in resin, bitumen or a similar substance, but it is difficult to determine through visual observation precisely what substance was used. While scientific analysis has not been carried out on most of the specimens, three examples housed in the Archaeological Museum in Krakow have been analysed (Klosowska 1997). The tests show that the substance thickly covering these mummies is neither bitumen nor resin, but rather a mixture of different adhesives, including vegetable gum and glue containing animal products. Such analysis has not yet been conducted for the corn-mummy specimens presented in this paper, thus, it is only for convenience that I refer to the substance applied to the linen wrappings as 'resin'.

Objects placed on most corn-mummies included a wax mask with a human face, divine beard and royal crown (either the *atef-* or White Crown). In some examples, wax fists holding wax royal sceptres were placed on the chest, and uraei and scarabs also made of wax were placed on or near the body. Some mummies have an erect phallus composed of a substance similar in appearance to that used in the manufacture of the mummies themselves, although the phallus is applied to the exterior of the wrapped body. Other contents of the coffins included small humanoid packages representing the Sons of Horus (four are usually present), as well as balls of earth and grain, all of which can provide further clues as to the possible provenance and meaning of the corn-mummies.

These coffins in which corn-mummies have often been found bear falcon-heads, and the lids are often inscribed and decorated with a range of vignettes. Aspects of these decorations, such as similarities in the texts and decoration, the colour scheme, composition, style and the subjects of depictions, as well as the overall shape of the coffins, can provide indications of the geographical and chronological context of particular mummies. In addition, the vignettes are suggestive of the symbolic meanings associated with the corn-mummies. Therefore, the study of the coffins is equally important to understanding the mummies themselves.

The various features taken into account in my analysis include the shapes of the coffins in which most corn-mummies have been found can also be informative. However, in some instances specimens differ markedly from the majority of examples, making comparative analysis and further understanding difficult. With the exception of the four examples discussed below, the inscriptions that occasionally occur on the coffin lids of some corn-mummies generally do not provide clues relating to provenance.

The catalogue

One of initial aims of this research is to compile a comprehensive catalogue of known corn-mummies. Raven (1982) previously published approximately 40 specimens, and in addition to these, a further 45 have been documented throughout the course of this research.

For the purpose of this paper I have selected examples of corn-mummies which best illustrate the corpus generally. These include corn-mummies, found both with and without coffins and unpublished and unprovenanced specimens for which a provenance may be suggested. Overall, I discuss specimens which derive from four different cemetery sites and whose stylistic features are illuminating in terms of understanding symbolic meaning and the range of traditions in corn-mummy manufacture and use.

(a) A possible Meidum corn-mummy

On 29 September 2002, a corn-mummy was sold at auction (Auction 81) at the Malter Galleries, Inc. in Los Angeles, California (Figure 1). The falcon-headed coffin is made of wood and measures 60 cm in length. It has a back pillar and narrow plinth and is decorated with representations and inscriptions in black on an ochre-coloured background. The falcon's head is adorned with a striated tripartite wig, and a beaded collar is depicted between the front lappets of the wig. Its large, round eyes are edged in black with the eyelashes and brows indicated. The cheeks are highlighted and the beak is short with a dotted line extending from it and over the throat. The chest area is occupied by a frame of stars surmounting two columns of inscriptions which translate as follows:

> Greeting to you, you the Heir, who comes from the marvellous god who is in the Netherworld, who comes as 'again child', who comes as the great god, who comes from the sky and shines on the earth as Orion (*s3ḥ*) when he follows him ... oh, Sokar, lord of *Sahti*'.

Two pairs of tenons and mortises, placed symmetrically on either side in the regions of the neck and lower limbs, were used to seal the coffin. The corn-mummy inside the coffin is slim, elongated and relatively small compared to the size of the coffin. The mummy is wrapped in black resin-soaked linen and is provided with a silver mask, of which the White Crown is part. The mask depicts a human face with small ears, eyes, eyebrows and an almost indiscernible nose.

According to the auction records, the provenance of this specimen is unknown. However, the short inscription on the lid of the coffin suggests that Meidum may have been the find site. This suggestion is based on the presence of the epithet of Sokar-Osiris, 'lord of *Sahti*', in the inscription. According to Gauthier (1925–1931, 5.43–44) and others (Grimal 1981, 81–83; Yoyotte 1963), Sahti is to be identified as Meidum. In the stela of Piankhy (Grimal 1981, 81–83), the probable fortress of Meidum (Moithymis) is called 'House of Sokar, lord of *sḥd*'.

The text on the coffin lid is of further interest in that it appears to be identical to a coffin published by Kurt (1998, 46–47). He refers to four corn-mummies, or rather to the coffins in which they were contained, noting that at that time the objects were in private collections in Germany. It is possible that this corn-mummy was in the private collection of a German collector but has since been auctioned to another private collector. These circumstances are mentioned in order to illustrate the difficulties scholars sometimes encounter in trying to trace unpublished artefacts and gather information on them, whether they are kept in private collections or museums.

(b) Corn-mummies of Wadi Qubbanet el-Qirud

Wadi Qubbanet el-Qirud (Valley of the Tombs of the Monkeys), a wadi located to the south-east of the Theban hills and about 2 km west of Medinet Habu, yielded numerous corn-mummies (Lortet 1906; Lortet and Gaillard 1907–1909, 2.247–248, 4.209). An example of these is currently in the British Museum (EA 60747; Taylor 2001, 212; Figure 2). The corn-mummy is 35 cm long, wrapped in black resin-coated bandages, and wears a bulbous head-

Figure 1. Corn-mummy in the Malter Galleries, Inc. with its falcon-headed coffin lid. (Photograph courtesy of Malter Galleries, Inc., Los Angeles, California, USA. Not to scale.)

Figure 2. Corn-mummy in the British Museum, EA 60747. (Author's photograph, courtesy of the Department of Ancient Egypt and Sudan, the British Museum. Not to scale.)

dress (presumably the White Crown), and a dark green wax mask with a human face, protruding ears, prominent lips, a long, pointed nose and divine beard. Remains of gold leaf are preserved on the beard, eyebrows, rims of the eyes and in the contours of the face.

Two similar specimens are housed in the Egyptian collection in the Oriental Museum of the University of Durham (North 96–97; Figure 3). Both these previously unpublished examples bear a remarkable resemblance to BM EA 60747 and other specimens which, based on the shape and dimensions of the mummy-form packages, are thought to have come from the Theban area. In comparison to these, each Durham corn-mummy bears a similarly erect phallus, a modelled and separately applied divine beard, a bulbous crown, and in particular, a stylistically-distinct, dark green wax mask with human ears, a long nose, and thick, elongated lips. Although the museum records do not contain information regarding the context of these objects, based on a comparative analysis of these various stylistic features, I suggest that both Durham corn-mummies belongs to the Wadi Qubbanet el-Qirud group.

(c) Corn-mummies from Tuna el-Gebel

Another unpublished corn-mummy and its coffin are located in the Royal Ontario Museum (Inv. no. 972.412; Figures 4 and 5). Purchased in 1972 from a private owner, the specimen consists of a slim wooden coffin characterised by a falcon's head and a thick rectangular plinth 48 cm long and 14 cm wide. The lower half of the coffin is plastered and painted in black, and the lid is decorated with a gilded background with gilded and red and blue painted details. The falcon head has a prominent beak and wears a blue tripartite wig with transverse straps on the front lappets. Gilding is preserved around the face and the details are painted in black. Between the front lappets of the wig, a bead necklace and an elaborate, colourful collar are depicted. Below these is a block frieze composed of vertical strips and bands in blue, red and gold paint, upon either side of which a *wsḫ n bik* motif is represented. The terminals of the *wsḫ n bik* decoration are composed of blue falcon heads surmounted by a gilded sun disc. In the centre, a blue lotus flower sits atop a small stylised, gilded naos. The lower part of the lid is occupied by a vignette on a blue background representing two gold uraei wearing the *atef-* and White Crowns, respectively. These are symmetrically arranged on either side of an *ankh* amulet painted gold. Underneath these, situated on the lower legs and feet of the coffin lid, are seven columns of inscriptions on alternating blue and gold backgrounds. The unusually shallow coffin contains a mummiform package wrapped in linen, covered by a linen shroud which is secured to the mummy at the head and feet. There is no trace of a mask or other objects which may have been placed in the coffin along with the mummy.

According to the museum's records the provenance of the corn-mummy is unknown. With regard to stylistic features, however, the coffin appears comparable to other specimens thought to have come from Tuna el-Gebel. The similarities between features of corn-mummy coffins from this region generally include the *wsḫ n bik* motif with terminals in the shape of a falcon's heads, the central lotus flower, the vignette in the lower part of the lid and columns of inscription referring to Book of the Dead (BD) Chapter 15B (Allen 1960, 79–80). I have yet to examine the specimen in the Royal Ontario Museum firsthand, and unfortunately museum photographs are somewhat blurry making a precise reading of the hieroglyphics impossible (see Figures 4 and 5). Nevertheless, certain signs can be made out which suggest that the text is similar to those found on other corn-mummy coffins from Tuna el-Gebel.

Figure 3. Corn-mummies in the Oriental Museum, North 96–97. Photograph North 96–97. (© The Oriental Museum, University of Durham. Not to scale.)

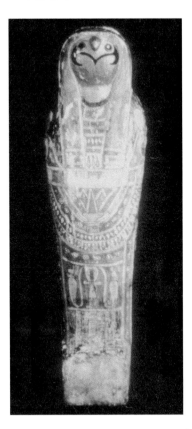

Figure 4. Falcon-headed coffin lid. Royal Ontario Museum, Inv. no. 972.412. (Photograph courtesy of the Royal Ontario Museum, Toronto, Canada. Not to scale.)

Figure 5. Coffin lid (Figure 4) next to the case containing the corn-mummy. Royal Ontario Museum, Inv. no. 972.412. (Photograph courtesy of the Royal Ontario Museum, Toronto, Canada. Not to scale.)

(d) Corn-mummies of Tehne el-Gebel

Corn-mummies which come from Tehne el-Gebel contribute further to understanding the extent and range of the corn-mummy tradition, and in particular offer insights into the interpretation of the symbolism embodied in these objects (discussed below).

A corn-mummy and coffin currently housed in the Egyptian Museum in Cairo (JE 36540; Figures 5 and 6) has previously been published by Kessler (1981, 267, pl. 9, 4) and discussed by Raven (1982, 22). However, the coffin as well as the mummiform package enclosed within were re-examined for this study. The coffin is made of wood, and the lower half is painted in ochre and the lid in black. Upon the latter a falcon head is depicted with a blue tripartite wig. The face of the bird is painted ochre, and traces of gilding are preserved. Other details of the lid decoration are painted in white and include a central column of inscriptions which reads: 'words spoken by Osiris, foremost of the West, the great god, lord of *bḥ(t)*; by Osiris, lord of *mr-nfr(t)*, given life for ever'. The inscription on the coffin mentions two titles of Osiris: 'lord of *bḥ(t)*' and 'lord of *mr-nfr(t)*'. These titles incorporate place names, both of which are thought to have been situated in the area of Tehne (Gauthier, 1925–1931, 2.4–5; 3.51–52; Kessler 1981, 269; Vandier 1961, 47–49). Indeed, the museum's records indicate that the specimen came from Tehne el-Gebel. The inscription is flanked by a row of divinities on each side. The figures include a human head wearing the *atef*-crown rising from a vessel-shaped element, and two ram-headed divinities with bodies resembling curved horns and three animal-headed genii. Interestingly, the arrangement and types of figures are similar to those depicted on a specimen from the Louvre discussed below.

Within the coffin of JE 36540 is a slightly ithyphallic, mummiform package wrapped in bandages and measuring 47.8 cm in length and 13 cm in width. The mummy wears a green wax mask which shows a well-delineated face with eyes painted in black and prominent human ears. The mummy also wears an *atef*-crown with a separately modelled and applied uraeus, as well as a divine beard modelled in black wax. A green wax fist holding a royal sceptre is placed on the chest. The coffin also contains four mummiform packages representing the Sons of Horus, each of which was also provided with a wax mask. In addition, the coffin held two linen-wrapped balls, one of which had a concave wax scarab placed on it.

A corn-mummy from Tehne el-Gebel, now at the Musée du Louvre, Paris (No. 12183; Figure 8), is of interest due to various features of its coffin. The mummy itself offers little insight, having lost its wax mask and royal sceptres (if it indeed had them), although it is accompanied by roughly made mummiform packages of the Four Sons of Horus. The coffin, measuring 58 cm in length and 21.5 cm in width, is made of sycamore wood painted an ochre colour and has a gilded falcon head which wears a tripartite wig. A beaded collar is depicted between the front lappets of the wig and on the chest there is a small *naos*-shaped pectoral which hangs on a bead necklace and contains a winged heart flanked by two genii. On either side is an elaborate *wsḥ n bik* motif with a terminal in the shape of a falcon head surmounted by a sun disc. Each is flanked by the Four Sons of Horus – two on either side, one above the other – each holding a *s3*-amulet and labelled with his name. Underneath, a kneeling figure of Nut with outspread wings holds a Maat feather in each hand. The whole is situated at the top of a column of inscription that reads: words spoken by him who is the foremost of the West, the great god, lord of *bḥ(t)*, lord of *mr-nfr(t)*. Each side of the coffin is decorated with a row of divinities which include four uraei, a divine head rising from a vessel-shaped object, two ram-headed divinities with bodies resembling curved horns, three animal-headed genii and a bird, probably a phoenix.

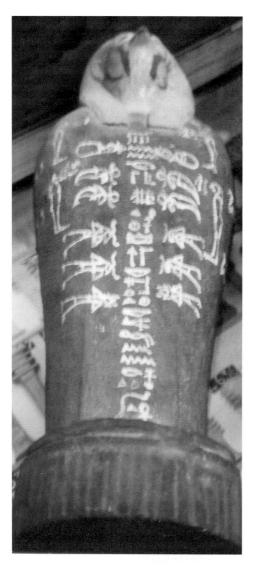 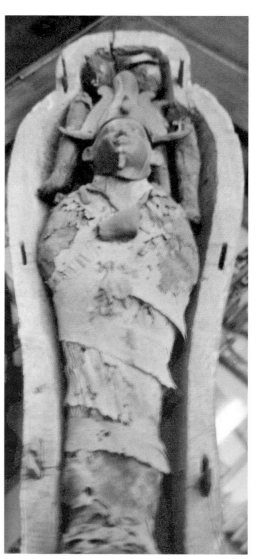

Figure 6. Falcon-headed coffin lid, Egyptian Museum, JE 36540. (Author's photograph, courtesy of the Egyptian Museum, Cairo. Not to scale.)

Figure 7. Coffin containing corn-mummy, Egyptian Museum, JE 36540. (Author's photograph, courtesy of the Egyptian Museum, Cairo. Not to scale.)

Figure 8. Coffin of corn-mummy in the Louvre, No. 12183. (Author's photograph, courtesy of the Musée du Louvre, Paris. Not to scale.)

Chronology

The chronological context of the corn-mummies presented above is not without difficulty given the common lack of archaeological data. The only reasonably firm date for a corn-mummy comes from a small roll of papyrus found by Lefebvre (1903, 230–231) beside one of the sarcophagi at Tehne el-Gebel. While the excavator dates it roughly to the 1st or 2nd century A.D., no further information is provided. Kessler's (1981, 263) examination of the inscriptions on the Tehne el-Gebel specimens in the Louvre and Cairo museums led him to suggest that the awkward rendering of the hieroglyphs and frequent errors in spelling, as well as graphic transposition, point to a Ptolemaic date.

For the corn-mummies with a poorly documented or unknown archaeological context, analysis of the stylistic evidence makes it possible to suggest general dates. Variations in the types of coffin and corn-mummy suggest that these objects were manufactured over a considerable period and particular features seem to be indicative of specific periods. For example, the presence of the plinth (which serves as a base for the coffin when positioned vertically), the back pillar, the small figures of protective deities arranged in symmetrical groupings and the wide variety of colour schemes are characteristic of the Third Intermediate Period (950–656 B.C.). Alternatively, the winged Nut figure depicted on the chest area of some coffin lids, as well as stylistic features of the masks are suggestive of the Late Period (664–305 B.C.). A late Ptolemaic or Roman Period date can be excluded on the basis of facial features that are uncharacteristic of those periods. Moreover, the masks placed on the Wadi Qubbanet el-Qirud corn-mummies feature a marked smile similar to 7th-century B.C. funerary masks. The elaborate collar placed low on the chest below the lappets of the wig, the *wsḫ n bik* motif with large falcon heads, and the presence of a central inscription flanked by figures of the Four Sons of Horus are characteristic of coffins dating to the 30th Dynasty and early Ptolemaic Period (305–30 B.C.). The polychrome decoration with the elaborate collars and the Nut figures are similar to Ptolemaic cartonnage and Ptah-Sokar-Osiris statues (Raven 1978–1979, 269). Thus, based on a comparative stylistic analysis, all the coffins seem to date to between the late Third Intermediate Period and the early Ptolemaic Period. At the present stage of the analysis, a narrower chronological delimitation is not possible, if at all.

The symbolism behind the corn-mummies and their relationship to Osiris

The decoration of the coffins and treatment of the mummy are important for understanding the context and meanings of these objects. Together they strongly suggest that corn-mummies were intended to represent the god Osiris. Grains of corn (either barley or wheat) were ground and mixed with earth into a 'dough' which was moulded or modelled into a shape resembling an ithyphallic figure of Osiris. The placement of various objects on the mummiform package, such as royal sceptres, the crown (*atef-* or White Crown) and the divine beard often incorporated into the wax mask, are all iconographic elements which relate to Osiris. The inscriptions on the coffins often relate directly to Osiris, giving his titles. Osirian themes are also manifest in the depictions on the coffins, as seen in the Louvre example discussed above. Raven (1982, 23) has noted a probable connection between the depiction of the head rising from the vessel-shaped element and the Osiris relic depicted on P. Jumilhac (Vandier 1961,

100–101, 252, pl. 3) which describes the religious beliefs and myths relating to the XVII Upper Egyptian nome to which Tehne el-Gebel belonged.

The presence of the phoenix in the vignettes can be understood in view of the Middle Kingdom assimilation of the phoenix, or *bnw*-bird, with Osiris as illustrated in Coffin Text (CT) spell 335 (Faulkner 1973, 260) and BD Chapter 17 (Faulkner 1985, 44–50). The phoenix is also associated with Osiris, where, according to BD Chapter 29B, it was the *bnw*-bird that took the deceased into the *duat* and aided his/her resurrection (Faulkner 1985, 55). Likewise, in Egyptian myth the deceased could be transformed into a phoenix; BD Chapter 83 gives a formula 'for being transformed into a phoenix' (Faulkner 1985, 80–81). Therefore, the *bnw* can be understood as symbolising regeneration, which, given the other Osirian attributes of the corn-mummies, seems to have been a key concept behind their manufacture.

The Osirian theme is further suggested by four inscribed balls of resin (E 12196–8, E 12202–3, E 12205 and E 12199) which were found by Lefebvre (1903, 229–230) along with the coffin in the Louvre; the coffin itself encased inside a pottery sarcophagus. Ziegler (1979), who analysed the balls in the Louvre, as well as those in the Cairo Museum, notes that they were made of earth, sand and resin. Various explanations have been suggested for the significance and meaning of these unique finds, including Lefebvre's (1903, 229–230) statement that these objects bore an inscription which gives the names of the Four Sons of Horus who were intended to provide protection, each being associated with a cardinal direction. Lortet and Gaillard (1909, 4.210), as well as Chassinat (1966–1968, 1.46), give an alternative explanation, suggesting that perhaps these balls were symbolic representations of the testicles of Osiris.

The inscriptions on these balls also mention four goddesses: Bastet, Uadjet, Sekhmet and Seshemet. These four deities are usually represented as felines, a form which may be symbolically associated with Osiris in two ways. Firstly, in many Egyptian contexts the lion was not only a symbol of the pharaoh, but also related to the sun god's power to defeat the forces of death (Houlihan 1999, 513–516). Moreover, felines also occur as symbols of resurrection on the funerary beds of the dead and the gods (De Wit 1951, 161–162), and Osiris himself is often depicted as lying on a lion bier. Secondly, the four lion goddesses served as protectors of Osiris. For example, in the temple of Seti I at Abydos, Seshemet is defined as 'destroyer of Osiris' enemies' (Derchain 1971, 17, doc. 7). In the Mammisi of Edfu, the four deities occur together and are invoked as the *bnnt* watching over the god (Chassinat 1939, 2, 1.9–10). Based on the protective role of these four goddesses in various contexts, I suggest that the presence of their names on the four balls placed in the Louvre coffin relates to the protection of Osiris who is symbolised by the corn-mummy.

The protective role of the four balls is further suggested in Brooklyn Museum (NY) Papyrus 47.218.138 (Goyon 1975) where, at the end of a magic formula to protect the king against serpents and reptiles, there is a brief note about a formula to be pronounced on four clay balls. The text reads:

Paroles à prononcer sur quatre boules d'argile. Jeter au sud, au nord, à l'ouest et à l'est. Réciter cette formule: nouée en forme de rouleau de papyrus et placée à son cou, elle le sauvera du désastre sur l'eau et sur terre, (car) c'est une grande protection, en vérité. Tu éviteras que n'importe qui puisse la voir … l'oraison sur les [quatre] boules d'argile qui assurent la protection d'Osiris, afin de détourner Seth et ses complices de tout lieu en qui est Osiris …

(Goyon 1975, 350)

The spell described on this papyrus is similar to the one shown on the lintel above the door of room IV of the Osiris chapel of Taharka at Karnak. Here the king is depicted in front of the Osirian *hn*-cenotaph striking four balls with a special stick in the direction of the four points of the compass (Leclant 1965, pl. 47). Given the apparent protective meanings of these balls in association with the cardinal directions, this scene was probably situated over the doorway for prophylactic purposes.

Further, wholly preserved in Metropolitan Museum Papyrus 35.9.21 (Goyon 1975) is a ritual for the protection of Osiris. The ritual involves the throwing of four balls toward the four points of the compass in order to protect Osiris against his enemies. The formula that must be vocalised on the four balls reads as follows:

> Graver le(s) nom(s) d'Amon et de Montou sur l'une, lancer vers le sud; de Shou et de Tefnout sur une autre, lancer vers le nord; de Neith et d'Ouadjyt sur une autre, lancer vers l'ouest; de Sekhment et Bastet sur une autre, lancer vers l'est.
>
> (Goyon 1975, 398)

Again, four balls associated with the cardinal directions and deities, two of which are also inscribed on the corn-mummy balls, are employed in a ritual for the protection of Osiris.

It is important to note some of the symbolic uses of corn in various periods and contexts in order to understand the possible emblematic connotations of the corn-mummies. In the most remote periods of Egyptian antiquity, wheat and barley were some of the first cereals grown in ancient Egypt (Darby *et al.* 1977, 460). Because of the great importance these products had in the life of Egyptians, from a very early period onwards they seem to have taken on symbolic meanings. Two main symbolic themes can be distinguished. Firstly, corn was regarded as food *par excellence,* and therefore it was related to the general idea of nourishment (Raven 1982, 7). Secondly, as a living substance, the growing cycle of cereals was often related to the cyclical pattern of life and death and often embodied the ideas of renewal and resurrection.

Some of the earliest examples of the symbolic meanings associated with cereals can be traced back to Egyptian Prehistory (Scharff 1947). For example, at the site of Merimda Junker (1930, 47–52) found six burials, dating to *c.*5000 B.C., which contained corn (species not specified) placed on or around the body, and especially in and near the mouth. The corn placed in these burials was not cooked or planted, but was interred in its raw state, causing Junker to suggest that it would have been inappropriate as nourishment for the deceased, therefore any symbolism would not have been associated with food. However, I am inclined to agree with Raven (1982, 9) who believes that because the corn was placed in and near the mouth, it was intended as a symbolic source of food for the deceased.

In the central chamber of the 2nd-dynasty mastaba 2498 at Saqqara, Quibell (1923, 1, 10, 45, pl. 25, 2) discovered a bed-like structure with a large quantity of corn placed in and around it. This corn, which was still in its husk, formed a layer 30 cm thick. Mastaba 2322 contained the same structure, and two rooms both contained a layer of corn (8 cm thick in one case). The corn was then covered by matting and sealed with a layer of mud upon which storage vessels were placed. While these rooms were intended as storerooms for burial equipment, they also seem to have held symbolic meanings related to the concept of corn as part of the provisions for the dead in the afterlife.

Several finds dating to the Middle Kingdom also suggest that corn was a symbol of rebirth and hoped-for rejuvenation. For example, a pottery vessel in the Petrie Museum (UC 45786; Figures 9 and 10) may have been used for the ritual sprouting of corn. The vessel consists of a roughly circular compartment (24.6 cm in diameter) and an elongated oval compartment divided into three sections by a pair of t-shaped dividers. A hole at the base of the circular compartment allowed water to drain into the three compartments and out a central drain hole to the exterior. The circular compartment still contains a dried, round mass of earth with roots and grains of barley preserved at the bottom. Presumably the roots are the remains of grain that was sprouted in the pot. Unfortunately, this find is unprovenanced, and its precise function and meaning remain uncertain.

A clearer example of the symbolic use of grain comes from Thebes where Petrie (1937, 7) found buried pans filled with soil containing the remains of germinated grain which had been buried near the entrance of a tomb. At Lahun, four or five rectangular and oval lumps of mud with traces of sprouted plant remains were discovered near the entrance of the small shaft which gave access to the pyramid of Senusret II (Petrie 1937, 8; Petrie *et al.* 1923, 14, pl. 15, 7). The mud cakes retained the shapes of the pots in which the soil and grain had been placed until the seeds had germinated. Apparently the soil and plants were removed from the pots before deposition. Petrie (1937, 8) suggests that these lumps of soil with grain sprouts were intended to promote the revivification of the dead, and that these finds demonstrate that the dead were regarded as being one with the corn-god Osiris. However, no explicit connection with Osiris is evidenced in the finds themselves.

What distinguishes the Middle Kingdom finds from the apparent symbolic use of corn at Merimda and Saqqara is that in the former case the corn was sown and allowed to germinate before being deposited in a funerary context. However, with reference to the corn-mummies, these Middle Kingdom examples of the probable symbolic use of corn do not provide any clear evidence of links to the cult of Osiris. Nevertheless, the funerary literature of this period contained spells equating the transformation of the dead with that of barley sprouting from the body of Osiris. In CT spell 268, the

Figure 9. View of the ceramic seed pot showing interior and exterior holes for drainage. Petrie Museum of Egyptian Archaeology, UC 45786. (Author's photograph, courtesy of the Petrie Museum of Egyptian Archaeology, University College London. Not to scale.)

Figure 10. View of the ceramic seed pot showing a ball of earth in the circular compartment and section with the t-shaped dividers. Petrie Museum of Egyptian Archaeology, UC 45786. (Author's photograph, courtesy of the Petrie Museum of Egyptian Archaeology, University College London. Not to scale.)

deceased becomes barley and is identified with the life-giving plant growing from the ribs of Osiris and with crops that nourishes humankind and the gods (Faulkner 1973, 205). In CT spell 330 entitled 'Becoming Neper' the deceased is guaranteed not to perish, because he/she has become an integral part of nature. The deceased is said to die and live as Osiris or as emmer, and live and grow as Neper (Faulkner 1973, 254–255). Thus, it seems likely that the practice of placing sprouted grain in the funerary context may have embodied symbolic meanings relating to rebirth and rejuvenation, but the relationship between these practices and the later manufacture and use of corn-mummies is unclear.

Pictorial evidence provides a more explicit connection between sprouting grain and Osiris and his regenerative powers. On the south wall of the Osiris Room at Philae (Bénédite 1893– 1895, 119–127, pls. 35–42), the dead body of Osiris is depicted with long budding stalks sprouting forth from it, and a priest waters the plants from a pitcher which he holds in his hand. The accompanying inscription reads: 'this is the form of whom one may not name, Osiris of the mysteries, who springs from the returning waters' (Bénédite 1893–1895, 119–127, pls. 35–

42). Here the symbolic connection is made clear, that the sprouting of plants from fertile, well-watered soil is equated with the revivification of Osiris. Therefore, in view of the form and contents of the so-called corn-mummies, I suggest that these objects represent a material expression of the concept of life springing from death – just as the new corn springs from the lifeless seed planted in the ground.

Conclusions

In this paper, several corn-mummies have been presented as examples of an important and interesting corpus of artefacts which, as a whole, have not been given sufficient consideration in the past. In the course of this research, I have encountered dozens of objects in Egyptian collections recorded or otherwise identified as 'falcon-mummies' or 'infant mummies' that, after examination, have proven to be corn-mummies. As the above discussion attempts to demonstrate, corn-mummies embody a range of symbolic meanings which centre on Osiris. Sprouting corn was one of the many symbols used to conceptualise the resurrection of Osiris. In addition to grain found in corn-mummies, the materials used for making the objects placed on and beside them, including resin, wax, silver and earth bore symbolic properties related to the supernatural or divine and the achievement of an afterlife and survival therein (Raven 1988). The colours used to decorate the Osirian packages and the coffins in which they were often deposited included black, blue, gold/yellow, red and green; colours which also held symbolic meanings related to concepts of fertility, regeneration and the renewal of life (Lucas 1962, 391–400). Moreover, the sun hymn from the Book of the Dead inscribed on the coffin lids of the Tuna el-Gebel corn-mummies addresses Re-Horakhte-Khepri in his aspect of the youthful sun at dawn bringing new life, thus reinforcing these concepts of rebirth. Together, the various attributes of the corn-mummies, their coffins and other contents, refer to Osiris and thus constitute an emblematic manifestation of rejuvenation and immortality in the next world.

University of Wales Swansea

Acknowledgements

I would like to express my gratitude to my supervisor, Prof. A. B. Lloyd, for his patience and valuable suggestions. I would also like to thank all those who have helped me to locate specimens of corn-mummies, often stored in collections gathering dust. My deepest thanks go to my parents and my friends for their encouragement and support.

References

Allen, T. G. 1960, *The Egyptian Book of the Dead: Documents in the Oriental Institute Museum at the University of Chicago*. University of Chicago Press, Chicago.

Bénédite, G. 1893–1895, *Le temple de Philae*. Leroux, Paris.

Chassinat, É. 1939, *Le mammisi d'Edfou*. Institut français d'archéologie orientale, Cairo.

Chassinat, E. 1966–1968, *Le mystère d'Osiris au mois de Khoiak, 1-2*. Institut français d'archéologie orientale, Cairo.

Darby, W. J., Ghaliounguim, P. and Grivetti, L. 1977, *Food: The gift of Osiris*. Academic Press, London.

Derchain, P. 1971, *El Kab 1: Les monuments religieux à l'entrée de l'ouady Hellal*. Fondation Égyptologique Reine Élisabeth, Brussels.

De Wit, C. 1951, *Le rôle et le sens du lion dans l'Égypte ancienne*. E. J. Brill, Leiden.

Faulkner, R. O. 1973, *The Ancient Egyptian Coffin Texts, 1-3*. Aris and Philips Ltd., Warminster.

Faulkner, R. O. 1985, *The Ancient Egyptian Book of the Dead*. Trustees of the British Museum, London.

Gauthier, H. 1925–1931, *Dictionnaire des noms géographiques contenus dans les textes hiéroglyphiques, 2-3, 5*. Institut français d'archéologie orientale pour la Société royale de géographie d'Égypte, Cairo.

Goyon, J. C. 1975, Les rélévations du mystere des quatre boules, *Bulletin de l'Institut français d'archéologie orientale du Caire* 75, 353–398.

Grimal, N.-C. 1981, *Etudes sur la propagande royale égyptienne 1, La stèle triomphale de Pi ('Ankh)Y au Musee du Caire*. Institut français d'archéologie orientale, Cairo.

Houlihan, P. F. 1999, Felines, in K. A. Bard (ed.), *Encyclopedia of the Archaeology of Ancient Egypt*, 512–516. Routledge, London.

Junker, H. 1930, Vorläufiger Bericht über die zweite Grabung der Akademie der Wissenschaften in Wien auf der vorgeschichtlichen Siedlung Merimde-Benisalâme vom 7.Februar bis 8.April 1930, *Anzeiger der Akademie der Wissenschaften in Wien, Philosophisch-historische Klasse* 5/13, 21–82.

Kessler, D. 1981, *Historische Topographie der Region zwischen Mallawi und Samalut*, 253–290. Reichert, Wiesbaden.

Klosowska, M. J. A. 1997, The Conservation and Technical Examination of Three Corn-mummies at the Archaeological Museum in Cracow, *Materialy Archeologiczne* 30, 17–23.

Kurt, D. 1998, Einige Inschriften auf Särgen des Korn-Osiris, *Göttinger Miszellen* 166, 43–50.

Leclant, J. 1965, *Recherches sur les monuments thébains, 2*. Institut français d'archéologie orientale, Cairo.

Lefebvre, M. G. 1903, Sarcophages égyptiens trouvés dans une nécropole gréco-romaine à Tehneh, *Annales du service des antiquités de l'Égypte* 4, 227–231.

Lortet, L. 1906, Momies de singes et nécropole du dieu Thot, *Bulletin de l'Institut d'Égypte* 4/6, 43–46.

Lortet, L. and Gaillard, C. 1907–1909, *La faune momifiée de l'ancienne Égypte, 2, 4*. Archives de Muséum d'Histoire Naturelle de Lyon, Lyon.

Lucas, A. 1962, *Ancient Egyptian Materials and Industries*. Harris, London.

Petrie, W. M. F. 1937, *Funeral Furniture and Stone Vases*. British School of Egyptian Archaeology, London.

Petrie, W. M. F., Brunton, G. and Murray, M. A. 1923, *Lahun, 2* British School of Archaeology in Egypt, London.

Quibell, J. E. 1923, *Excavations at Saqqara, 1912–1914: Archaic mastabas*. Institut francais d'archéologie orientale, Cairo.

Raven, M. J. 1978–1979, Papyrus-sheaths and Ptah-Sokar-Osiris Statues, *Oudheidkundige Mededelingen iut het Rijksmuseum van Oudheden te Leiden* 59/60, 251–296.

Raven, M. J. 1982, Corn-mummies, *Oudheidkundige Mededelingen iut het Rijksmuseum van Oudheden te Leiden* 63, 7–33.

Raven, M. J. 1988, Magic and Symbolic Aspects of Certain Materials in Ancient Egypt, *Varia Aegyptiaca* 4, 237–242.

Scharff, A. 1947, Frühe Vorstufen zu "Kornosiris", *Forschungen und Fortschritte* 21/23, 38–39.

Taylor, J. H. 2001, *Death and the Afterlife in Ancient Egypt*. British Museum Press, London.

Vandier, J. 1961, *Papyrus Jumilhac*. Centre National de la Recherche Scientifique, Paris.

Wasylikova, K. and Jankun, A. 1997, Identification of Barley from the Ancient Egyptian Corn-mummies in the Archaeological Museum in Cracow, *Materialy Archeologiczne* 30, 13–15.

Yoyotte, J. 1963, Études géographiques, 2: Les localités méridionales, *Revue de l'Égyptologie* 15, 98–104.

Ziegler, C. 1979, À propos du rite des quatre boules, *Bulletin de l'Institut français d'archéologie orientale du Caire* 79, 437–439.

The Lisbon Mummy Project: The employment of non-destructive methods in mummy studies

Álvaro Figueiredo

Introduction

During research in Lisbon for a PhD (Institute of Archaeology, University College London) on the palaeoepidemiology of Roman period (30 B.C.E.–395 C.E.) populations in Portugal and Egypt, I became aware of the fact that the Egyptian mummies in the Museu Nacional de Arqueologia (MNA) had never been the subject of a comprehensive study. Although their present display in the mummification section of the Egyptian Rooms of the Museum resulted in the study of the objects associated with them (*i.e.* cartonnage coffins and linen shrouds), a basic scientific examination of the specimens, such as standard X-ray analysis, was never carried out. This situation called for the urgent creation of a research project to study the mummies. Following the example of similar studies (David and Tapp 1992; Harris and Wente 1980; Melcher *et al.* 1997; Taylor 1995), and inspired by the pioneering work carried out by the team of the Manchester Museum Mummy Project (David 1979), such a project has been created. The Lisbon Mummy Project will have a multidisciplinary approach in the study of the human and animal mummies, and their associated artefacts, and will employ non-destructive analytical methods. The Project will include international specialists from the MNA, the Institute of Archaeology (University College London), Instituto Português de Arqueologia (Lisbon), the British Museum (London), the American University in Cairo and the University of L'Aquila (Italy).

Methods and aims of the project

The research methodologies to be employed in this study will be non-destructive and will rely primarily on the radiographic examination of the specimens. This will be achieved through the use of conventional flat plate radiography and computed axial tomography to derive the maximum possible information concerning sex, age, stature, biological affinity, dietary reconstruction and palaeopathology. Radiography will allow visual access to the interior of the mummies without the need to unwrap or dissect them, and the restricted use of endoscopy will permit sampling of human tissue and embalming materials from the interior of the bodies. These will then be prepared for histological, genetic, palaeobotanical and radiocarbon analyses.

The cultural context of human and animal mummification will be addressed, whilst conservation and stabilisation of the mummies and associated artefacts will also take place. Finally, the project aims to promote the understanding of the bioarchaeology of ancient Egypt amongst the scientific community and the wider public. To achieve this we hope to present the results of the Lisbon Mummy Project in a series of research articles and through the organisation of a conference and exhibition.

The historical background of the collection

The Museu Nacional de Arqueologia houses an important collection of Egyptian antiquities collected by various travellers to Egypt during the 19th and early 20th centuries (Araújo 1987; 1990–1992; 1993–1994; Guedes 1993–1994). In 1909, the Museum director, Leite de Vasconcelos, attended the World Archaeological Congress in Cairo and returned with various artefacts (including prehistoric stone tools and Graeco-Roman ceramics) presented to him by Evaristo Breccia (Dawson and Uphill 1995, 63), the director of the Graeco-Roman Museum in Alexandria. These objects formed the beginnings of the Egyptian Collection, which was subsequently greatly enlarged with the addition of objects acquired by Queen Amelia of Portugal during her visit to Egypt (Figure 1) and Palestine in 1903.

Figure 1. The Portuguese Royal party at Giza, 1903. Queen Amelia can be seen in the centre of the group, seated on a camel. The men in uniform are staff of the Portuguese Consulate in Cairo. (Photograph courtesy of the Museu Nacional de Arqueologia.)

Whilst in Cairo, she was the guest of Khedive Abbas Hilmi II, who presented the royal party with a gift of Egyptian antiquities for the King of Portugal's private collection. With the declaration of the Portuguese Republic in October 1910, ownership of this collection reverted to the state, eventually finding its way to the MNA. Gifts from private collections – especially those belonging to the last Duke of Palmela – added considerably to the Museum's collection of Egyptian antiquities.

At present, the Museum has 560 artefacts of Egyptian provenance, representing all the main phases of ancient Egyptian civilisation (Araújo 1993). Of these, around 300 objects are exhibited in the Egyptian Rooms of the Museum, making it the largest collection of its kind in Portugal. The exhibition, arranged according to subject (*e.g.* sculpture, daily life and funerary), displays objects of a highly diverse nature, ranging in time from the Prehistoric to the Coptic Periods. Whilst flint tools represent the Mesolithic, objects such as palettes, pottery, mace heads and flint knives illustrate the Predynastic Period (*c.*5000–3050 B.C.E.). There are also a number of stone vases, pottery and objects of daily use, such as footwear, combs and jewellery dating from the Old Kingdom (2663–2195 B.C.E.) to the New Kingdom (1550–1069 B.C.E.). Funerary relief sculpture and various pieces of statuary dating from the Middle Kingdom (2066–1650 B.C.E.) to the New Kingdom are also exhibited, together with some interesting examples of wooden funerary models dated to the First Intermediate Period (2195–2066 B.C.E.) and Middle Kingdom (2066–1650 B.C.E.), as well as wooden funerary statuettes dating from the Late Period (525–323 B.C.E.) and Ptolemaic Period (304–30 B.C.E.). Coffins, coffin fragments, canopic equipment, inscribed funerary cones, scarabs, ushabtis and amulets, together with the mummies, complete the section on funerary practices. A number of Late Period bronzes also form part of the collection. The Ptolemaic Period is represented by objects such as votive stelae, terracotta figurines, pottery, glass and coins. The exhibition of the collection ends with Coptic period (after 395 C.E.) pottery, ostraca, papyri and textiles.

Materials of study

As for the focus of the Lisbon Mummy Project, it will examine the Museum's entire collection of ancient Egyptian mummified remains, which comprises two human and six animal mummies, as well as a sandstone canopic vessel containing organic matter. One of the human mummies (MNA 217; Figure 2), is enclosed in a painted cartonnage coffin characteristic of the Third Intermediate Period (1070–712 B.C.E.), probably belonging to the 22nd Dynasty (948–743 B.C.E.). The deceased is identified by the name Irtierw, at the end of an *ḥtp dí nsw* inscription painted vertically along the front of the coffin between its legs.

The head of the anthropoid coffin wears a large black wig, framing the face which is painted red-brown and once wore a false beard (now lost). A large floral pectoral is depicted on the chest and shoulders. The body of the coffin is covered with representations of funerary deities arranged horizontally and painted on a white background. The upper portion shows a stylised representation of the Osiris sanctuary at Abydos surmounted by the winged solar disc, crowned by two *kachuti* plumes. On both sides of the sanctuary are represented, in two registers, the deities responsible for the protection of the body and its internal organs. In the upper register to the left are Isis and Selqet, and on the opposite side, Nephthys and Neith. Thoth is represented in the second register on the left, followed by Imseti and Duamutef, and opposite Horus who is followed by Hapy and Qebehsenuef. They all face towards the sanctuary in adoration. In the middle of the coffin is a large representation of a falcon with outstretched wings. The vertical inscription that stretches from this point down to the area between the feet of the coffin is surrounded on either side by large winged figures of Isis and

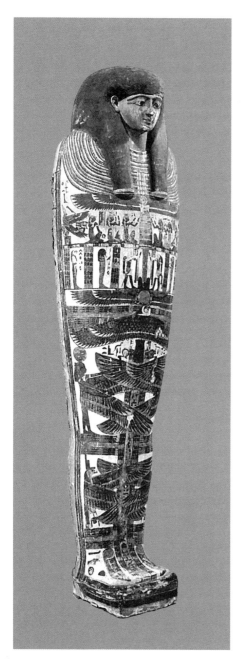

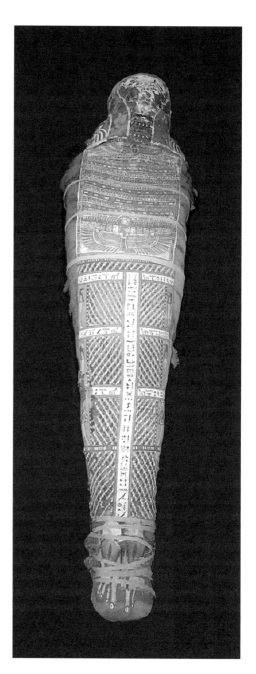

Figure 2. The cartonnage coffin of Irtierw dated to the Third Intermediate Period (1070–712 B.C.E.), provenance unknown. MNA 217. (Photograph courtesy of the Museu Nacional de Arqueologia.)

Figure 3. Mummy dated to the Ptolemaic Period (304–30 B.C.E.), provenance unknown. MNA 215. (Photograph courtesy of the Museu Nacional de Arqueologia.)

Nephthys, first in human and then in bird form. The foot base of the coffin was closed by a wooden board with a painted representation of the Apis bull in its centre. This has now been removed and is undergoing restoration. The back of the coffin is almost entirely covered by a large *djed* pillar, painted on a white background and surmounted by the upper portion of the body of Osiris. The hieroglyphic inscription identifies him as 'Osiris, Lord of Busiris'.

The second human mummy (MNA 215, Figure 3) is an unnamed individual bearing a cartonnage mask and dates to the Ptolemaic Period. It is still fully wrapped in linen bandages with a painted linen shroud decorated with a short *ḥtp dí nsw* inscription and representations of Isis, Nephthys and the Four Sons of Horus. The external wrappings are damaged in the area of the right shoulder and feet.

The canopic vase (MNA 221–222, Figure 4), made of sandstone with traces of black paint, dates to the early Late Period. Its human-headed lid represents Imseti, one of the Four Sons of Horus. With the lid, it measures approximately 26.5 cm in height; the middle of the vessel is about 13 cm in width. Organic material of a black appearance, probably the remains of internal organs, is still preserved in the interior of the vessel.

The animal specimens consist of four juvenile crocodile mummies and two bird mummies. One of the crocodile specimens (MNA 231) still has some resin-impregnated linen bandages intact, while the other three (MNA 232, 233 and 234) appear to have been unwrapped in the recent past. They date to the Ptolemaic and Roman Periods and may have come from Kom Ombo, a cult centre dedicated to the crocodile god Sobek.

The bird mummies include a wrapped falcon (MNA 230, Figure 5), and a sealed pottery coffin (MNA 235) that probably contains an ibis. The falcon mummy, which dates from the Late or Ptolemaic Period, has lost part of its outer wrappings and seems to have been mummified in a standing position, in a manner resembling representations of Horus and other bird deities. The pottery coffin resembles specimens from the catacombs at Tuna el-Gebel (Hermopolis), which – like the ibis itself – were sacred to the god Thoth (El-Mahdy 1989, 162; Ikram and Dodson 1998, 135–136).

Radiographic analysis

Petrie (1898, pl. 37) was the first Egyptologist to examine Egyptian mummies using radiography. This approach became more common from the 1960s onwards (Dawson and Gray 1968; Gray 1973), culminating in the work on the royal mummies in the Egyptian Museum, Cairo (Harris and Wente 1980), and the Manchester Mummy Project (David 1979; Isherwood *et al.* 1979; 1984). Radiography allows for the examination of the interior of a mummy without the need to unwrap or dissect it and usually provides valuable bioarchaeological and cultural information about the specimen.

The first step of the Lisbon Mummy Project involves the X-raying (conventional flat plate radiography) of the human and animal mummies. Since both human mummies are still fully wrapped, the X-ray plates will reveal the bodies' internal arrangements, state of preservation and the presence of objects – such as amulets and pectoral ornaments – located within the wrappings or the body cavity. Computed axial tomography (CT) will then be used to obtain detailed information about the mummies' interior. These images will give detailed information on the nature of the cartonnage, linen bandaging, body packing, embalming substances (such as resin), amulets, soft tissue, organ packages (if present) and the skeleton (Brown and Wood

1999; Filer 1997; 1998; 2002; Melcher *et al.* 1997; Pickering *et al.* 1990; Ruhli and Boni 2000; Stanworth *et al.* 1986). Information on the presence of embalmer's incisions, subcutaneous packing, removal of the brain, position of the arms, the use of artificial eyes (Gray 1971; 1972; Ikram and Dodson 1998) and organ packages inside the body will also be investigated. This information

Figure 4. Sandstone canopic vessel (7th/6th century B.C.E.), provenance unknown. MNA 221–222. (Photograph courtesy of the Museu Nacional de Arqueologia. Not to scale.)

is important as mummy preparation methods can provide valuable data on the social status of the individuals, as well as their age and date. Past CT studies have also been able to determine if a body was restored in antiquity, as was sometimes necessary after damage due to disturbances such as tomb robbing (David 1979; Tapp 1979).

Figure 5. Falcon mummy. Late Period (525–332 B.C.E.) or Ptolemaic (304–30 B.C.E.), provenance unknown. MNA 230. (Photograph courtesy of the Museu Nacional de Arqueologia. Not to scale.)

Individuals will be sexed on the basis of pelvic and cranial morphology (Buikstra and Ubelaker 1994), although if genitalia are preserved, these will be visible in CT scans. Age estimates will be determined using standard methods (Buikstra and Ubelaker 1994), while stature will also be estimated from the X-rays and CT scans. CT scans also permit the study of dental pathology, developmental disorders, bone trauma, parasite infection, physical abnormalities and other indicators of health or disease.

It is anticipated that the high resolution of CT images (Brown and Wood 1999) will permit the detection of parasites, such as *Schistosoma haematobium* which has been identified in the kidneys (Ruffer 1910) and bladder (Isherwood *et al.* 1979) of mummified remains, and skeletal lesions caused by certain diseases (Sandison and Tapp 1998); all without the need to unwrap or dissect the remains.

Endoscopic examination and contents of the canopic vessel

The interior of a mummified body may also be examined using endoscopes (Tapp and Wildsmith 1986; 1992; Tapp *et al.* 1984), which can be inserted into a body through natural orifices and *post-mortem* damage (*e.g.* embalmer's incisions), although this is only possible if such openings are exposed and accessible. This technique is inappropriate for the mummy of Irtierw as it is still fully wrapped and encased in cartonnage (Figure 2). Endoscopy will therefore only be used for the Ptolemaic mummy (Figure 3), as access to the thorax and possibly the abdomen can be obtained through a breach in the wrappings over the right shoulder. In addition to providing an opportunity to examine the body's interior, endoscopic techniques also permit the removal of small tissue samples for further analysis (Tapp 1992; Tapp and Wildsmith 1986). Mummified tissue can be re-hydrated and stained for detailed analysis by both light and scanning electron microscopy (Curry *et al.* 1979; Lewin and Cutz 1976), while immunological tests may also reveal the presence of specific antigens such as those responsible for schistosomiasis and malaria (Deelder *et al.* 1990; Miller *et al.* 1993; Taylor 1995). Samples of embalming agents (such as resin) and packing materials (such as sawdust, linen and mud) may also be retrieved for further study. Insects may also be present, such as the remains of carrion beetles (*Dermestes frischii* and *Dermestes ater*) as found in previous studies (Curry 1979; Taylor 1995), which may provide information on the duration of exposure before mummification. Finally, the analysis of pollen samples and plant remains may assist in determining the season of the individual's death.

Histological (Tapp 1992) and chemical techniques will be employed in identifying the contents of the canopic jar (Figure 4). According to the iconography of the lid (representing the human-headed Imseti), remains of a mummified liver package should be found inside. However, while the four organ packages – placed in canopic vessels or inside the body – ought to contain the remains of the liver, lungs, stomach and intestines, previous research indicates that the contents do not always correspond to the correct organ package. For example, of the four packages found within a mummy (PUM II) in the University of Pennsylvania Museum of Archaeology and Anthropology (Cockburn *et al.* 1998), three contained pieces of lung, while the fourth contained a mixture of intestine and spleen.

The animal mummies

While there were numerous motives for ancient Egyptian animal mummification (Ikram and Dodson 1998, 131–136), the animal remains in the Lisbon collection seem to have been mummified as votive offerings. From the Late Period onwards several animal species were mummified at special cult centres and bought by pilgrims who offered the mummies to the gods. These were buried in catacomb-like structures sacred to the deity with whom they were associated, the practice becoming especially popular during the Ptolemaic and Roman Periods. It has been estimated that around 10,000 birds were buried annually in the bird catacombs at Saqqara (Aufderheide 2003, 399–400; Ikram and Dodson 1998, 135), while the catacombs at Tuna el-Gebel are thought to contain over four million bird burials (El-Mahdy 1989, 162).

The animal mummies in the Lisbon collection will also be studied using the same range of techniques applied to the human specimens in order to accurately determine species, as well as additional information such as age, pathology and cause of death (Filer 1995). The latter is especially important since it is now generally accepted that some of the animal species that were presented as votive offerings, were reared, killed and mummified especially to serve that ritual purpose.

Mummification techniques will also be addressed, with particular attention being paid to the bird mummies as previous studies have shown some of these to be 'fakes', containing only a few bones, feathers, reeds, wood, or even pottery (Ikram and Dodson 1998, 135–136). In such cases, the elaborate external wrappings were made up to look like the mummy of a bird.

Conservation

One of the main aims of the project entails the stabilisation and conservation of the mummified tissues and associated materials. Intervention will take place only where it is deemed necessary by the team of conservators, and consideration will be given to the reversibility of any process carried out. Work will begin with a general assessment of the state of preservation of the materials before handling by the team. Both human mummies will require conservation before being returned to their exhibition cases. The cartonnage coffin of Irtierw needs particular attention. In the recent past a cut was made along the sides and across the back of the coffin in order to gain access to the mummy in its interior. The wooden board covering the foot end of the coffin has also become separated and, as mentioned above, has already been removed for conservation. Once the radiographic study is complete, the board will be returned to its original position.

The Ptolemaic mummy also needs urgent conservation to its outer wrappings, which have suffered damage around the area of the right shoulder and feet. Some elements – the tarsals – have become detached and have been stored separately. During conservation they will be returned to their original position in the mummy. The condition of the textiles will be assessed, and where there are areas of deterioration that may suffer further damage, these may be repaired with a supportive textile backing.

Conclusion

Outlined in the present paper are the main research objectives of the Lisbon Mummy Project. By employing a combination of non-destructive analytical techniques, coupled with a limited range of invasive techniques, the project will provide the maximum possible information concerning each individual's life history, as well as the cultural aspects surrounding the practice of human and animal mummification in ancient Egypt. Although not original (this work is inspired by and closely follows previous research projects in the field of mummy studies), the project is innovative in the sense that it is the first of its kind ever to be carried out in Portugal, and will provide a framework for future research projects on mummy studies. The results of the Lisbon Mummy Project will be made available to the scientific community and wider public, and through them we hope to make a valuable contribution to the understanding of the bioarchaeology of ancient Egypt.

Institute of Archaeology, UCL

Acknowledgements

I would like to thank Dr. Luis Raposo, Director of the Museu Nacional de Arqueologia, for his continuing support of the Lisbon Mummy Project, and the Fundação para a Ciência e a Tecnologia (Portugal). Thanks are also due to my colleagues and team members, Daniel Antoine and Lawrence Owens, for their useful comments on sections of this paper.

References

Araújo, L. M. 1987, A colecção de antiguidades egípcias do Museu Nacional de Arqueologia e Etnologia, *O Arqueólogo Português* 5, 241–257.

Araújo, L. M. 1990–1992, Cinco cones funerários egípcios no Museu Nacional de Arqueologia, *O Arqueólogo Português* 8/10, 341–355.

Araújo, L. M. 1993, *Antiguidades Egípcias, I*. Museu Nacional de Arqueologia, Lisbon.

Araújo, L. M. 1993–1994, Paletas egípcias pré-dinásticas do Museu Nacional de Arqueologia, *O Arqueólogo Português* 11/12, 391–402.

Aufderheide, A. C. 2003, *The Scientific Study of Mummies*. Cambridge University Press, Cambridge.

Brown, K. R. and Wood, H. 1999, The Utility of Minimal CT Scanning in the Study of Two Egyptian Mummy Heads, *International Journal of Osteoarchaeology* 9, 199–204.

Buikstra, J. E. and Ubelaker, D. H. 1994, *Standards for Data Collection from Human Skeletal Remains*. Arkansas Archaeological Survey, Fayetteville, Arkansas.

Cockburn, A., Barraco, R. A., Peck, W. H. and Reyman, T. A. 1998, A Classic Mummy: PUM II, in A. Cockburn, E. Cockburn and T. A. Reyman (eds.), *Mummies, Disease and Ancient Cultures*, 69–90. Cambridge University Press, Cambridge.

Curry, A. 1979, The Insects Associated with the Manchester Mummies, in A. R. David (ed.), *The Manchester Museum Mummy Project*, 113–118. Manchester University Press, Manchester.

Curry, A., Anfield, C. and Tapp, E. 1979, Electron Microscopy of the Manchester Mummies, in A. R. David (ed.), *The Manchester Museum Mummy Project*, 103–111. Manchester University Press, Manchester.

David, A. R. (ed.), 1979, *The Manchester Museum Mummy Project*. Manchester University Press, Manchester.

David, A. R. and Tapp, E. (eds.), 1992, *The Mummy's Tale*: *The scientific and medical investigation of Natsef-Amun, priest in the temple of Karnak*. Manchester University Press, Manchester.

Dawson, W. R. and Gray, P. H. K. 1968, *Catalogue of Egyptian Antiquities in the British Museum 1: Mummies and human remains*. British Museum Press, London.

Dawson, W. R. and Uphill, E. P. 1995, *Who Was Who in Egyptology* (3rd ed., revised by M. L. Bierbrier). Egypt Exploration Society, London.

Deelder, A. M., Miller, R. L., de Jonge, N. and Krijger, F. W. 1990, Detection of Schistosome Antigen in Mummies, *Lancet* 335, 724-725.

El-Mahdy, C. 1989, *Mummies, Myth and Magic in Ancient Egypt*. Thames and Hudson, London.

Filer, J. M. 1995, Attitudes to Death with Reference to Cats in Ancient Egypt, in S. Campbell and A. Green (eds.), *The Archaeology of Death in the Ancient Near East*, 38–40. Oxford, Oxbow Books.

Filer, J. M. 1997, Revealing Hermione's Secrets, *Egyptian Archaeology* 11, 32–34.

Filer, J. M. 1998, Revealing the Face of Artemidorus, *Minerva* 9.4, 21–24.

Filer, J. M. 2002, Ancient Bodies, but Modern Techniques: The utilisation of CT scanning in the study of ancient Egyptian mummies, in R. Arnott (ed.), *The Archaeology of Medicine*, 33–40. Oxford, Archaeopress.

Gray, P. H. K. 1971, Artificial Eyes in Mummies, *Journal of Egyptian Archaeology* 57, 125–126.

Gray, P. H. K. 1972, Notes Concerning the Position of the Arms and Hands of Mummies with a View to Possible Dating of the Specimen, *Journal of Egyptian Archaeology* 58, 200–204.

Gray, P. H. K. 1973, The Radiography of Mummies of Ancient Egyptians, *Journal of Human Evolution* 2, 51–53.

Guedes, N. C. 1993–1994, A múmia Ptolemaica do Museu Nacional de Arqueologia, memória do Museu de História Natural do Marquês de Angeja, *O Arqueólogo Português* 11/12, 367–390.

Harris, J. E. and Wente, E. F. (eds.), 1980, *An X-ray Atlas of the Royal Mummies*. University of Chicago Press, Chicago.

Ikram, S. and Dodson, A. 1998, *The Mummy in Ancient Egypt: Equipping the dead for eternity*. Thames and Hudson, London.

Isherwood, I., Fawcitt, R. A. and Jarvis, H. 1984, X-raying the Manchester Mummies, in A. R. David and E. Tapp (eds.), *Evidence Embalmed*, 45–64. Manchester University Press, Manchester.

Isherwood, I., Jarvis, H. and Fawcitt, R. A. 1979, Radiology of the Manchester Mummies, in A. R. David (ed.), *The Manchester Museum Mummy Project*, 25–64. Manchester University Press, Manchester.

Lewin, P. K. and Cutz, E. 1976, Electron Microscopy of Ancient Egyptian Skin, *British Journal of Dermatology* 94, 573–576.

Melcher, A. H., Holowka, S., Pharoah, M. and Lewin, P. K. 1997, Non-Invasive Computed Tomography and Three-Dimensional Reconstruction of the Dentition of a 2,800 Year Old Egyptian Mummy Exhibiting Extensive Dental Disease, *American Journal of Physical Anthropology* 103, 329–340.

Miller, R. L., De Jonge, N., Krijger, F. W. and Deedler, A. M. 1993, Predynastic Schistosomiasis, in W. V. Davies and A. M. Walker (eds.), *Biological Anthropology and the Study of Ancient Egypt*, 54–60. British Museum Press, London.

Petrie, W. M. F. 1898, *Deshasheh 1897*. Egypt Exploration Fund, London.

Pickering, R. B., Conces, D. J., Braunstein, E. M. and Yurco, F. 1990, 3-Dimensional Computed Tomography of the Mummy Wenuhotep, *American Journal of Physical Anthropology* 83, 49–55.

Ruffer, M. A. 1910, Note on the Presence of Bilharzia Haematobia in Egyptian Mummies of the Twentieth Dynasty (1250–1000 B.C.), *British Medical Journal* 1, 16.

Ruhli, F. J. and Boni, T. 2000, Radiological Aspects and Interpretation of Post-Mortem Artefacts in Ancient Egyptian Mummies from Swiss Collections, *International Journal of Osteoarchaeology* 10, 153–157.

Sandison, A. T. and Tapp, E. 1998, Disease in Ancient Egypt, in A. Cockburn, E. Cockburn, and T. A. Reyman (eds.), *Mummies, Disease and Ancient Cultures*, 38–58. Cambridge University Press, Cambridge.

Stanworth, P., Wildsmith, K. and Tapp, E. 1986, A Neurosurgical Look Inside the Manchester Mummy Heads, in A. R. David (ed.), *Science in Egyptology*, 371–374. Manchester University Press, Manchester.

Tapp, E. 1979, The Unwrapping of a Mummy, in A. R. David (ed.), *The Manchester Museum Mummy Project*, 83–94. Manchester University Press, Manchester.

Tapp, E. 1992, The Histological Examination of Mummified Tissue, in A. R. David and E. Tapp (eds.), *The Mummy's Tale: The scientific and medical investigation of Natsef-Amun, priest in the temple of Karnak*, 121–131. Manchester University Press, Manchester.

Tapp, E. and Wildsmith, K. 1986, Endoscopy of Egyptian Mummies, in A. R. Davis (ed.), *Science in Egyptology*, 351–356. Manchester University Press, Manchester.

Tapp, E. and Wildsmith, K. 1992, The Autopsy and Endoscopy of the Leeds Mummy, in A. R. David and E. Tapp (eds.), *The Mummy's Tale: The scientific and medical investigation of Natsef-Amun, priest in the temple of Karnak*, 132–153. Manchester University Press, Manchester.

Tapp, E., Stanworth, P. and Wildsmith, K. 1984, The Endoscope in Mummy Research, in A. R. David and E. Tapp (eds.), *Evidence Embalmed*, 65–77. Manchester University Press, Manchester.

Taylor, J. H. 1995, *Unwrapping a Mummy: The life and death of Horemkenesi*. British Museum Press, London.

Plying the Nile: Not all plain sailing

Angus Graham

Introduction

It is often asserted that travel on the Nile within the valley in ancient Egypt was straightforward (Vinson 1994, 7). The prevailing wind from the north or north-west meant sails could be used to propel vessels southwards/upstream, and vessels travelled northwards with the aid of the current and oars – a view often supported by the Pharaonic terms 𓏏𓏏𓏏𓈖𓏭 *ḫnti* 'to sail upstream or southwards' and 𓂋𓏭 *ḫdi* 'to travel downstream or northwards' (Faulkner 1962, 195, 199; Gardiner 1957, 498–499). The so-called Qena bend and cataracts are usually cited as the only areas of difficulty in journeying on the Nile (Kees 1961, 98–99; Vinson 1994, 7–8). It has been suggested that either time-consuming traversing or laborious rowing was required to navigate the stretch of river from Nag' Hammadi to Qena (Kainopolis) (Kees 1961, 99). In the case of the cataracts, the various methods employed throughout history to overcome these obstacles are well documented; from dragging up the rapids, to canals and even a slip-way several kilometres in length (Roccati 1982, 185, 197; Vandersleyen 1971; Vercoutter *et al.* 1970, 13–15).

The evidence for travel on the Nile from the Pharaonic, Ptolemaic, Roman and Byzantine Periods, as well as evidence from the early modern travellers from the 16th to the end of the 19th centuries, will be explored in order to dispel this notion that – except for the two issues mentioned – travel on the Nile in the Dynastic Period was uncomplicated. The evidence also demonstrates that many of the difficulties experienced in the Pharaonic Period remained real into modern times.

In December 1873, Amelia Edwards experienced the disdain of her boat's captain as her party chose to forgo the opportunity of travelling upon a favourable wind to stay a further night at el-Bedrashein. As they were about to depart the following morning, the wind fell to calm and the only way to make progress was by tracking, with nine crew harnessed to a rope and towing the boat against the current from the river bank (Edwards 1877, 107–108). The following morning the wind was a southerly one and the crew tracked up to Beni Suef, from where they struggled against a strong current and a head wind to haul the boat round the bend in the river and keep the *dahabiyah* off the bank with punting poles. "Driven back again and again, but still resolute, our sailors, by dint of sheer doggedness, get us round the bad corner at last" (Edwards 1877, 113). This tough day for the crew was followed by a night where local guards slept soundly on the bank of the Nile while both the boats were boarded by a man swimming up to the boats only to be fired upon and chased away by the crew (Edwards 1877, 113–114). For the following "three days and nights the adverse wind continued to blow with such force that the men could not even track against it". One of these three days saw them experience their first sandstorm that "tore the river into angry waves and blotted out the landscape as it came" (Edwards 1877, 114–115). At Luxor a stormy night saw the collapse of:

> … a huge slice of the bank … thundering like an avalanche upon [their] decks; whereupon Reïs Hassan, being alarmed for the safety of the boat, hauled us up to a little sheltered nook a few hundred yards higher. Taking it altogether, we had not had such a lively night since leaving Benisouef!
>
> (Edwards 1877, 229)

Edwards' vivid description encapsulates some of the difficulties to be discussed. This paper will investigate two main aspects: the physical environment, namely the weather, annual cycle and morphology of the Nile, and how these were addressed through social organisation and human toil. Secondly, human intervention is examined in the shape of crime and corruption and the measures put in place to prevent and control them.

Physical Environment

(a) Winds and storms

Thunderstorms in modern Egypt are infrequent. The Mediterranean coast is the most susceptible with the highest incidence occurring in the area of Alexandria. It has an average of seven days of thunderstorms per year, whilst at Cairo it is 1.8 days on average every year, and at Aswan thunderstorms occur on average one day every 10 years. Although the frequency is low, these thunderstorms can be very violent and accompanied by heavy rainfall and hail (Griffiths and Soliman 1972, 88).

The modern climate should not be used as direct evidence of the climate during the Pharoanic and the other periods under discussion as numerous studies have discussed the climatological changes and cycles that have occurred during the Holocene period that affected Egypt (*e.g.* Hassan and Stucki 1987, 44–46; Petite-Maire *et al.* 1997, 299). They do, however, remain instructive and it appears that storms in ancient times may have been similarly infrequent. One particular violent storm is the subject of a stele found at Karnak dated to the reign of Ahmose (Vandersleyen 1967, 133, 155–157). The Pharaonic sources reveal an ambivalent attitude towards storms. They were seen as a metaphor for the strength of the king, and wind and hail were described in the Pyramid Texts as aiding the deceased king's ascent to the sky (Verhoeven 1986, 860). Conversely, they were also a metaphor for danger and confusion (Verhoeven 1986, 860). The reality was that storms could cause serious damage to ships.

The Ptolemaic text P. Magd. 37+11 (W. Chr. 442) describes a grain ship travelling to Thebes that was caught in a storm at Aphroditopolis (Atfih) and lost its yards. It then had to be towed with great difficulty into the harbour of Arsinoe (Medinet el-Fayum) (Vinson 1998, 40, 155–156). Still worse, in P. Hibeh I, 38 (252–251 B.C.E.), a ship is recorded as listing and then sinking during a storm near the harbour of Aphroditopolis (Grenfell and Hunt 1906, 179–180). According to Vinson (1998, 40), the 26th-ynasty demotic text P. Berlin P13615 mentions a wrecked ship during an expedition to Nubia in the reign of Amasis.

Turning to the climatic normal, it is commonly argued that the prevailing wind was from the north or north-west (Degas 1994, 144; Hurst 1952, 173), and this has been explained by the weather systems and the fact that the wind is channelled down the Nile Valley (Besançon 1957, 19). Degas (1994, figs. 5–7) reveals a more complex picture of wind direction, but then glosses over these in his attempt to show the feasibility of Herodotus' (II.9) generally disputed description of a journey from Memphis to Thebes in only nine days (Lloyd 1976, 57–59).

The climatological records of the 20th century show a complex picture of wind direction that varies according to place, time of day and year (Ministry of Public Works

1922; 1938). Records of el-Minya from 1907 to 1934 support the notion of a dominant northerly wind, from 31% in February to 56% in September. If we add to this the north-easterly and north-westerly winds, we have means ranging from 73% in February to almost 99% of all winds in September coming from these directions. It was rarely calm at el-Minya and the monthly mean force of these winds varied from about 5 to 12 km/h (Ministry of Public Works 1938, xi, 51). Many of these winds would have provided slow progress against a current velocity of over 6 km/h during the inundation and of about three km/h during the dry months (Willcocks 1904, 16, 121). Besançon (1957, 19) states that in the summer the winds are quiet until mid-morning and reach up to 20 km/h in the afternoon. This would affect when travel was undertaken during any one day.

At other places the normals do not present such a supporting picture. At Helwan the south-westerly, southerly and south-easterly winds accounted for one third of all wind during the months of December and January from 1904 to 1934 (Ministry of Public Works 1938, 43). At 8 a.m. during the months of November to February one would have experienced a southerly wind on average every fourth day at Beni Suef in the early 1900s (Ministry of Public Works 1938, 49). At Asyut the westerly wind dominates for 11 months of the year closely followed by the north-westerly wind (Ministry of Public Works 1938, 53). The *khamsin*, a wind from the Sahara, made travel both difficult and potentially dangerous. It occurs from March to early June and is caused by depressions moving eastwards along the North African coast or the southern Mediterranean. These draw the hot, dry air from the Sahara to the coast and generally affect Lower Egypt, but can also traverse Middle Egypt. They normally reach a speed of 45 km/h and are laden with dust and sometimes sand (Besançon 1957, 19–20; Giles 2003; Hurst 1952, 171). A *khamsin* recorded in March 1946, which uprooted trees and sank a number of boats in the Nile, reached a speed of 100 km/h (Besançon 1957, 20). These recent climatological records are again only indicative of the variability of winds in ancient Egypt.

In Pharaonic times the language not only included words for the four winds from the north, east, south and west (Kurth 1986, 1267), but also for the favourable wind, *mꜣꜥw* (Erman and Grapow 1928, 23,15) and the head wind, *sbjt* (Erman and Grapow 1930, 89,1). From as early as the Old Kingdom tomb scenes, we have examples of commands to the crew to steer the vessel with the wind (Erman 1919, 55–56). The four cardinal winds each had different attributes and qualities and none is associated with evil (Kurth 1986, 1266–1267; see also Kemboly this volume, 91–93, 101-102). Captains and crew may have called upon various gods associated with the creation of the different winds to aid their journey and to Amun who had the ability to drive back the adverse wind (Derchain-Urtel 1984, 756; Kurth 1986, 1268).

Many travellers in the Roman Period mention adverse weather conditions when they travelled. P. Oxy. XIV. 1682 is a letter from the 4th century C.E. from a man to his 'sister' stating that since her departure the winds have been against them and that he is now sending someone with the letter to enquire of her journey and safety (Grenfell and Hunt 1920, 143–144).

What is known is that wind is channelled by valleys. Wind channelling has been observed in various geomorphological environments from straits (Overland 1984) to valleys, as well as anthropogenic environments such as so-called 'urban canyons' produced by parallel rows of buildings. Studies of the effects of airflow on urban canyons suggest that when the wind direction is oblique to the canyon axis, within-canyon flow is influenced considerably by an induced flow along the canyon (Johnson and Hunter 1999,

3998). Numerous factors contribute to the channelling effect, not least the valley geometry with the width of the valley, height and steepness of the valley sides being important factors, together with the angle of the valley to the wind and the strength of the wind (Egger 1988, 104, 106, 108; Johnson and Hunter 1999, 3998). I would suggest that the Nile valley channels the wind to a certain degree and that this varies locally according to the various factors mentioned, for example the Eocene limestone cliffs rising to 200–500 m between Esna and el-Minya would contribute to a greater effect than the more open valley margins north of el-Minya (Butzer 1999, 572).

The Qena bend is usually cited as being problematic because of the approximate east-west course of the valley from Qena to Nag Hammadi, and thus the supposed prevailing north-west wind would not aid navigation upstream (*e.g.* Kees 1961, 98–99). This argument may be somewhat overstated when we consider the channelling effect of the valley. The 20th-century annual means of wind direction at Nag Hammadi and Qena both reveal a dominant westerly wind with the north-westerly second in prominence at both towns (Ibrahim 1968, fig. 32). It is not the direction of the valley that should be considered solely, but the relationship between the course of the valley and that of the Nile.

(b) Navigation, ship design and propulsion

Any channelling effect is favourable for some stretches of the river and not others. Recent maps of the Nile Valley exhibit areas with large meanders that have sections that are perpendicular to the valley, for example, just north of Asyut, around Sohag and in the area of Balabish (see Figure 1). In the region of Hiw the crew would have to sail north on an upstream journey as the river flows in a southerly direction (Baines and Malek 2000, 71, 109; Egyptian General Survey Authority 1991, sheets NG 36 J2b, NG 36 J4a). While sufficient data does not exist to accurately assess the sinuosity of the river at any particular time during the Pharaonic Period, Butzer (1976, 34) has suggested that it may have been even more sinuous than it is now based upon records from the last 200 years.

The windward performance of a ship is influenced by numerous factors such as the sail, rigging, and the ability of the hull to prevent drift to leeward through the use of a keel and the profile of the hull of the vessel (McGrail 1987, 111–115; Wachsmann 1998, 253). The square sail was used throughout the Pharaonic Period and was designed to travel primarily with the wind from the stern or close to it, whereas the later sails were more efficient into the wind (Casson 1995, 243–245, 273; McGrail 1987, 223; Wachsmann 1998, 253). McGrail (2001, 32–33) argues that the forward position of the mast, often seen in 6th-dynasty depictions, would restrict them to sailing with the wind 45 degrees either side of dead astern. However, various types of rigging shown in Old Kingdom tomb scenes lead him to suggest that the vessels could be sailed with the wind forward of the stern sector and perhaps even on the beam, that is, 90 degrees from the direction of travel. Although numerous changes and innovations were made to sails and rigging during the Pharaonic Period (McGrail 2001, 31–33, 47; Wachsmann 1998, 248–253), Bowen's (1962, 57) suggestion that the New Kingdom ships could sail into the wind seems unlikely to have occurred in practice. The presence of a keel on Egyptian vessels is doubtful with the only evidence of a projecting central strake at the stem and stern known from some New

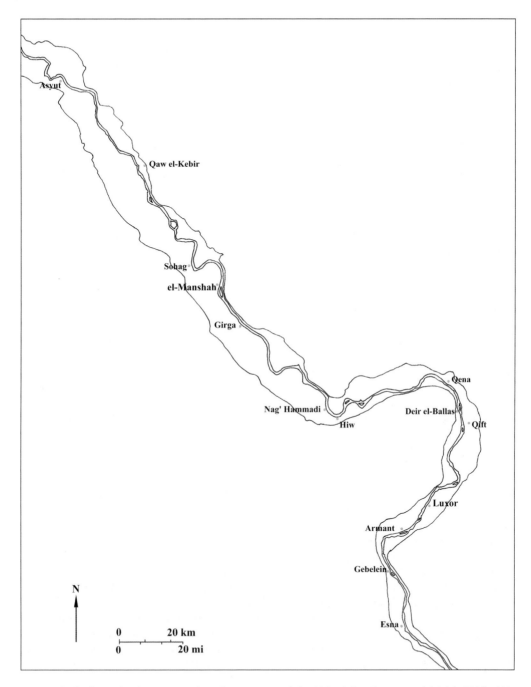

Figure 1. Outline of cultivation and modern course of the Nile (after Baines and Malek 2000, 109; Egyptian General Survey Authority 1991, NG 36 sheets).

Kingdom models and depictions (*cf.* Hocker 1998, 245–246; Jones 1990, 54; Landström 1970, 107; Ward 2000, 141). Even if such a central strake did protrude below the waterline, the apparent tradition of a rounded lower hull form would have provided little resistance to leeway (lateral motion). In practice one would often have to traverse the river back and forth, especially in the months just prior to the rise of the Nile when the river would have been reduced to half its ordinary breadth (Said 1993, 96), each time being pushed sideways by the wind. This would be exacerbated when travelling upstream, such that one would not gain any ground on each traverse. The wind on the beam would have caused considerable leeway and it seems optimistic that Pharaonic vessels could have used such a wind. Although the ability of the Egyptian vessels to sail at least 45 degrees from dead astern gave them some scope for coping with the meanders of the river, an adverse wind meant either stopping or propulsion by other means: rowing or towing.

Depictions of large rowing crews and textual sources for rowers and rowing units are generally found in the context of funerary, ceremonial, official, special-purpose and, in particular, military vessels (Dürring 1995, 162–163; Vinson 1998, 146–147). Depictions of cargo vessels rarely have rowing crews and, if they do, they are usually small (Vinson 1998, 151–152). However, the *Instructions of Amenemope* seem to suggest that a passenger should be prepared to take an oar and help if necessary when the boat is in distress (Vinson 1998, 149–150). Rowing had replaced paddling as the means of propulsion on larger craft by about the 5th Dynasty (Casson 1995, 18; Jones 1995, 68, fig. 61).

Towing is known throughout Pharaonic history (Vinson 1998, 155). It is common to see religious vessels being towed, either by other boats under oar or by men on the river banks in temple and tomb scenes (Kemp 1989, 206; Moussa and Altenmüller 1977, pls. 8, 12; Vandier 1969, 729, 895, 904–905, 1000–1002; Vinson 1998, 155). Evidence of towing in non-funerary contexts does exist however, for example during the Ramesside Period in the so-called 'Ship's Log', P. Leiden I 350 v. III, 9, 15 we have a 'chief of the towing men' and the 'towing men' (Janssen 1961, 33, 35). Herodotus (II.29, 96; Lloyd 1976, 117) mentions it as a common form of propulsion going upstream and through the cataracts. Towing along the banks of the Delta was still seen in the 20th century C.E. (MacLeish 1966, 776). Towing along a straight levee may have been a straightforward affair, but towing around a bend was a different matter. The greater the angle between the tow-rope and direction of travel, the more inefficient the task becomes. This would suggest that towing on the outside of the bend is not practical, certainly when travelling upstream, as the boat would be in the thalweg. Towing on the inside of the bend may also have been problematic during the dry season when the boat was forced out away from the bank due to the exposed point bar, and thus creating a large angle and requiring great effort or a very long tow-rope to reduce the angle. As Janssen (1961, 49–50) points out, towing a boat into a strong head wind in the Delta for about 25 miles a day would have been an arduous task.

During April and May and into June when the river was at its lowest, certain places along the Nile may have been relatively shallow and grounding on sandbanks was a real possibility (Bonneau 1964, 22–23; Said 1993, 96–97; Willcocks and Craig 1913, 136–137, table 64). P. Oxy. XVI. 1862, from the 7th century C.E., mentions a payment of expenses at the harbour until the Nile rises, at which time the writer will take the goods to the monastery by boat (Grenfell *et al.* 1924, 50–51). Wilbour, during his travels in the 1880s, experienced problems of grounding on sandbanks as early as January and February (Capart 1936, 49, 350, 368, 519). At el-Badrashein on 30 March 1889, we find Wilbour grounded on a sandbank and then caught up in congestion with 30 vessels all in the deeper water. It took them three hours to push their way through (Capart 1936, 531). Some three years earlier, again at el-Badrashein in March, Wilbour used the services of a local pilot (Capart 1936, 382). A similar navigational role is known from the Pharaonic Period.

The role of a bow lookout on the vessel, *iry-ḥꜣ.t* and *ꜥš-ḥꜣ.t,* is well attested. These terms have often been translated as 'pilot' (*e.g.* Faulkner 1962, 25, 49; Jones 1988, 64, no. 67, 71, no. 90; Lesko and Lesko 1982, 90; 1984, 93). However, the evidence suggests that these people were not pilots in the modern sense, *i.e.* local experts taken on a vessel temporarily to assist the crew in navigating waters unfamiliar to them (Vinson 1998, 9, n. 1). The former term is known from the Middle Kingdom through to the Ptolemaic Period (Jones 1988, 64, no. 67) and the latter, literally 'crier/caller at the front', is known from the New Kingdom onwards (Jones 1988, 71, no. 90). The bow lookout is depicted in tomb scenes from Old Kingdom onwards (*e.g.* Boreux 1925, fig. 179b) and present on model boats from the Middle Kingdom onwards (*e.g.* Winlock 1955, pl. 33, 35–37, 40–41, 51). Despite the shallow draught of even the largest of Pharaonic vessels (Landström 1970, 128–129), many bow lookouts were often depicted with sounding poles to test the depth of the water (Jones 1990, 60). The textual sources reveal that the role of lookout was to observe both the weather and the water, and was used as a metaphor for diligence in both literary sources and tomb inscriptions (Säve-Söderbergh 1946, 86; Vinson 1998, 11, 12–14). The bow lookout's role was as important as that of the steerer, with the two working together to detect and avoid obstacles, eddies and whirlpools (Kees 1961, 100; Vinson 1998, 11). Most Ramesside examples of bow lookouts show a man at the bow with a long sounding-pole and often turned towards the stern to shout (*ꜥš*) to the steerer (Vinson 1998, 11). The bow lookout was part of the crew who travelled on the boat throughout its journey. In the Roman Period it has been suggested that a port charge may have been for the services of a pilot (Vinson 1998, 69, n. 80).

Security on the Nile – crime, prevention and punishment

Difficulties and dangers of travelling on the Nile came not only from natural sources, such as the climate and the dynamics of the river, but in the shape of human actions. We have already had a brief glimpse of thieves attempting to board Amelia Edwards' boat. The following sections will firstly consider infrastructures to protect shipping, and then crime and its prevention.

(a) Physical and social infrastructure protecting shipping

In the Pharaonic Period we have evidence of infrastructure and measures to protect vessels, as well as their crew and cargo. In Nubia, the Middle Kingdom system of forts built between the first and second cataracts are believed to have had considerable functional differentiation with some providing people to aid river traffic through areas of rapids and to protect shipping (Adams 1977, 183–187, 192; Lawrence 1965, 72; Smith 1991, 131–132). A spur wall in the girdle wall at the Middle Kingdom fort of Mirgissa was probably intended to protect a small harbour and also provide protection for shipping, both from the prevalent wind and sudden attack (Vercoutter 1967–1968, 274).

The title 'Overseer of all police patrols on water and on land' is known from a fragmentary 11th-dynasty stela from Deir el-Ballas (Boston 25.680; Dunham 1937, 35). The duties of those who held this title may have included regulating river traffic and acting as immigration control officers in border areas (Jones 1995, 82). The latter activity of security would also have been carried out by the *phrt* or 'frontier patrols' (Faulkner 1953, 41). Guarding of waterways is also attested in the New Kingdom. The biographical text of Amenhotep, the son of Hapu, suggests that the Delta was guarded on both sides to watch the movements of the Bedouin, and the banks of the mouths of the Nile were guarded by troops restricting movements in and out of Egypt during the reign of Amenhotep III (Säve-Söderbergh 1946, 59; Varille 1968, 41). Harbour and canal guards are also attested in P. Harris. Ramesses III provided companies of guards to watch the harbour of the Heliopolitan (*Ity*) canal and watchmen to police the canal (Grandet 1994a, 261 (28,6–28,8); 1994b, 121–125). It is, however, not explicit what the protection is from.

Protection of shipping was not restricted to the Pharaonic Period. During the Ptolemaic Period it is clear that navigation on the Nile was controlled by river guards and there were also guard posts on the river, some of which also served as toll stations taxing the boats (Hauben 1985, 184; Reddé 1986, 403; Thompson 1988, 62). Sometime during the reign of Ptolemy Philopator or Ptolemy Epiphanes, a special force of soldiers was placed on board the river police ships in order to protect the safety of the commercial traffic on the waterways in collaboration with the river guards (Rostovtzeff 1940, 370, 373–374; 1941, 715). P. Tebtunis 919 and 920 (Hunt *et al.* 1938, 193), dated to the early part of the 2nd century B.C.E., refer to uprisings and robbery and reveal a lack of security (Rostovtzeff 1941, 715). It is at this time that the regular river police were unable to guarantee the safety of river transport, and rebels and brigands succeeded in disturbing the transportation of grain to Alexandria (Rostovtzeff 1941, 715; Van't Dack and Hauben 1978, 61). Late in the reign of Epiphanes we have the first mention of the royal navy on the Nile under the command of the *dioecetes* to assure the safety of communications on the river and the canals (Rostovtzeff 1941, 715; Van't Dack and Hauben 1978, 61). In the second half of the 2nd century B.C.E., as well as infantry and cavalry, the special force of troops on river police boats were stationed at Ptolemais (el-Manshah), which enforced the authority of the *epistrategos* and Theban *strategos*. On board these boats, loyal troops could easily move around in order to quash revolts (Van't Dack and Hauben 1978, 61). In the first two centuries C.E. it is clear that the river patrol had stations at Thebes (Luxor) and Syene/Elephantine, as well as Alexandria. Other stations remain questionable. There were admittedly many guard posts on the Nile where taxes were levied, but nothing indicates that the river patrol exerted its control at these places (Reddé 1986, 288–289).

(b) Crime and its prevention by royal decree and commercial contract

The *Decree of Horemheb* describes the denunciation of the act of requisitioning boats from those who were carrying out service to the Pharaoh. The penalty for those caught acting against the decree was to have their noses cut off and then be sent to Tjarou (Kruchten 1981, 28, 30, 48, 50, 74, 75, 206–207). It is clear from this edict that such activities were considered to be damaging to the operation of the state. This is the only complete statement of normative measurements for the state as a whole (Kruchten 1981, 209). The later Ramesside decrees are attempts to protect particular temple property and staff from interference by others. The Nauri decree aimed at protecting the property and employees belonging to Seti I's temple at Abydos whilst in Nubia (Gardiner 1952, 24; Griffith 1927, 200; Kitchen 1993a, 44, §1, §2; Kitchen 1993b, 51). This included the protection of boats from interference in general, and specifically, by the fortress commander and other military commanders in Kush from the taking any of the cargo, or from the taking of crew members to carry out other work, (Griffith 1927, pl. 41 ll.33, 48–50, pl. 42 ll.83–97; Kitchen 1993a, 44 §4, 46 §11A–B, 48–49 §25–30). A similar edict existed at Elephantine from the reign of Ramesses III (Griffith 1927, 207–208) and fragments of other Ramesside protective decrees are known at Iuny (Hermonthis/Armant) (Kitchen 1996, 469; Kitchen 1999, 460–461; Mond and Myers 1940, 161) and Hermopolis (el-Ashmunein) (Kitchen 1993a, 106; Kitchen 1993b, 102–103). Such decrees that protected individual institutions from the demands of others date back to the Old Kingdom (Kemp 1989, 238).

P. Hibeh 198, a royal ordinance from the reign of Ptolemy Philadelphus, reveals attempts to regulate security measures on transport routes and waterways (Turner and Lenger 1955, 76; Zilliacus *et al.* 1979, 141). The ordinance states that all malefactors should be caught and turned in, and those who harbour them or their stolen goods will be subject to the same penalties (Bagnall 1969, 85–92; Turner and Lenger 1955, 98–102). It also establishes preventative measures designed to minimise the dangers (Bagnall 1969, 93–96; Turner and Lenger 1955, 102–103). A ban on sailing at night was imposed with the exception of vessels sent in haste (possibly messengers from the king), which were given an escort. Vessels were also required to moor at appointed places overnight suggesting a real threat to shipping. If a vessel failed to do this due to a storm or other factor, they were to inform the police, who would then send a guard to protect them.

The requisitioning of transport, boats and beasts of burden by the military was a common abuse in Roman Egypt and throughout the Roman Empire (Mitchell 1976, 106). The practice was so deep-rooted that the repeated orders to cease and desist by the prefect of Egypt, and even emperors, failed to curb it (Lewis 1983, 173–174). In 19 C.E., upon his visit to Alexandria, Germanicus issued an edict in reaction to the malpractice of his own entourage stating that transport would be paid for accordingly and that those who did not do so would be dealt with by his secretary or himself personally (Lewis 1983, 173; Mitchell 1976, 114).

The difficulties and dangers, and the duties placed upon the ship's captain to minimise risk are also attested in Ptolemaic and Roman period commercial shipping contracts (Meyer-Termeer 1978, 55, 60; Vinson 1998, 41, 83). One such freight contract, P. Oxy. Hels. 37, from 176 C.E. (Zilliacus *et al.* 1979, 138–142), reveals that the measures taken by the early Ptolemies remained largely intact during the Roman Period and that if the crew kept to the contract, they would not be liable for losses on the journey. It states that the ship's captain:

> ... shall provide the ship equipped for sailing with a sufficient crew ... not sailing by night nor during a tempest, and anchor every day at the designated and safest anchorages at the proper hours, unless, which shall not happen, there should be a cause of *vis maior*, brought about by fire starting from the land or storm or an onslaught of criminals. If you give evidence of this, you and your crew shall be free from liability.
>
> (Zilliacus *et al.* 1979, 139–140)

(c) Criminal and crime, and the fears and actions of crew and passengers

Plying the Nile was obviously considered risky, as illustrated by the following sources. The diaries and writings of travellers to Egypt from the 16th to the end of the 19th century reveal that robbery was not confined to the sea and its ports, but occurred along the Nile, particularly in the Delta (Nibbi 1985, 30). Many experiences were similar to that of Edwards', with thieves swimming up to the boat at night in an attempt to board it, steal and perhaps kill the passengers (Brejnik and Brejnik 1972, 39 (54–55); Van de Walle 1975, 413 [12]). There were also incidences of attack by another vessel during the night, for example during Johann Wild's travels from 1606 to 1610 (Volkoff 1973, 101 (16–17)). Jean Palerne Forésien states on his travels in 1581 that robbery and piracy from Damietta to Cairo had been so bad that there was a bounty for the heads of those involved, and travellers journeyed through the Delta in groups of boats for safety (Sauneron 1971, 45–46 (26–27), 217 (168)). Christophe Harant, travelling in 1581, explains that by igniting a number of lighters for firing guns all around the boat, one could give the impression that the boat was well armed, which served to deter would-be attackers (Brejnik and Brejnik 1972, 39 (54–55)). Such acts of attack and robbery are not surprising in the context of the 16th century Mediterranean in which piracy is described as endemic (De Souza 1999, 240).

Travellers in Roman and Byzantine Egypt often viewed travel as a serious undertaking and it was done as a matter of necessity. Kotsifou (2000, 58–59, 62) discusses some of the precautionary measures taken, such as the use of oracles and prayers – the practice of offering prayers for one's safe return home to the family was also used in the Pharaonic Period (Wente 1967, 32, 55, 56). Travellers also hired the services of professional escorts and state guards. However, there is evidence of guards sometimes taking advantage of their positions by delaying travellers and extorting money from them. A fragmentary edict from a prefect in the 2nd century C.E. orders an immediate cessation of such activities (Kase 1936, 9).

P. Loeb 1, a demotic document from the Persian Period, deals with the journey of a vessel to Nubia to collect grain. The crew had been ordered to unload the grain at the first cataract and store it, presumably until a team arrived to move the cargo past the cataract. The letter expresses concern that this will attract bandits who will attempt to steal the cargo (Vinson 1998, 125).

In the Roman Period peasant farmers, ground down by excessive taxation, brutal tax collectors and poor harvests, took flight. This flight from one's registered place of abode automatically resulted in outlawry (Given 2004; Lewis 1993, 101). A few of these fugitives gravitated to the big cities, especially Alexandria, in an attempt to disappear with impunity, but most ended up in the swamps of the Delta or in the hills along the edges of the Nile Valley. Lake Mareotis, south of Alexandria, was particularly attractive because of the many hiding places in the marshes and the rich traffic coming past on its way to the southern harbour of Alexandria (Haas 1997, 37). Lewis (1983, 203–205) argues that banditry remained endemic in Roman Egypt and whilst the government never succeeded in completely eradicating brigandage, their numbers remained small. It was a tough life separated permanently from family and capture meant certain death. The acts of robbery witnessed in the historical sources are reflected in the literature of the day by the 2nd-century C.E. romancer, Achilleus Tatios. He describes a Delta full of brigands who use the papyrus as cover for planning ambushes (Lindsay 1968, 233).

So why use the Nile?

This paper has looked at a number of factors adversely affecting travel upon the Nile in order to demonstrate that it was not all plain sailing. A great deal of toil would have been involved in the rowing or towing of vessels against the wind or current, or both, and at times it was simply not possible to make progress. Despite the changes in boat technology over the millennia, the experiences and potential difficulties and dangers that the weather had to offer remained broadly similar during the periods in question, and the annual cycle of the Nile remained largely unchanged until the construction of the Aswan dams. A possibly more sinuous Nile may have exacerbated some of these difficulties in the past. Whilst the paper has not made any attempt at a quantitative assessment of these experiences, we have an annual cycle with which everyone who plied the Nile knew and worked, along with social organisations that included bow lookouts and pilots.

The human element has many similarities through time: the requisitioning of vessels by those in authority was clearly a problem in the Pharaonic Period, as well as later ones, and decrees were issued in an attempt to stop such activities; the boarding of vessels with intent to steal was a danger encountered at various times. These, however, need to be placed within their differing political, social and economic contexts, something that has largely been outside the scope of this paper. The measures put in place to contend with such problems also differed. The ban on travelling at night imposed early in the Ptolemaic Period and continuing through the Roman Period does not appear to have been a measure used during the Pharaonic Period, although there is little evidence for travel at night (Janssen 1961, 44; Vinson 1998, 41, n. 95). In the case of the early modern travellers, travel at night is known to have occurred in order to take advantage of favourable winds (Capart 1936, 475).

Despite these difficulties, the Nile was the central medium of transport and communication through the Nile Valley and Delta until the arrival of the motor vehicle. Perhaps the main benefit was the far greater carrying capacity of vessels, from the 54 tonne capacity of Khufu's royal ship (Khufu I) (Lipke 1984, 102–103) to the grain vessels of the New Kingdom (Gardiner 1941, 47, 49; Vinson 1998, tables 2.1, 3.1) and Ptolemaic and Roman Periods at over 160 tonnes (Bagnall 1993, 35, 37; Vinson 1998, 158), compared to that of overland travel by sled, donkey, oxen and later by camel and carts (Arnold 1991, 58, 63–64; Bagnall 1985; 1993, 38–39). When the weather and the Nile were favourable, considerable distances could be achieved by boat. The use of desert routes between points on the Nile required supplies for both the people and animals involved in the transport, whereas the river bank provided a place where goods could readily be exchanged for provisions (Kemp 1989, 253–255, fig. 86). The boat also provided a ready-made shelter for the crew and passengers. Many of the human interferences occurring on water are equally attributable to land; from the Middle Kingdom 'Tale of the Eloquent Peasant' (Parkinson 1997, 59–60) to the 15th-century traveller Meshullam Ben R. Menahem and his party being robbed by their guide and camel-driver between Alexandria and Rosetta (Nibbi 1985, 32–33). Textual sources from the Roman Period show that some viewed the river as a safer alternative to the road, whilst others preferred to travel overland (Kotsifou 2000, 60–61).

Travel on the Nile was an essential part of the functioning of the state and society until recent times that was not always easy and was sometimes held in trepidation by the traveller. However, we see the tangible results of countless journeys on the Nile in the landscape today, from pyramids to cities.

Institute of Archaeology, UCL

Acknowledgements

I would like to thank Dr. Sally-Ann Ashton, University of Cambridge, as well as the anonymous reviewer for numerous valuable comments and advice on this paper. My thanks also go to Dr. Michael Given, University of Glasgow, who provided many helpful comments on the text and kindly allowed me to draw upon his forthcoming work. I am very grateful to Dr. Alistair Manning, Metrological Office, Exeter, UK, for his comments in the discussion of the meteorological aspects of the paper.

References

Adams, W. Y. 1977, *Nubia: Corridor to Africa*. Allen Lane, London.

Arnold, D. 1991, *Building in Egypt: Pharaonic stone masonry*. Oxford University Press, New York and Oxford.

Bagnall, R. S. 1969, Some Notes on P. Hib. 198, *The Bulletin of the American Society of Papyrologists* 6, 73–101.

Bagnall, R. S. 1985, The Camel, the Wagon, and the Donkey in Later Roman Egypt, *The Bulletin of the American Society of Papyrologists* 22, 1–6.

Bagnall, R. S. 1993, *Egypt in Late Antiquity*. Princeton University Press, Princeton.

Baines, J. and Malek, J. 2000, *Cultural Atlas of Ancient Egypt*. Checkmark Books, New York.

Besançon, J. 1957, *L'homme et le Nil*. Gallimard, Paris.

Bonneau, D. 1964, *La Crue du Nil, divinité égyptienne, à travers mille ans d'histoire (332 av.–641 ap. J.-C.) d'après les auteurs grecs et latins, et les documents des époques ptolémaïque, romaine et Byzantine*. C. Klincksieck, Paris.

Boreux, C. 1925, *Études de nautique égyptienne: l'art de la navigation en Égypte jusqu'à la fin de l'Ancien Empire*. Institut français d'archéologie orientale, Cairo.

Bowen, R. L. 1962, Egyptian Sail in the Second Millennium B.C., *The Mariner's Mirror* 48, 52–57.

Brejnik, C. and Brejnik, A. (eds.), 1972, *Voyage en Egypte de Christophe Harant de Polžic et Bezdružic, 1598*. Institut français d'archéologie orientale, Cairo.

Butzer, K. W. 1976, *Early Hydraulic Civilization in Egypt: A study in cultural ecology*. The University of Chicago Press, Chicago and London.

Butzer, K. W. 1999, Nile Valley, Geological Evolution, in K. A. Bard and S. B. Shubert (eds.), *Encyclopedia of the Archaeology of Ancient Egypt*, 571–573. Routledge, London.

Capart, J. (ed.), 1936, *Travels in Egypt [December 1880 to May 1891]: Letters of Charles Edwin Wilbour*. Brooklyn Museum, Brooklyn.

Casson, L. 1995, *Ships and Seamanship in the Ancient World*. Johns Hopkins University Press, Baltimore and London.

Degas, J. 1994, Navigation sur le Nil au Nouvel Empire, in B. Menu (ed.), *Les problèmes institutionnels de l'eau en Égypte ancienne et dans l'Antiquité mediterranéenne*, 141–151. Institut français d'archaéologie orientale, Cairo.

Derchain-Urtel, M.-T. 1984, Die Schwangere im Ozean?, in F. Junge (ed.), *Studien zu Sprache and Religion Ägyptens: Zu Ehren von Wolfhart Westendorf überreicht von seinen Freunden und Schülern, Band 2: Religion*, 753–761. F. Junge, Göttingen.

De Souza, P. 1999, *Piracy in the Graeco-Roman World*. Cambridge University Press, Cambridge.

Dunham, D. 1937, *Naga-ed-Dêr Stelae of the First Intermediate Period*. Oxford University Press, London.

Dürring, N. 1995, *Materialien zum Schiffbau im alten Ägypten*. Achet Verlag, Berlin.

Edwards, A. B. 1877, *A Thousand Miles up the Nile*. Longmans, Green and Co., London.

Egger, J. 1988, Ekman Flow over Valleys, *Geophysical and Astrophysical Fluid Dynamics* 41, 103–127.

Egyptian General Survey Authority, 1991, *Egyptian Series 1:50000, Edition 1*. Egyptian General Survey Authority in co-operation with FINNIDA, Finland.

Erman, A. 1919, *Reden, Rufe und Lieder auf Gräberbildern des Alten Reiches*. Verlag der Akademie der Wissenschaften, Berlin.

Erman, A. and Grapow, H. 1928, *Wörterbuch der ägyptischen Sprache, Zweiter Band*. J. C. Hinrichs'sche Buchhandlung, Leipzig.

Erman, A. and Grapow, H. 1930, *Wörterbuch der ägyptischen Sprache, Vierter Band*. J. C. Hinrichs'sche Buchhandlung, Leipzig.

Faulkner, R. O. 1953, Egyptian Military Organisation, *Journal of Egyptian Archaeology* 39, 32–47.

Faulkner, R. O. 1962, *A Concise Dictionary of Middle Egyptian*. Griffith Institute, Oxford.

Gardiner, A. 1941, Ramesside Texts Relating to the Taxation and Transport of Corn, *Journal of Egyptian Archaeology* 27, 19–73.

Gardiner, A. 1952, Some Reflections on the Nauri Decree, *Journal of Egyptian Archaeology* 38, 24–33.

Gardiner, A. H. 1957, *Egyptian Grammar: Being an introduction to the study of hieroglyphs*, (3rd edition). Griffith Institute, Oxford.

Giles, B. 2003, *BBC Weather. Weather A-Z: The Khamsin*. http://www.bbc.co.uk/weather/features/alphabet32.shtml. Date accessed: 5 June 2003.

Given, M. 2004, *The Archaeology of the Colonized*. Routledge, London.

Grandet, P. 1994a, *Le Papyrus Harris (BM9999), 1*. Institut français d'archéologie orientale, Cairo.

Grandet, P. 1994b, *Le Papyrus Harris (BM9999), 2*. Institut français d'archéologie orientale, Cairo.

Grenfell, B. P. and Hunt, A. S. (eds.), 1906, *The Hibeh Papyri I. Nos. 1–171*. Egypt Exploration Society, London.

Grenfell, B. P. and Hunt, A. S. (eds.), 1920, *The Oxyrhynchus Papyri XIV, Nos. 1626–1777*. Egypt Exploration Society, London.

Grenfell, B. P., Hunt, A. S. and Bell, H. I. (eds.), 1924, *The Oxyrhynchus Papyri XVI, Nos. 1829–2063*. Egypt Exploration Society, London.

Griffith, F. L. 1927, The Abydos Decree of Seti I at Nauri, *Journal of Egyptian Archaeology* 13, 193–208.

Griffiths, J. F. and Soliman, K. H. 1972, The Northern Desert (Sahara), in J. F. Griffiths (ed.), *World Survey of Climatology Volume 10: Climates of Africa*, 75–131. Elsevier, Amsterdam.

Haas, C. 1997, *Alexandria in Late Antiquity: Topography and social conflict*. Johns Hopkins University Press, Baltimore.

Hassan, F. A. and Stucki, B. R. 1987, Nile Floods and Climatic Change, in M. R. Rampino, J. E. Sanders, W. S. Newman and L. K. Königsson (eds.), *Climate: History, periodicity, and predictability*, 37–46. Van Nostrand Reinhold, New York.

Hauben, N. 1985, The Guard Posts of Memphis, *Zeitschrift für Papyrologie und Epigraphik* 60, 183–187.

Herodotus. *The Histories*, (trans. by A. De Sélincourt, 1954). Penguin, Baltimore.

Hocker, F. M. 1998, Appendix: Did Hatshepsut's Punt ships have keels?, in S. Wachsmann (ed.), *Seagoing Ships and Seamanship in the Bronze Age Levant*, 245-246. Chatham Publishing, London.

Hunt, A. S., Smyly, J. G. and Edgar, C. C. (eds.), 1938, *The Tebtunis Papyri, 3/2*. Cambridge University Press, London.

Hurst, H. E. 1952, *The Nile: A general account of the river and the utilization of its waters*. Constable, London.

Ibrahim, E. E. E. 1968, *Aspects of the Geomorphological Evolution of the Nile Valley in the Qena Bend Area*. Unpublished thesis, University of Newcastle upon Tyne.

Janssen, J. J. 1961, *Two Ancient Egyptian Ship's Logs: Papyrus Leiden I 350 verso and Papyrus Turin 2008+2016*. E. J. Brill, Leiden.

Johnson, G. T. and Hunter, L. J. 1999, Some Insights into Typical Urban Canyon Airflows, *Atmospheric Environment* 33, 3991–3999.

Jones, D. A. 1988, *A Glossary of Ancient Egyptian Nautical Titles and Terms*. Kegan Paul International, London and New York.

Jones, D. A. 1990, *Model Boats from the Tomb of Tut'ankhamun*. Griffith Institute, Oxford.

Jones, D. A. 1995, *Boats*. British Museum Press, London.

Kase Jr., E. H. (ed.), 1936, *Papyri in the Princeton University Collections, 2*. Princeton University Press, Princeton.

Kees, H. 1961, *Ancient Egypt: A cultural topography*. Faber and Faber, London.

Kemp, B. J. 1989, *Ancient Egypt: An anatomy of a civilization*. Routledge, London and New York.

Kitchen, K. A. 1993a, *Ramesside Inscriptions. Translated and Annotated: Translations, 1: Ramesses I, Sethos I and Contemporaries*. Blackwell, Oxford and Cambridge, Mass.

Kitchen, K. A. 1993b, *Ramesside Inscriptions. Translated and Annotated: Notes and Comments, 1: Ramesses I, Sethos I and Contemporaries*. Blackwell, Oxford and Cambridge, Massachusetts.

Kitchen, K. A. 1996, *Ramesside Inscriptions. Translated and Annotated. Translations, 2: Ramesses II, Royal Inscriptions*. Blackwell, Oxford and Cambridge, Massachusetts.

Kitchen, K. A. 1999, *Ramesside Inscriptions. Translated and Annotated: Notes and Comments, 2: Ramesses II, Royal Inscriptions*. Blackwell, Oxford and Cambridge, Massachusetts.

Kotsifou, C. 2000, Papyrological Evidence of Travelling in Byzantine Egypt, in A. McDonald and C. Riggs (eds.), *Current Research in Egyptology 2000*, 57–64. Archaeopress, Oxford.

Kruchten, J.-M. 1981, *Le Décret d'Horemheb: Traduction, commentaire épigraphique, philologique et institutionnel*. Éditions de l'Université de Bruxelles, Brussels.

Kurth, D. 1986, Wind, in W. Helck and E. Otto (eds.), *Lexikon der Ägyptologie, 6: Stele – Zypresse*, cols. 1266–1272. Otto Harrassowitz, Wiesbaden.

Landström, B. 1970, *Ships of the Pharaohs: 4000 years of Egyptian shipbuilding*. Allen and Unwin, London.

Lawrence, A. W. 1965, Ancient Egyptian Fortifications, *Journal of Egyptian Archaeology* 51, 69–94.

Lesko, L. H. and Lesko, B. S. 1982, *A Dictionary of Late Egyptian, 1*. B.C. Scribe Publications, Berkeley, California.

Lesko, L. H. and Lesko, B. S. 1984, *A Dictionary of Late Egyptian, 2*. B.C. Scribe Publications, Providence.

Lewis, N. 1983, *Life in Egypt Under Roman Rule*. Clarendon Press, Oxford.

Lewis, N. 1993, A Reversal of a Tax Policy in Roman Egypt, *Greek, Roman and Byzantine Studies* 34, 101–118.

Lindsay, J. 1968, *Men and Gods on the Roman Nile*. Frederick Muller, London.

Lipke, P. 1984, *The Royal Ship of Cheops*. National Maritime Museum, Greenwich.

Lloyd, A. B. 1976, *Herodotus Book II: Commentary 1–98*. E. J. Brill, Leiden.

MacLeish, K. 1966, Abraham, the Friend of God, *National Geographic* 130, 739–789.

McGrail, S. 1987, *Ancient Boats in N.W. Europe: The archaeology of water transport to AD 1500*. Longman, London and New York.

McGrail, S. 2001, *Boats of the World: From the Stone Age to Medieval times*. Oxford University Press, Oxford.

Meyer-Termeer, A. J. M. 1978, *Die Haftung der Schiffer im griechischen und römischen Recht*. Terra, Zutphen, Netherlands.

Ministry of Public Works, 1922, *Climatological Normals for Egypt and the Sudan, Candia, Cyprus, and Abyssinia*. Ministry of Public Works, Physical Department, Cairo.

Ministry of Public Works, 1938, *Climatological Normals for Egypt and the Sudan, Cyprus and Palestine*. Ministry of Public Works, Physical Department, Cairo.

Mitchell, S. 1976, Requisitioned Transport in the Roman Empire: A new inscription from Pisidia, *Journal of Roman Studies* 66, 106–131.

Mond, R., and Myers, O. H. 1940, *Temples of Armant: A preliminary survey*. Egypt Exploration Society, London.

Moussa, A. M. and Altenmüller, H. 1977, *Das Grab des Nianchchnum und Chnumhotep*. Philipp von Zabern, Mainz am Rhein.

Nibbi, A. 1985, *Wenamun and Alashiya Reconsidered*. DE Publications, Oxford.

Overland, J. E. 1984, Scale Analysis of Marine Winds in Straits and along Mountainous Coasts, *Monthly Weather Review* 112, 2530–2534.

Parkinson, R. B. 1997, *The Tale of Sinuhe and Other Ancient Egyptian Poems, 1940–1640 BC.* Clarendon Press, Oxford.

Petite-Maire, N., Beufort, L. and Page, N. 1997, Holocene Climate Change and Man in the Present Day Sahara, in H. N. Dalfes, G. Kukla and H. Weiss (eds.), *Third Millennium BC Climate Change and Old World Collapse,* 297–308. Springer-Verlag, Berlin.

Reddé, M. 1986, *Mare nostrum: Les infrastructures, le dispositif et l'histoire de la marine militaire sous l'Empire romain.* École française de Rome, Rome.

Roccati, A. 1982, *La littérature historique sous l'Ancien Empire égyptien.* Éditions du Cerf, Paris.

Rostovtzeff, M. 1940, ΠΛΟΙΑ ΘΑΛΑΣΣΙΑ on the Nile, in *Études dédiées à la mémoire d'André M. Andréadès,* 367–376. Publiées par un comité d'amis et d'élèves sous la présidence de K. Varvaressos, Pyrsos, Athens.

Rostovtzeff, M. 1941, *The Social and Economic History of the Hellenistic World, 2.* Clarendon Press, Oxford.

Said, E. 1993, *The River Nile, Geology, Hydrology, and Utilization.* Pergamon Press, Oxford.

Sauneron, S. 1971, *Voyage en Égypte de Jean Palerne, Forésien, 1581.* Institut français d'archéologie orientale, Cairo.

Säve-Söderbergh, T. 1946, *The Navy of the Eighteenth Egyptian Dynasty.* A.-B. Lundequistska Bokhandeln, Uppsala.

Smith, S. T. 1991, Askut and the Role of the Second Cataract Forts, *Journal of the American Research Center in Egypt* 28, 107–132.

Thompson, D. J. 1988, *Memphis Under the Ptolemies.* Princeton University Press, Princeton.

Turner, E. G. and Lenger, M.-Th. 1955, *The Hibeh Papyri II: Edited with translations and notes.* Egypt Exploration Society, London.

Van de Walle, B. (ed.), 1975, *Voyage en Egypte de Vincent Stochove, Gilles Fermanel, Robert Fauvel, 1631.* Institut français d'archéologie orientale, Cairo.

Vandersleyen, C. 1967, Une tempête sous le règne d'Amosis, *Revue d'Égyptologie* 19, 123–159.

Vandersleyen, C. 1971, Des obstacles que constituent les cataractes du Nil, *Bulletin de l'Institut français d'Archéologie orientale* 69, 253–266.

Vandier, J. 1969, *Manuel d'archéologie égyptienne, Tome 5: Bas-reliefs et peintures. Scènes de la vie quotidienne.* Éditions A. et J. Picard, Paris.

Van't Dack, E. and Hauben, H. 1978, L'Apport égyptien à l'armée navale lagide, in H. Maehler and V. M. Strocka (eds.), *Das Ptolemäische Ägypten: Akten des internationalen Symposions 27. – 29. September 1976 in Berlin,* 59–94. Philipp von Zabern, Mainz am Rhein.

Varille, A. 1968, *Inscriptions concernant l'architecte Amenhotep fils de Hapou.* Institut français d'archéologie orientale, Cairo.

Vercoutter, J. 1967–1968, Excavations at Mirgissa – 3, *Kush* 15, 269–279.

Vercoutter, J., Elhai, H., Hesse, A., Karlin, C., Maley, J. and Vila, A. 1970, *Mirgissa 1.* Direction Générale des Relations Culturelles, Scientifiques et Techniques, Ministère des Affaires Étrangères avec le concours du Centre National de la Recherche Scientifique, Paris.

Verhoeven, U. 1986, Unwetter, in W. Helck and E. Otto (eds.), *Lexikon der Ägyptologie, 6: Stele – Zypresse,* cols. 860–861. Otto Harrassowitz, Wiesbaden.

Vinson, S. 1994, *Egyptian Boats and Ships.* Shire Publications Ltd., Princes Risborough.

Vinson, S. 1998, *The Nile Boatman at Work.* Philipp von Zabern, Mainz am Rhein.

Volkoff, O. V. (ed.), 1973, *Voyages en Egypte de Johann Wild, 1606–1610.* Institut français d'archéologie orientale, Cairo.

Wachsmann, S. 1998, *Seagoing Ships and Seamanship in the Bronze Age Levant.* Chatham Publishing, London.

Ward, C. A. 2000, *Sacred and Secular: Ancient Egyptian ships and boats.* Published for Archaeological Institute of America, Boston, MA by The University Museum, University of Pennsylvania; Kendall/Hunt Publishing Company, Philadelphia.

Wente, E. F. 1967, *Late Ramesside Letters.* Oriental Institute of the University of Chicago, Chicago.

Willcocks, W. 1904, *The Nile in 1904.* E. and F. N. Spon, London.

Willcocks, W. and Craig, J. I. 1913, *Egyptian Irrigation, I.* E. and F. N. Spon, London.

Winlock, H. E. 1955, *Models of Daily Life in Ancient Egypt from the Tomb of Meket-r' at Thebes.* Harvard University Press, Cambridge, Massachusetts.

Zilliacus, H., Frösén, J., Hohti, P., Kaimio J. and Kaimio, M. (eds.), 1979, *Fifty Oxyrhynchus Papyri (P.Oxy.Hels.).* Societas Scientiarum Fennica, Helsinki.

The Spitting Goddess and the Stony Eye: Divinity and flint in Pharaonic Egypt

Carolyn A. Graves-Brown

Introduction

Flint is often considered to be a utilitarian stone, neither rare nor particularly beautiful, commonly used for the manufacture of weapons and tools until at least the New Kingdom (1550–1069 B.C.). This paper attempts to demonstrate that flint also held symbolic meanings and was closely associated with celestial serpents, transfiguring fire and solar lions. Born from the dangerous and mysterious deserts, *Feuerstein* was a perfect weapon of the gods and particularly apt for the fiery and furious deities who embodied the Eye of Re.

These associations will be explored in texts, and to a lesser degree in pictorial evidence, by first looking at the general context of flint and then examining its relationship with particular deities. The evidence shows that flint appears in the same fuzzy metaphoric set as fire, lions, storms, and snakes, and displays certain attributes of divinity, including the polarised attributes of protection and danger. The ways in which specific deities may be associated with flint evoke multivocal metaphoric messages which can be divided into three groups: avatars of the Eye of Re, storm gods and doorkeepers. While in individual instances it could be argued that references to flint are arbitrary, general patterns do seem to emerge. Indeed, this is what one might expect of embedded implicit ideas rather than explicit ideology.

To understand which particular deities correlate with flint, that is, the connection between flint and religion in the narrowest sense, we must employ textual evidence. This is not without difficulties, however. One of the words for flint, *ds*, is also a word for 'knife' (Erman and Grapow 1971, 5.485–486). I suggest that perhaps the *ds*-knife bore the qualities of flint in concept, even when metal was also used. However, here the assumption that a knife is made of flint is limited to only those instances where the stone determinative is used, where *ds* is used as an adjective, or where the text is so early in date as to suggest that it was more likely that stone rather than metal was used. A stone knife was likely to have been made of flint since, although knives are also known in other materials (*e.g.* rock crystal in the Early Dynastic Period), flint is, archaeologically, by far the most common type of stone used in knife manufacture. Depictions of butchery scenes in Old Kingdom (2686–2181 B.C.) tombs clearly show the sharpening of a stone, not a metal knife, and recent excavations have shown that even in the New Kingdom flint tools are common (Giddy 1999, 227). Therefore, in the analysis of early texts, including the Pyramid Texts, I have assumed that references to knives refer to flint knives.

One might argue that the association of particular deities with the flint knife was based on their general association with the form of the knife and that the reference to a particular stone is immaterial. While I have some sympathies with this argument, I believe that generally the stone determinative is very deliberately placed in the text. In fact, it appears that, textually, references to flint knives increase as the archaeological evidence declines; not a pattern one would expect if the material were irrelevant.

As for understanding the symbolic relationships between flint and other entities, Aufrère's (1983, 13–14) exploration of the affiliation of gods and minerals demonstrates that deities were seen as extracting power from the Eastern Desert, from whence minerals derive, and that stone, including flint, was created by the Eye of Re or Horus. Given that the desert is often cited in texts as the home of serpents and lions, a metonymical link may be anticipated between flint and these creatures, or deities who take their forms or bear their attributes.

Spitting and licking serpents of flint

Snakes appear to generally correlate with knives in several ways. Both were apotropaic as suggested by protective figures carrying snake wands or magical knives (*e.g.* the figures on apotropaic 'wands'). As we shall see, snakes were also associated with flint. The snake on the mountain of Bakhu is described in Coffin Texts (CT) II.160, 375b ff and Book of the Dead (BD) 108 and 111 – all versions of the same spell:

> … there is a snake on the top of that mountain, 30 cubits in his length; 3 cubits from his foreside on are flint. I know the name of this snake: 'who is on his mountain, who is in his flame' is his name.
>
> (Borghouts 1973, 114)

A very similar snake is recounted in P. Turin 1993 2,4–6:

> I am purified by it – just as they did for their father Re-Horakhty, on the big mountains of *Bȝhw* when the great *mḥy* snake appeared, in the front side of whose form the *mꜥbȝ* spear is, of one cubit of flint.
>
> (Borghouts 1973)

Bȝhw was a mythical place in the East (Posener 1965, 76) and was associated with danger and difficulty, as well as creation. The snake is identified as Apophis, firstly, because of its role as an archenemy of Re. Secondly, its title *imy nsr.f* 'he who is in his flame' is later linked to Apophis in Edfu I, 62,9 (Borghouts 1971, 207–208; 1973, 114, n. 7). Interestingly, *inr*, 'stone', is also given as a name of Apophis (Aufrère 1991, 98–99). As we shall see, it is more usual for instruments of Re, not his enemies, to have flinty associations.

Another description of a flint snake occurs in spell 108 of the Papyrus of Nu, BM EA10477 (Lapp 1997, pl. 22): ⟨hieroglyphs⟩ *m ds wbḫ n bšw*. That the flint is bright and light is suggested by *wbḫ* meaning 'shining', 'bright', etc. *Bšw*, written with other determinatives, can mean to 'break out', 'erupt', and 'spit' or 'vomit' and can refer to the uraeus flame. Thus, the phrase may be translated as 'of light coloured, shiny, spitting flint'; conjuring images of the spitting uraeus. The link between flint and snakes can also be observed in scenes involving fearsome goddesses, daughters of Re, and uraeus entities which may be depicted as spitting serpents or human-headed spitting deities. For example, a painting from the tomb of Seti I (Piankoff 1954, fig. 86) depicts snake- and lioness-headed goddesses and four other knife-wielding goddesses spitting into pits; the spittle resembling Old Kingdom depictions of spalls from the sharpening of flint knives. Alternatively, the allusion may be to the spalling of heated flint, whereby hot fragments are 'spat' out. Such heating may have taken place either in the process of firing a quarry surface or through heat treatment to improve flaking quality, the latter being attested as early as the Predynastic Period (5500-3100 B.C.; Holmes 1989, 459–464).

In the Pyramid Texts, flint knives are described in ophidian terms, *e.g.* Utterance 228 (228) (I use Sethe's (1969) transcriptions for the Pyramid Texts throughout the paper.): [hieroglyphs] *pri nm s3b w3d r s ʿm nf i nsb n.f* 'the parti-coloured knife, which is green, has gone forth thereat and it has swallowed for itself that which it has licked'. Fire and snakes are both described as having licking and consuming abilities. Ritner (1993, 97–98) believes *nsb* or 'licking' parallels the 'spitting' of snakes. In a similar text, PT Utterance 290 (431), the knife is described as 'black', a colour associated with fertility or, again, as 'parti-coloured'. This provokes the question of whether or not colours used to describe knives might also be allusions to the colours of snakes.

The translation with regard to colour is not without difficulty. Green, *w3d* can mean 'fresh', possibly alluding to the *wd3t* eye. Divine snakes, like the knife, may be described as *s3b*. Horus Behedeti was described as *s3b šwt* or 'multicoloured of plumage' and celestial cows and dog-faced guardians of the portals of the other-world were also referred to as *s3b*. Perhaps the word may be understood as 'colourful', relating to celestial images of 'brightness'. Alternatively, the description 'parti-coloured' may have denoted ideas of liminality, of both light and dark. Parallels for this are known among the Nuer, where skins of spotted felines are among liminal objects used to heal the wounds of initiates (Beidelman 1968, 121; Turner 1991, 142). The notion of pied divinity is also common to the Dinka (Lienhardt 1961, 14, 46). In ancient Egyptian culture, spotted skin was worn by liminal beings, *e.g. Sem*-priests and the transfigured dead, and, until the Middle Kingdom (2055–1650 B.C.), was placed over coffins. Thus, textual references to the parti-coloured nature of the knife may allude to celestial and possibly liminal meanings, as well as snake imagery.

The question must then be raised, why should snakes be associated with flint? Like flint, snakes are of the earth. Re passes through a snake in the underworld. Snakes, like flint, are found in the desert. Their spitting may recall the spalls of flint tool manufacture. Finally, each (as will be discussed further below) can be either associated with protection or danger.

Lions

Lions, too, are associated with flint via references to claws of flint or as wielders of flint knives. Kees (1965, 108, n. 4) states that the claw is used as a metaphor for knife as implied in PT 1212 where the 'claw of Madfet' is used against enemies of the king. In an inscription of Seti I, Pachet sharpens her claws of stone. As will be discussed, in an inscription from the Temple at Edfu the Horus lion is said to have flint arms.

The lion and flint also appear to be linked through their common solar and desert associations. The lion and lioness were considered to be creatures of the desert and were linked metonymically with minerals. They were also solar animals and lioness goddesses (for Sekhmet see below) and were envisaged as the raging, wandering (solar) Eye which must, like mined flint, be brought back from the desert.

Fire

Fire itself was often paralleled with flint in religious texts. From the 19th Dynasty, *iw nsrsr* 'the Lake of Fire' could be substituted for *iw dsds* 'the Lake of (Two) Knives'. In addition, flint and fire were both described in texts as 'sharp' (Zandee 1960, 152); they could 'lick' (*nsb*), they could both 'consume' (Eyre 2002, 173), and both were 'struck' (*sḫt*) in manufacture (Erman and Grapow 1971, 4.467). An example of their parallel use in text occurs in P. Bremner-Rhind 25,7:
𓊬𓄿𓏏𓀜𓂝𓏛𓂋𓏛 'a fire shall cut you with its (flint) knife' (Faulkner 1937, 170).

The ability of *Feuerstein* to produce sparks, particularly when struck with meteoric iron, would probably have been familiar to the Egyptians. The occasional emission of sparks in the manufacturing of flint tools must have been noticed. Additionally, the use of flint scrapers by sculptors against certain hard stones produces an acrid burning smell. There is therefore little wonder that flint was associated with fire.

Thus far, I have attempted to show how flint was associated within the metaphoric set – snakes, lions, and fire. Below I shall discuss how specific gods may be associated with this set, but first I briefly explore further reasons why flint was used to emphasise divinity.

Tools of divinity – weapons of death, instruments of protection

Flint may be characterised as both protective and dangerous. The lethal sharpness of flint is well known to knappers, a quality predisposing its suitability as an effective weapon. However, the material was also protective, as suggested by a miniature Early Dynastic (3100–2686 B.C.) flint knife found by Petrie (1902, 24, pl. 51) in the town of Abydos, presumed to have amuletic/protective qualities since it is too small to have been functional. Miniature polished flint knives have also been found in the tomb of Tutankhamun (Murray and Nutall 1963 19, 620/62 and 63). Early Dynastic amuletic flint *psš-kf* knives are also known (*e.g.* BM EA37279; Petrie 1902, 24, pl. 51, 22; Spencer 1980, 101 (755), pl. 79). Later amuletic *psš-kf* made from other materials are also attested (Roth 1992). (It is worth noting that amuletic flint is to some degree poorly documented, since when the stone is particularly attractive or highly polished, Egyptologists tend to call it 'chalcedony'.) An ivory object, apparently imitating a flint blade, inscribed with the name of the 1st-dynasty king Aha was found at Abydos (Petrie 1901, 21, pl. 36). Amuletic flints of non-knife forms occur at Deir el-Medina, presumably of New Kingdom date (Bruyère 1933, 7). A pendant of 'roughly ground and pierced' black flint was found at Tanis possibly dating to the Ptolemaic Period (332–30 B.C.; Petrie 1885, 34). In these last two cases at least, it seems that the material and not the form was the protective element. Further evidence for the symbolic nature of flint comes from the Edfu mineral lists which include the stone as an amuletic material (Edfu 6.1 l.4–5; Aufrère 1983, n. 47).

Several other texts make reference to flint which suggests that in certain contexts it was imbued with protective qualities. From the Second Beth-Shan Stela of Seti I (Kitchen 1993, 13) comes a description of the king: 'Spreading his wings (firm) as flint …'. Although this passage may be variously interpreted, wings, like flint, may be considered protective as demonstrated by frequent depictions of female winged goddesses protecting the deceased.

Another example of the protective role of flint is suggested in the First Hittite Marriage Stela of Ramesses II:

Sovereign of the Two Lands like Atum
Wall of flint around the Nile-land …

(Kitchen 1996, 87)

Similarly, CT 1072 reads: 𓀀𓂋𓏏𓏤𓏛𓇋𓅱 *iw sn kȝi m inb nw ds nt* [*m*] *R-sṯȝw pn ḥr mw ḥr tȝ* 'They have high walls of flint in Rosetau upon water and upon land'. The protective character of the town walls seems to be emphasised here, but the references to flint may be symbolic since flint walls, as such, have not yet been attested archaeologically. However, two conical flint and limestone tumuli surrounded by Roman burials were found by Petrie *et al.* (1896, 34) near the 18th-dynasty town near Naqada, an area where flint and limestone are abundant. (Due to the size of these tumuli they were not excavated and at present remain undated.) The protective nature of flint may also be attested at Dendera where flint was also used to cover graves, for example, at a 17th-dynasty tomb excavate by Petrie (1900, 22), although, it could be argued that this was simply the use of a material that was readily available.

Nevertheless, the protective properties of flint are implied in various 'medical' papyri. The Brooklyn Papyrus 47.218.48 and 85 (lines 31 and 72a) prescribes the use of a flint knife against snake bites (Sauneron 1989, 27, 97). P. Ebers (673 83, 20–22; 375 59, 20–21; 412 62, 14–15; 875 109, 2–11, etc.; Wreszinski 1913) prescribes the use of flint spalls, particularly black flint, for various ailments including those of the eye, as well as a flint knife for excising a worm. P. Ramesseum V (Nr. XVII; Nr. XX) similarly prescribes the use of black flint (Deines *et al.* 1958, 32). While Miller (1989) and others believe that the choice of flint may have been predicated upon its practical sterile quality rather than some magical protective essence, Bouchet-Bert (1998), discusses the 'superstitious' views of the Egyptians. Perhaps both played their part – functionality and ideology need not be mutually exclusive.

The tool of the sun god

In the foregoing, I have discussed the association of flint with divine snakes, fire and lions, and the attribution of protective qualities to this stone. Here, I am concerned with how these aspects of flint relate to specific deities. I will first examine its connections with the sun god and then show that flint was also a suitable weapon for Re and Horus, as well as the fiery goddesses of the Eye, such as Sekhmet and Isis.

It seems that in certain contexts flint was viewed as a solar stone, and could be interchanged with quartz which also embodied solar meanings. The textual and iconographic correlation of the arrow with the Eye of Re, the sun-beam 'laser' has been explicated by Brunner-Traut (1956). The solar significance of quartzite, which became particularly salient during the heliocentric periods, is perhaps partly suggested by the many quartz and quartzite arrowheads found in Pharaonic tombs. Likewise, flint arrowheads are common and occur even as late as the New Kingdom, *e.g.* from the tomb of Tutankhamun (McLeod 1982), from the Memphite area (Giddy 1999, 227, 229–243, pl. 52), Qantir (Tillman 1986, 86–87, pl. 24–25), and from the tomb of Maiherpei at Thebes (Daressy 1902, 33–36, pl. 11). Perhaps, then, flint was used as an ideological substitute for quartz. *Ds* is, after all, the label beside a quartz object on the amulet board in the Berlin Museum (20 600; Harris 1961, 138).

The following texts portray the flint knife as a magically efficacious solar weapon of Re. The first is one of a number from the Bremner Rhind Papyrus, 27,21: 'Re triumphs over Apep in the presence of the Great Ennead, and the flint knife shall be stuck fast in his head in the presence of Re every day' (Faulkner 1933, 21; 1937, 173). Another occurs in P. Salt 825: 'A knife of flint from Eastern Behdet is brought. It came forth from Re to repel his enemies by means of it' (Derchain 1965, 139 and 7, col. 6/5). The writing of *ds* in these texts employs the stone determinative, or states explicitly that flint was the material from which the knife was made. Roth (1992, 138–140) suggests that the *psš-kf* in its early (flint) form may have been used to cut the umbilical cord, thereby symbolising the killing of the Apophis snake. Likewise, for the ritual 'trampling of the fish' at the Festival of Edfu, an execration rite against the enemies of the sun god, flint was also employed (Meeks and Favard-Meeks 1996, 181).

Horus

Horus, like Re, had solar associations and likewise was associated with flint. Horus held the title, 'Lord of the Knife' (Wilson 1997, 1208) and as god of Letopolis was portrayed as a snake fighter (Borghouts 1971, 209). As mentioned above, flint knives were used as weapons against snakes, thus, we might expect examples which link Horus with flint. BD Chapter 125b, 7 (Allen 1974, 98) reads: 'Oh flinty-eyed one who has come forth from Letopolis, I have not done crooked things'. Naville (1886, 292) gives 24 versions of the spell of which two mention flint. His transcription of BM 9900 is given here as the most complete published rendering of the phrase: *i ir. ty.fy m ds*. A 21st-dynasty Cairo papyrus of *B3k-n-mw.t* (Seeber 1976, pl. 31) contains the same hieroglyphic composition. The alternative version of 'two eyes of flint' is *i ir.ty.fy m ḥt* or 'two eyes of flame'. Thus, fire and flint, both of which have similar properties as we have seen, are used to characterise Horus' eyes.

At Edfu, *ꜥf mi ds* 'his arm is like flint' occurs in a passage describing Horus: 'his arm is like flint, he chases after foes and attacks them with his claws (in the form of a lion)' (Chassinat 1931, 127,11). Here again, Horus is associated with flint and its qualities as a weapon. Linked to this is the imagery of the attacking lion, associated elsewhere with flint as the material of which the lion's claws are made.

Fiery goddesses – the eye of the sun god

Various knife- and bow-wielding goddesses were also associated with flint, particularly lioness-headed deities associated with the Eye of Re, or Eye of Horus. As Junker (1917, 150–151) points out, the Eye could be represented as a knife or the uraeus, or as Hathor or Sekhmet. The identification of flint with the goddesses of the Eye emphasised their knife wielding, leonine, ophidian, fiery and desert connections.

(a) Sekhmet

In texts the goddess Sekhmet was associated with flint, as well as fire, lions and the desert. Often portrayed in leonine form, she bore the following epithets: 'Lady of the Eastern Desert'

(Germond 1981, 106; Sethe 1923); 'mistress of fire' who can shoot flame from her eyes (Borghouts 1973, 136); and 'Knife of the King' (Morschauser 1991, 140), a designation whose meaning may be further understood via an epithet of Horus, the god of kingship, 'Lord of Sekhmet'. Taken together, perhaps this goddess can be understood as embodying the slaying knife of Horus (Wilson 1997, 288). Thus, Sekhmet is characterised by the metaphorically-linked elements of lions, the desert, eyes, fire and knives; all of which may assume a common link in their association with flint.

Further, the Ptolemaic Book of Hours (BM EA10569) describes a deity as 'Flint Knife of Sakhmis' (Faulkner 1958, 17). Although Faulkner's translation does not specify whether or not the *ds*-knife was flint, his transcription clearly shows the stone determinative: *ds nw Šḥmt*. Similarly, the god, 'The bearer of the flint knife' is linked with Sekhmet (hieroglyphs from Gauthier 1925–1931, 140; presumably the original text was meant to begin). P. Jumilhac mentions two flint knife-carrying demons, *ḫȝtyw* and *šmȝyw* (Vandier 1962, 130, pl. 18, 7). These beings are often connected with Sekhmet (Wilson 1997, 705–706, 1008–1009). Thus, there is another possible link between Sekhmet and flint knives through her association with these demons.

CT 311 reads: 'Sekhmet is she who wielded the Viper-Mountain knife on the night of the great battle ...' (De Buck 1947, 67; Faulkner 1978, 228). The mountain itself was associated with flint, *e.g.* BD 31a: 'My teeth are of flint. My teeth are of Viper (Cerastis) Mountain' (Naville 1886, 100). Kees (1965) discusses the meaning of 'Viper Mountain' noting that it first appears in the Pyramid Texts in connection with claws and teeth and is associated with gods such as *ʿȝnti*, *Mʿti.t* and *Pʿḥt*. There is also a suggestion that Viper Mountain as *ȝtf.t* may be associated with *itfȝ-wr* 'the great (flint) saw' of PT 627. These various texts demonstrate then, that in addition to being associated with flint knife-wielding demons, Sekhmet herself carried a knife, which, if not made of flint itself, was associated with a locality which had links to this type of stone.

(b) Isis

Isis too was characterised by attributes common to flint and was associated with the Eye of Re. Kees (1925, 4) discusses how Isis of the Edfu version of the Horus myth was depicted as a knife with legs. She is known as the 'fiery one' (*ȝsb.t*) in BD spell 69, and in Plutarch's account suckled a child with fire to immortalise him (Darnell 1995, 91). On Egyptian coffins, Isis also appears as a snake that is spitting, a behaviour which, as mentioned above, is related to sharp flint spalls produced when knapping flint.

Isis is also related to flint, albeit indirectly, in a text from the tomb of Ramesses VI (Piankoff 1942, 24, 95) which describes the constellation of the Great Bear: 'as to this Foreleg of Seth, it is in the northern sky, tied to two mooring posts of flint by a chain of white gold (electrum)'. The text goes on to say that the Foreleg is given into the charge of Isis in her hippopotamus form. The two mooring posts may represent Isis and Nephthys, as described in the Pyramid Texts (*e.g.* Utterance 720 (2239); Faulkner 1969, 310). A possible explanation for why the posts were described as being made of flint may be found in BD spell 153 which alludes to the Lake of the Two Knives: 'I sit in the bark (of Re), I cross the Pool of the Twin Knives to the northern sky' (Allen 1974, 152). The reference to knives may relate to the mooring posts as well as Isis, given that Isis can also take the form of a flint knife.

Alternatively, in the *Adventure of Horus and Seth,* Isis is said to have been transformed into a headless block of flint (Horus and Seth 9,10): [hieroglyphs] *iw nn wn w m di s st dȝdȝ(w) n ds* 'I did not give to her a head of flint' (Gardiner 1981, 50). The mooring post in flint may thus allude to Isis herself being transformed into flint. The association of Isis with the hippopotamus was possibly another reference to her flint-like qualities. In the text from the tomb of Ramesses VI, Isis is associated with the northern sky, a celestial association that was also attributed to the hippopotamus goddess, Taweret. In addition, hippopotamus goddesses were frequently described as being fiery (Darnell 1995), an attribute which, as discussed, can be related to flint. Thus, even though Isis is named in this text, perhaps it was her manifestation as a hippopotamus, and thereby the qualities of Taweret, that together were being evoked. Additionally, the text alludes to the inundation so perhaps Isis-Sothis is invoked here. Finally, it may be that the presence of flint in the constellation alludes to the metonymic relationship between meteoric iron (the Foreleg of Seth) and flint (the *psš-kf* knife) in the *Opening of the Mouth Ceremony,* and has nothing to do with Isis.

The connections between Isis and flint and related associations are expressed in text and image in multiple ways. However, due to the layering and overlapping of meanings in Egyptian ideology and religion, as well as the laconic nature of the evidence, these metaphorical associations emerge as a complex web of relationships rather than a simple one to one correlation, thereby making clearer understandings difficult.

Storm gods

The connection between flint and storms is documented in ancient Egyptian sources, but cross-cultural parallels are also attested, particularly in relation to thunderbolts (Blinkenberg 1911; Saintyves 1936). Similar associations have been suggested by Wainwright (1932; 1963) for Seth, Min and Thoth who exhibit flint-related characteristics as gods associated with storms, *e.g.* BD spell 95 and possibly spell 125. Seven versions of spell 95,4 are cited by Naville (1886, 213), one of which, P. Berlin 3002, uses the stone determinative for the word knife: [hieroglyphs] *rwd.i ds imy ꜥ Ḏhwti m nšni* 'I steady the knife in the hand of Thoth in storms' (Allen 1974, 77).

Naville (1886, 324–325) gives two versions of spell 125,25 where the stone determinative was used (Papyrus of *twri*, Louvre III, 93 L3092; the tomb of Ramesses IX at Thebes). The Papyrus of Ani (BM EA10470) also incorporates the stone determinative (Budge 1913, 590): [hieroglyphs] *dꜥm n ds rdi tȝw rn.f* 'A sceptre of flint, Breath/North wind Giver is its name'. Allen (1974, 100) translates the passage in full: 'And what didst thou find on it, on the shore of the *mꜥȝt* (-lake)?' A sceptre of flint; Breath Giver is its name'. This type of sceptre, *dꜥm,* is similar to the word *dꜥ* meaning storm and is often written: [hieroglyphs], perhaps as a play on words.

That the Egyptians perceived a link between flint and storms is not exclusive to their culture; a belief in the celestial origin of flint is prevalent in a number of cultures (Blinkenberg 1911; Brown 1995, 30; Saintyves 1936; Taçon 1991; Thompson 1972). Nevertheless, the Egyptian textual evidence for this connection appears to be limited to the above examples;

research thus far has only yielded results for Seth and Thoth, as far as their capacity as 'storm gods' is concerned. Interestingly, no flint/storm associations have been found for Min.

Thoth and Seth

In addition to the connection between storms and flint mentioned above in BD spell 95, Thoth has additional associations which relate him to flint. For example, Aufrère (1991, 258) quotes an instance where Thoth-Re is referred to as *sḥtp nsrt* and Wilson (1997, 288) notes the association of Thoth (and Horus) with the *wdзt* knife. However, in the latter example, flint is not mentioned explicitly, but may be implied based on the hypothesis that the symbolic meanings associated with flint become embedded and presenced *vis-à-vis* the form of the knife.

Links between Thoth and flint are also suggested in his associations with the word(s) *mds/m ds*, used alternatively as a noun, adjective or verb (Kees 1925, 3). The phrase *m ds* (*mds*) *pr m št* occurs in PT 1999 (Sethe 1969, 483) and possibly in BD spell 149,1 (Naville 1886, 416). In the former Thoth's name is mentioned explicitly, and in the second text he may be implied via one of his titles, 'Great of Magic'. However, this association is not entirely certain since this title is also shared by the cobra goddess. Of more certainty is Thoth's association with the *mds*-knife in the form of the crescentic lunar avenging knife, a weapon also equated with the uraeus snake, the Eye of Horus and a flame (Kees 1925). More generally, the phrase *m ds*, is accorded different translations, sometimes as *mds*, 'keen' or 'cutting [one]' (*e.g.* Allen 1974, 292). Alternatively it may be rendered *m ds* 'with flint' or 'sharp knife' (*e.g.* Faulkner 1969, 288). The words *mds/m ds* may include the stone determinative emphasising its origins as *m ds* 'with flint' (Kees 1925, 2–5). When translated as 'powerful' *mds* can take the flame determinative. Nevertheless, with regard to *mds* and possible flint associations, only those texts which exhibit the stone determinative are included in this analysis.

The most direct links between Thoth and flint centre on his *use* of the (flint) knife. PT Utterance 477 (962) reads: ⟨hieroglyphs⟩ *dm ds.k ḏḥwty nšm mds* 'Sharpen your knife, O Thoth, which is keen and cutting ...' (Faulkner 1969, 165). Further, Thoth is characterised as the wielder or bearer of knives or flint objects, while Seth is mentioned as the source thereof. For example, Utterance 665 (1906) reads: 'Thoth comes to you with the knife which came forth from Seth ...' (Faulkner 1969, 275). In Utterance 674 (1999) *ds* is used as an adjective which may be translated as flint: ⟨hieroglyphs⟩ *mзs tp ʿwy Ḏḥwti m ds pr m Štš* 'The *mзs* upon the arms of Thoth are of flint which came forth from Seth'. However, Faulkner (1969, 288) translates *mзs* as 'spines' and *ds* as 'sharp' and Kees (1925) translates *mзs* as 'knife', based on PT 1560c where the feathers on Thoth's shoulders are described as being like knives. Seth is also mentioned in connection with a (flint) knife in Utterance 665 (1906): 'Thoth comes to you with the knife which came forth from Seth ...' (Faulkner 1969, 275). Similarly, BD spell 149,1 (Naville 1886, 416; P. Burton, BM EA9900) reads: ⟨hieroglyphs⟩ *wr ḥkзw m ds pr m Štš* 'Great of Magic, the sharp one (*mds*) which came forth from Seth' or as Allen (1974, 145) translates it: 'the keen one who escaped from Suty'. Thus, Seth seems to be related to the flint *ds* knife and to Thoth.

Returning to the latter deity, the Sanctuary of Thoth is mentioned with reference to flint. The Middle Kingdom P. Westcar (P. Berlin 3033 9,5) reads: 'There is a chest of flint in the building called 'inventory' in On'. The chest contains the number of the secret chambers in the sanctuary of Thoth (Gardiner 1925). The fact that the chest is made of flint may relate to its protective nature, or perhaps to its solar qualities, both of which in other contexts are attributed to flint. Alternatively, it may be because the chest was in a Sanctuary of Thoth that was made from a material associated with the god.

Anubis

Anubis was also associated with flint, although primarily through knives. In P. Jumilhac Anubis was said to take on the form of a snake and wield knives of flint (*dmwty n ds*) against an enemy (Vandier 1962, 125, pl. 13). Elsewhere in the text the demons, *ẖ3tyw* and *šm3yw*, use flint knives on the orders of Anubis (Vandier 1962, 130, pl. 18). It is worth noting that these are the demons who, as we have seen, were associated with Sekhmet (Wilson 1997, 705–706; 1008–1009), who was also a wielder of flint knives. On a door jamb of the Ptolemaic temple of Hibis in the Kharga Oasis, a jackal-headed god carrying two knives is labelled: 𓏞𓈖𓂋𓇋𓆱 *ḥry-ds*, 'he who is over his flint knives' (Bull and Hall 1953, pl. 10). Perhaps Anubis' associations with flint knives had to do with his status as a protective deity, and/or an aspect reflected in his role of 'divine midwife', guardian of a gateway to Rosetau (DuQuesne 1991).

Doorkeepers: Flint and protection

Another category of protective beings who seem to be both directly and indirectly associated with flint are the doorkeepers mentioned in the Book of the Dead. These guardians are variously described as fiery, ophidian, parti-coloured and knife-wielding, attributes that were characteristic of flint and other protective deities associated with flint.

An example of doorkeepers described as *mds ḥr*, using the stone determinative, comes from spell 144 which refers to the Keeper of the 4th Gate in the Papyrus of Iouiya (Cairo 51189, Naville 1908, pl. 19, 20). Likewise, in the same spell the Keeper of the 7th Gate is described as *mds*, which in one version, P. Brockelhurst II, includes the stone determinative (Naville 1886, 369). Elsewhere doorkeepers are described as employing flint directly. One of many examples is spell 145,v which describes the guardian of the 21st Portal as *(dmt ds r mdt n.s)*, 'She Who Sharpens Flint to Speak for Her' (P. BM EA10554; Allen 1974, 125, 276). A stone determinative is also apparent in the Greenfield Papyrus (BM 10544; Budge 1913, pl. 58). Spell 146, a version of 145, introduces the Keeper of the 4th Portal as the Lady 'Mighty of Knives'. Naville (1886, 371) cites seven versions of this spell, one of which (Leyden T6) gives *ḥr-m-3ḥ-bit* with the stone determinative, perhaps meaning 'Mighty of Flint Knives'. The stone determinative is also present in the Book of the Dead of Hori (Berman 1999, 370–371): 𓊪𓏞𓂋𓇋𓊖 *sḥmt(i) dsw*. The Keeper of the 4th Portal in the tomb of Sennedjem has the same hieroglyphic combination (Bruyère 1959, 58–59). While the directness of the relationship of these doorkeepers with flint varies, the general association of flint with knives and the protective aspects of both are themes which run throughout the names, titles, and other descriptions of the doorkeepers of the afterlife.

Conclusion

As we have seen, flint embodied a constellation of metaphors related to protection, protective deities and doorkeepers of the other-world, as well as possessing serpent-like attributes of spitting and licking. This stone was also noted for its brilliance and thus associated with the cardinal direction of the East, placing it firmly within the metaphoric set of instruments of Re, of fiery goddesses and snakes. Perhaps less clearly, but still plausibly, it was also a material associated with storm gods.

There are, however, some exceptions to the patterns discussed above. For example, the users of flint knives may also include threatening demons as exemplified by the demotic Papyrus IX, 'The Petition of Petêse in the Reign of Darius', from the John Rylands Library Manchester: 〔hieroglyphs〕 *iw.f n ds n ḥnbw* 'he shall belong to the knife of the slaughterers' (Griffith 1909, 2.pl. 4 and 3.250; Morschauser 1991, 109). Clearly the pattern is not always straightforward. Nevertheless, I have attempted to show that for the ancient Egyptians this humble stone held meanings which were not purely utilitarian.

While lithics are traditionally considered separate from the world of religion, it is now generally recognised that technology cannot be divorced from other social realms (Dobres 2000; Lemonnier 1986; Michael 2000; Pfaffenberger 1992). As Piankoff (1974, 6) states, "For the Egyptians every so-called "physical" fact of life had a symbolic meaning, and at the same time every symbolic act of expression had a "material" background; both were equally true and real".

Egypt Centre, University of Wales Swansea and Institute of Archaeology, UCL

Acknowledgements

All work depends upon the efforts of others. My special thanks to my husband, Paul Graves-Brown, for his extensive encouragement, suggestions and editorial input, to V. A. Donohue for his helpful conversation, to Terence DuQuesne for drawing to my attention the jackal headed deity at Hibis, and finally, to Wendy Goodridge for moral support.

References

Allen, T. G. 1974, *The Book of the Dead, or, Going Forth by Day: Ideas of the ancient Egyptians concerning the hereafter as expressed in their own terms.* University of Chicago Press, Chicago.

Aufrère, S. 1983, Caractères Principaux et Origine Divine des Minéraux, *Revue d'Égyptologie* 34, 3–21.

Aufrère, S. 1991, *L'Univers minéral dans la pensée égyptienne, 1.* Institut français d'archéologie orientale, Cairo.

Beidelman, T. O. 1968, Some Nuer Notions of Nakedness, Nudity and Sexuality, *Africa* 38, 113–167.

Berman, L. M. 1999, *The Cleveland Museum of Art: Catalogue of Egyptian art.* Hudson Hills Press, New York.

Blinkenberg, C. 1911. *The Thunderweapon in Religion and Folklore: A study in comparative archaeology.* Cambridge University Press, Cambridge.

Borghouts, J. F. 1971, Excurses II: The *s3b.t*-snakes, in J. F. Borghouts (ed.), *The Magical Texts of Papyrus Leiden. Papyrus I.348.* Rijksmuseum van Oudheden te Leiden, 200–209. E. J. Brill, Leiden.

Borghouts, J. F. 1973, The Evil Eye of Apophis, *Journal of Egyptian Archaeology* 59, 114–150.

Bouchet-Bert, L. 1998, The Question of *dkr* and Sterile Blades in P. Ebers 875, *Journal of Egyptian Archaeology* 84, 224–228.

Brown, A. G. 1995, Beyond Stone-Age Economics: A strategy for contextual lithic analysis, in A. J. Schofield (ed.), *Lithics in Context: Suggestions for the future direction of lithic studies*, 27–37. Lithic Studies Society, London.

Brunner-Traut, E. 1956, Atum als Bogunschütze, *Mitteilungen des Deutschen Archäologischen Instituts Abteilun Kairo* 14, 20–28.

Bruyère, B. 1933, *Rapport sur les fouilles de Deir el Médineh (1930).* Institut français d'archéologie orientale, Cairo.

Bruyère, B. 1959, *La tombe no. 1 de Sen-Nedjem à Deir el Médineh.* Institut français d'archéologie orientale, Cairo.

Budge, E. A. W. 1913, *The Greenfield Papyrus in the British Museum: The funerary papyrus of princess Nesitanebtashru, daughter of Painetchem II and Nesi-Khensu, and priestess of Amen-Ra at Thebes, about B.C. 970.* British Museum, London.

Bull, L. and Hall, L. F. (eds.), 1953, *The Temple of Hibis in the El Khargeh Oasis, 3: The decoration.* The Metropolitan Museum of Art, New York.

Chassinat, E. 1931, *Le Temple d'Edfou, 6.* Institut française d'archéologie orientale du Caire, Cairo.

Daressy, G. 1902, *Fouilles de la Vallée des Rois (1898-1899).* Catalogue Général des Antiquités Égyptiennes du Musée du Caire, Cairo.

Darnell, J. C. 1995, Hathor Returns to Medamûd, *Studien zur Altägyptischen Kultur* 22, 47–94.

De Buck, A. 1947, *Coffin Texts, 4.* University of Chicago Press, Chicago.

Deines, H., Grapow, H. and Westendorf, W. 1958, *Gundriss der Medizin der Alten Ägypter: Übersetzung der Medizinischen Texte, 4/1.* Akademie Verlag, Berlin.

Derchain, P. 1965, *Le Papyrus Salt 825 (B.M. 10051).* Palais des Académies, Brussels.

Dobres, M-A. 2000. *Technology and Social Agency.* Blackwell, Oxford.

DuQuesne, T. 1991, *Jackal at the Shaman's Gate.* Darengo Publications, Oxford.

Erman, A. and Grapow, H. (eds.), 1971, *Wörterbuch der Aegyptischen Sprache, 4-5.* Akadamie Verlag, Berlin.

Eyre, C. 2002, *The Cannibal Hymn: A cultural and literary study.* Liverpool University Press, Liverpool.

Faulkner, R. O. 1933, *The Papyrus Bremner-Rhind BM No. 10188.* Édition de la Fondation égyptologique Reine Élisabeth, Brussels.

Faulkner, R. O. 1937, The Bremner-Rhind Papyrus III, *Journal of Egyptian Archaeology* 10, 166–185.

Faulkner, R. O. 1958, *An Ancient Egyptian Book of Hours (Pap. British Museum 10569).* Griffith Institute, Oxford.

Faulkner, R. O. 1969, *The Ancient Egyptian Pyramid Texts.* Clarendon Press, Oxford.

Faulkner, R. O. 1978, *The Ancient Egyptian Coffin Texts.* Aris and Phillips, Wiltshire.

Gardiner, A. H. 1925, The Secret Chambers of the Sanctuary of Thoth, *Journal of Egyptian Archaeology* 11, 2–5.

Gardiner, A. H. 1981 [1932], *Late Egyptian Stories.* Édition de la Fondation égyptologique Reine Élisabeth, Brussels.

Gauthier, H. 1925–1931, *Dictionnaire des Noms Géographiques Contenus dans les Inscriptions Hiéroglyphiques.* Institut français d'archéologie orientale pour la Société royale de géographie d'Égypte, Cairo.

Germond, P. 1981, *Sekhmet et la Protection du Monde.* Editions de Belle-Lettres, Geneva.

Giddy, L. 1999, *Kom Rabi'a: The New Kingdom and post-New Kingdom objects.* Egypt Exploration Society, London.

Griffith, F. Ll. 1909, *Catalogue of the Demotic Papyri in the John Rylands Library, Manchester: With facsimiles and complete translations, 2-3.* University Press, Manchester.

Harris, J. R. 1961, *Lexicographical Studies in Ancient Egyptian Minerals.* Deutsche Akademie Der Wissenschaften Zu Berlin Insut Für Orientforschung, Berlin.

Holmes, D. L. 1989, *The Predynastic Lithic Industries of Upper Egypt: A comparative study of the lithic traditions of Badari, Nagada and Hierakonpolis, 2.* British Archaeological Reports, Oxford.

Junker, H. 1917, *Die Onurislegende.* Hölder, Vienna.

Kees, H. 1925, Zu den Ägyptischen Mondsagen, *Zeitschrift fur Ägyptische Sprache und Altertumskunde* 60, 1–15.

Kees, H. 1965. Der angebliche Gauname „Schlangenberg", *Mitteilungen des Deutschen Archäologischen Instituts, Abteilung Kairo* 2, 103–109.

Kitchen, K. 1993. *Ramesside Inscriptions Translated and Annotated: Translations, 1.* Blackwell, Oxford.

Kitchen, K. 1996, *Ramesside Inscriptions Translated and Annotated: Translations, 2.* Blackwell, Oxford.

Lapp, G. 1997. *The Papyrus of Nu.* British Museum Press, London.

Lemonnier, P. 1986, The Study of Material Culture Today: Toward an anthropology of technical systems, *Journal of Anthropological Archaeology* 5, 147–186.

Lienhardt, G. 1961, *Divinity and Experience: The religion of the Dinka.* Clarendon Press, Oxford.

McLeod, W. 1982, *Self Bows and Other Archery Tackle from the Tomb of Tutankhamun.* Griffith Institute, Oxford.

Meeks, D. and Favard-Meeks, C. 1996, *Daily Life of the Egyptian Gods,* (trans. by G. M. Goshgarian). John Murray, London.

Michael, M. 2000, *Reconnecting Culture, Technology and Nature: From society to heterogeneity.* Routledge, London.

Miller, R. 1989, *Dqr,* Spinning and Treatment of Guinea Worm in P. Ebers 875, *Journal of Egyptian Archaeology* 75, 249–254.

Morschauser, S. 1991, *Threat-Formula in Ancient Egypt: A study of the history, structure and use of threats and curses in ancient Egypt.* Halgo, Baltimore.

Murray, H. and Nuttall, M. 1963, *A Handlist to Howard Carter's Catalogue of Objects in Tut'ankhamun's Tomb.* Griffith Institute, Oxford.

Naville, E. 1886, *Das Ägyptische Totenbuch der XVIII bis XX Dynastie, 2.* A. Asher, Berlin.

Naville, E. 1908, *The Funeral Papyrus of Iouiya.* Constable, London.

Petrie, W. M. F. 1885, *Tanis.* Egypt Exploration Fund, London.

Petrie, W. M. F. 1900, *Dendereh 1989.* Egypt Exploration Fund, London.

Petrie, W. M. F. 1901, *The Royal Tombs of the Earliest Dynasties, 2.* Egypt Exploration Fund, London.

Petrie, W. M. F. 1902, *Abydos, 1.* Egypt Exploration Fund, London.

Petrie, W. M. F. and Quibell, J. E. 1896, *Naqada and Ballas.* B. Quaritch, London.

Pfaffenberger, B. 1992, Social Anthropology of Technology, *Annual Review of Anthropology* 21, 491–516.

Piankoff, A. 1942, *Le Livre du Jour et de la Nuit.* Institut français d'archéologie orientale, Cairo.

Piankoff, A. 1954, *The Tomb of Ramesses VI.* Pantheon Books, New York.

Piankoff, A. 1974. *The Wandering of the Soul.* Princeton University Press, Princeton.

Posener, G. 1965, Sur l'Orientation et l'Ordre des Points Cardinaux Chez les Égyptiens, in S. Schott (ed.), *Göttinger Vorträge vom Ägyptologischen Kolloquium der Akademie am 25. und 26. August 1964,* 69–78. Nachrichten der Akademie der Wissenschaften in Göttingen. Philogische-historische Klass, Göttingen.

Ritner, R. K. 1993, *The Mechanics of Ancient Egyptian Magical Practice.* Oriental Institute of the University of Chicago, Chicago.

Roth, A. M. 1992, The *Psš-kf* and the 'Opening of the Mouth' Ceremony: A ritual of birth and rebirth, *Journal of Egyptian Archaeology* 78, 113–147.

Saintyves, P. 1936, *Pierres Magiques: Bétyles, Haches-Amulettes et Pierre de Foudres. Traditions Savantes et Traditions Populaires.* Émile Nourry, Paris.

Sauneron, S. 1989, *Un Traite Égyptien d'Ophiologie. Papyrus du Brooklyn. 47.218.48 et 85.* Institut français d'archéologie orientale du Caire, Cairo.

Seeber, C. 1976, *Untersuchungen zur Darstellung des Totenrichts im Alten Ägypten.* Deutscher Kunstverlag, Berlin.

Sethe, K. 1923, Zu den Sachmet-Statuen Amenophis III, *Zeitschrift für ägyptische Sprache und Alterumskunde* 58, 43–44.

Sethe, K. 1969, *Die Altägyptischen Pyramidentexte: Nach den Papierdrüken und Photographien des Berliner Museums*. Georg Olms, Heidelsheim.

Spencer, A. J. 1980, *Catalogue of Egyptian Antiquities in the British Museum, 5: Early Dynastic objects.* British Museum Press, London.

Taçon, P. S. C. 1991, The Power of Stone: Symbolic aspects of stone use and tool development in Western Arnhemland, Australia. *Antiquity* 65, 192–207.

Thompson, J. E. S. 1972, *Maya History and Religion*. University of Oklahoma Press, Norman.

Tillman, A. 1986, Ein Steingerätinventar des neuen reiches aus Qantir/Piramess (Ägypten) Vorbericht, *Archäologisches Korrespondenzblatt* 16, 149–155.

Turner, T. 1991, "We are Parrots", "Twins are Birds": Play of tropes as operational structure, in J. W. Fernandez (ed.), *Beyond Metaphor: The theory of tropes in anthropology*, 121–158. Stanford University Press, Stanford.

Vandier, J. 1962, *Le Papyrus Jumilhac*. Centre National de la Recherche Scientifique, Paris.

Wainwright, G. A. 1932, Letopolis, *Journal of Egyptian Archaeology* 18, 159–172.

Wainwright, G. A. 1963, The Origin of Storm-Gods in Egypt, *Journal of Egyptian Archaeology* 49, 13–20.

Wilson, P. 1997, *A Ptolemaic Lexikon: A lexicographical study of the texts in the temple of Edfu.* Uitgeverij Peeters en Department Oosterse Studies, Leuven.

Wreszinski, W. 1913, *Der Papyrus Ebers: Umschrift, Übersetzung und Kommentar.* J. C. Hinrichs, Leipzig.

Zandee, J. 1960, *Death as an Enemy According to Ancient Egyptian Conceptions.* E. J. Brill, Leiden.

From the Cradle to the Grave: Anthropoid busts and ancestor cults at Deir el-Medina

Nicola Harrington

Introduction

A group of enigmatic artefacts known as 'anthropoid' or 'ancestor' busts form the topic of this paper which considers their place in the domestic and funerary religion of ancient Egypt, particularly at the New Kingdom settlement of Deir el-Medina. Characteristic features of the busts are analysed for the information they provide on gender and function. This paper argues that anthropoid busts may represent individual deceased family members in an idealised form and supports the view that the busts were part of an ancestor cult in New Kingdom Egypt. The concept of gendered space is also discussed within the context of household cults and, in view of the location and use of domestic busts, the light this may shed on the social status of women during this period.

During 30 years of excavation at the artisan's village of Deir el-Medina, Bruyère (1939, 168) discovered around 75 freestanding stone sculptures which he termed '*bustes de laraires*', but which are now commonly known as anthropoid or ancestor busts. Another 80 busts have been recovered, from sites including Abydos, Amarna and Saqqara, but many are unprovenanced (Keith-Bennett 1981, 46; Romero 1999, 282). At their most basic, the busts have human heads, often with wigs, but no other physical features are delineated below the shoulders, which slope towards a slightly wider base. Traces of polychrome decoration in the form of floral collars and lotiform pendants are found on some examples. A variety of materials, including sandstone, granite, wood, faience and clay were used in their manufacture (Romero 1999, 282), though the majority were carved from limestone (Figures 1 and 2).

The busts seem to be the product of gradual religious changes that became apparent in the 18th Dynasty, a period which also saw greater emphasis on solar theology (Allen 1989, 89), and the manufacture of solar-related artefacts, such as stelephorous statues (*cf.* Friedman 1985, 93–94). The explicit labelling of the *ꜣḫ iḳr* (or 'powerful spirits', see below) on stelae also began at this time, although the actual concept of *ꜣḫ iḳr* and stelae depicting the deceased holding lotus flowers in the traditional *ꜣḫ iḳr* pose had existed from the Old Kingdom (2696–2181 B.C.) onwards (Schulman 1986, 303, 316). It is possible that, though not directly responsible for their emergence, the so-called Amarna revolution was a catalysing factor in the production of both stelae and busts (*cf.* Schulman 1986, 318), and the latter may be linked to the human-headed stelae depicted in the First Hour of the Amduat, which "allude to the commanding power of the [sun] god, who communicates all that is necessary for those in the afterlife through his directives" (Hornung 1999, 34, 43–44, figs. 14 and 15). The artisans of Deir el-Medina, being responsible for the construction and decoration of the royal tombs, would obviously have had access to religious texts such as the Amduat, which is first attested in the early 18th Dynasty. However, this explanation does not account for the busts' tripartite wigs, which are absent on the bearded Amduat figures, and the non-uniformity of the busts' shapes (Keith-Bennett 1981, 45).

There are no direct precedents for anthropoid busts, which are first attested from around the reign of Amenhotep II (*c.*1400 B.C.), except perhaps for the decoration on a Middle Kingdom coffin (Keith-Bennett 1981, 49; Romero 1999, 282). The 'bust' depicted on the stele of Hetepmontu, dated to about the 13th Dynasty (Lines 2001), is more likely to be a damaged or deliberately truncated version of Gardiner's (1957, 447) sign A52 . Contemporary comparative material is limited, with human-headed heart amulets (Andrews 1994, fig. 61), the 'mannequin' of Tutankhamun (Einaudi 1998, 230), and the 18th-dynasty feminoform

Figure 1. A typical 19th-dynasty 'female' limestone anthropoid bust with painted broad collar and tripartite wig. Dimensions: 26.2 cm high x 15.5 cm wide. Brooklyn Museum, New York; Edwin Charles Wilbour Fund, cat. no. 54.1. (© Nicola Harrington.)

vases providing the closest parallels. The latter are a specific group of burnished terracotta vessels with carefully moulded female faces and wigs, and large black-painted lotiform pendants or collars. They also bear platform crowns that form the neck and spout of the bottle, with no other physical features indicated (*e.g.* Hayes 1959, 195, fig. 110; Roveri N.D., 45). Most are unprovenanced and their function is unclear, though it seems reasonable to suggest that they had a specific cultic function based on their uniformly high quality and distinctive appearance.

Figure 2. Wooden 'female' anthropoid bust, which was originally covered in gesso. 18th Dynasty(?), from Medinet el-Fayum. UC 16550. (Courtesy of the Petrie Museum of Egyptian Archaeology, UCL.)

Characteristics of the busts

Despite the work of Keith-Bennett (1981), Friedman (1985), Boreux (1932) and Kaiser (1990), the busts remain enigmatic. This is largely a result of the fact that, from a corpus of 150, only four busts bear inscriptions (Friedman 1985, 82). The busts seem to have required no formal identification to the ancient Egyptians, as visual recognition within specific contexts would have been sufficient, particularly if their main function was within a domestic environment. A similar interpretation for pre-18th-dynasty *ȝḥ ikr* stelae has been suggested:

> Since the *akh* was clearly a supernatural being, and since … the figures shown on stelae receiving offerings and prayers in fact represented *akhw*, then it becomes obvious that there was no real need to identify them as such with captions, for everyone who looked at the stelae immediately knew what these figures were.
>
> (Schulman 1986, 317)

Literacy, especially among women, although certainly higher at Deir el-Medina than elsewhere in contemporary Egypt, appears to have been limited (Bryan 1986, 17–25; Janssen 1992, 89–91). There would be little gain in having busts labelled if those to whom they were most significant could not read the inscriptions (Meskell 2002, 129), and given the levels of illiteracy, the majority would have turned to oral requests for immediate help in preference to the services of scribes (Baines and Lacovara 2002, 22; Meskell 2002, 187).

In ancient Egypt, hair was an indication of gender and social status, and as Robins (1999, 63–64) points out, hairstyles were designed to reinforce the "gender distinction inherent in Egyptian society", and could also indicate timelessness associated with the dead. In the rare double busts, gender is distinguished iconographically; the male heads have caps or are shaven, and some have beards, whereas women wear tripartite wigs and collars (*e.g.* Demarée 2002, 138, cat. 79; Keith-Bennett 1981, 70, figs. 15–17; Figure 3). This distinction between male and female deceased figures is never seen in mummy masks or coffins (with the obvious exception of the Osirian false beards; Robins 1999, 68), or the double shabtis that are also attested in the 18th Dynasty (Markoe 1996a, 54; Trapani 1998, 1172; Wildung and Schoske 1984, 134), which calls into question the busts' supposed development from mummiform objects (Romero 1999, 282; Roveri 1988, 149, cat. 90). As the vast majority of busts have non-striated tripartite wigs, it is likely that they represent women, providing a parallel to the *ȝḥ ikr n Rˁ* stelae mostly dedicated to men. The two artefact types are combined on a unique stela now in the British Museum which shows a female(?) figure before three busts, two *en face* and carved in raised relief (Bierbrier 1982, fig. 69).

A pair of finely carved yellow limestone busts discovered in TT 373 at Dra Abu el-Naga (Habachi 1976, 84; Porter and Moss 1960, 433–434) present an exception to the pattern outlined above. This tomb was constructed in the 19th Dynasty for the royal scribe Amenmose, and the busts represent his mother, Mutemonet, the sistrum player of Amun, Mut and Khonsu (BM EA 1198; Egyptian Antiquities Organisation 1978, 93; Shaw and Nicholson 1995, 32) and his father, and the official, Paendjerty (Luxor J. 147). Both busts, which stood about 50 cm high (Habachi 1976, 84), bear striated wigs and three vertical columns of inscription on the front identifying each individual and providing their titles. These busts seem to be purely funerary; this function is expressed by the striated wigs which are normally associated only with deities and found on anthropoid coffins and shabtis (Fazzini 1996, 134; Robins 1999, 68), and by their inscriptions and find context. It seems that the busts of Paendjerty and Mutemonet shared a niche at the entrance of TT 373, opposite statues of the tomb owner (Habachi 1976, 85). Perhaps Amenmose's parents were presenced in the medium of the busts to guide their son through the dangers of the afterlife.

Another bust (Metropolitan Museum 66.99.45), possibly also intended directly for a tomb, stands 41.5 cm tall and bears a painted striated wig and a floral collar (Kaiser 1990, pl. 61, fig. 1). It is more cylindrical in shape than the majority of busts, and is in this sense more akin

Figure 3. Limestone male bust with beard and traces of a painted broad collar. UC 16553. (Courtesy of the Petrie Museum of Egyptian Archaeology, UCL.)

to anthropoid coffins. As the majority of busts have an average height of 23–25 cm (Bothmer 1987, 27), it is possible that such large artefacts form a distinct group intended for inclusion in the tomb. This theory is supported by a unique scene in the 18th-dynasty tomb of Horemheb at Sheikh Abd el-Qurna (TT 78) which shows two life-size bearded busts being carried in a funerary procession (Janssen and Janssen 1996, 54, fig. 20). In previous studies, some scholars (*e.g.* Kaiser 1990, 271–272) have attributed male gender to busts with red-painted faces (Fiore-Marochettti 2002, 142–143, cat. 87). However, some categories of female figure are normally painted red, such as nursing mothers on ostraca, so-called fertility figurines (Andreu 2002b, 115; Pinch 1983, 410) and feminoform vases (Bourriau 1982a, 102–103). Female deities, including Hathor and Mut, were portrayed with either red or yellow skin, reflecting their solar aspects and their roles in birth and rebirth. In the Turin Love Songs, "the body of the desired woman is figured as a bountiful sycamore tree, ripe and laden with fruit, redder than red jasper" (Meskell 2002, 130). Hathor is both Lady of the Sycamore (Figure 4) and Lady of the Vulva, the latter being a title inscribed on a bust (Pinch 1993, 219). According to Meskell (2002, 132), red has "symbolic resonances of power and magic", and it was "added to female statuettes that promoted sexuality and fertility in domestic and mortuary spheres".

The 18th Dynasty onwards saw a greater percentage of red/brown, as opposed to yellow, female figures, the obvious examples being statues of Queens Tiye, Nefertiti, Ankhsenamun (Ankhsenpaaten), and the royal princesses from the Amarna Period (Arnold 1996a, 50, 57–58, 71; 1996b, 87, 96, 115; 1996c, 120; Murnane 1999, 180, fig. 139). Private examples from the 18th and 19th Dynasties include the shabti of Kai-neferu, the group statues of Nefersekheru and Neye, and tomb scenes such as those of Userhat and Sennedjem (Kampp-Seyfried 1998, 254, 261; Markoe 1996b, 149).

Figure 4. Sennedjem and Iyneferti receive water from Hathor, Lady of the Sycamore, who wears a turquoise tripartite wig. Whilst the deity's face, arms and breast are yellow, the rest of her body is painted red and green, in contrast to the worshippers whose skin is uniformly red/brown. Interestingly, Iyneferti is portrayed with darker skin than her husband, 19th Dynasty, Tomb of Sennedjem (TT 1), Deir el-Medina. (© Nicola Harrington.)

Other features, such as earrings, were not necessarily gender-specific, but although men were rarely shown wearing earings in tomb paintings or elsewhere, women are frequently shown with them, particularly in funerary contexts. The platform crown found on some busts (Bruyère 1939, pl. 21; Holden 1982, 300, fig. 409) is normally associated with female royalty and divinity, and with clay female fertility figurines (*e.g.* Andreu 2002c, 244, cat. 193; Bruyère 1939, 139); it may be another device to emphasise the divine status of the deceased individual.

The choice of the lotus as part of the adornment on several busts is significant (*e.g.* Bruyère 1939, 172, fig. 67) as floral collars, along with lotus buds and blossoms, are symbols of regeneration and rebirth (Meskell 2002, 176). The feminoform vases mentioned above, stylistically part of the same tradition as the busts, are also recognisable by these pendant blossoms (Bourriau 1982a, 102–103, fig. 84). On the New Kingdom stela of Henout (Friedman 1994, 109; Vandier D'Abbadie 1946, 135), the dedicatee is shown pouring water into a large lotiform vessel on the floor before a bust on a plinth (Figure 5). Actual vessels of this type are

Figure 5. Stela of Henout, showing the dedicatee libating and burning incense before a bust with a lotiform collar, New Kingdom, from Abydos (after Vandier D'Abbadie 1946, 135).

known from several sites including Deir el-Medina (Bourriau 1982b, 146–147), and evidence suggests that these containers were used in the presence of deities, as illustrated by the stelae of Hormose and Iuy (Robins 1997, 448).

Analysis of the main features of the busts indicates certain trends. Large busts (over 25 cm high) form a distinct group, probably manufactured specifically as funerary equipment. Amulets and small faience busts (*e.g.* UC 2400, UC 2401a and 2401b; Petrie 1974, pl. 17, figs. 277–278; Thomas 1981, pl. 55, nos. 711–712; Figure 6) are also distinct from the limestone examples, which were probably created for use within the home. The lack of inscriptions on the busts or the domestic niches in which at least some of them stood (Friedman 1985, 83; 1994, 115; Meskell 2002, 114) suggests that their identification was closely linked to their location. Taken individually, features such as colour, collars and earrings were not gender-specific. Collectively, however, these features in combination with the non-striated tripartite wigs, the fact that most did not have beards, and that the inscriptions name the 'mistress of the house' and Hathor, support the theory that the majority of busts may be identified as representing female ancestors (*akhw*) – counterparts to the predominantly male *3ḫ iḳr n R*ᶜ stelae discussed below.

Figure 6. Faience amuletic busts wearing tripartite wigs and broad collars, New Kingdom, unprovenanced. UC 2401a and 2401b. (Courtesy of the Petrie Museum of Egyptian Archaeology, UCL.)

The ancestors (akhw) and the role of busts in the domestic environment

The *akh* itself was the powerful spirit of the deceased individual who could act as a mediator between mortals and the gods, and offerings were made to the *akhw* in return for guidance (Janssen and Janssen 1996, 56). P. Sallier IV states: "Make a funerary offering to the *akhw* in your house; make an offering to the gods" (Friedman 1985, 96). Many stelae and offering tables (Bruyère 1939, 166, fig. 63) are labelled *3ḫ iḳr n Rꜥ* 'powerful/effective spirit of the sun god', or according to Schulman (1986, 320), "the spirit which is effective on behalf of Re", and on some stelae this title is prefixed with 'the Osiris'. Osiris, as the deity with whom the sun god merged in the night (Hornung 1999, 42), the god of the dead and the place where the solar journey began, was also associated with the niche that provided the *akhet* horizon where the dead were reborn daily with Re/Horus (*cf.* Friedman 1985, 91; 1986, 100–101). The niche may also have been linked with Mut and Hathor as the '*Akhet*-eye' of Re (Troy 1997, 303; see also the disembodied head of Mut with a figure of Taweret on a Deir el-Medina stele dedicated by a Chantress of Amun; Capel 1996b, 130, no. 62).

The *akh* was a living entity, the spirit of an individual, thus the *akhw* were depicted in statues and stelae in human form (*cf.* McDowell 1992, 97; Schulman 1986, 307–308, 311, 316), as the Book of the Dead Papyrus of Iouiya explicitly states: "I have come forth as an *akh iqr* ... *I shall be seen in my human form forever*" (Friedman 1994, 114, author's emphasis). It seems reasonable to interpret the majority of the busts as depicting a person during their lifetime, or at least as they would appear in tomb decoration. This hypothesis is supported by incidental features, such as the fact that some busts bear nicked earlobes indicating that earrings were normally worn (Bothmer 1987, 27, 29; Demarée 2002, 142, cat. 86).

The solar aspect of the busts, suggested by their probable identification as *3ḫ iḳr n Rꜥ*, the lotus decoration and use of paint, is one of the keys to understanding their function as catalysts for the regeneration of life. The endless succession of sunrises and sunsets paralleled many other constant cycles, the most obvious being birth, death and rebirth. However, as Meskell (2002, 69) notes, it was the "continuous cycle of conception, pregnancy, and birth [that] preoccupied women from puberty to menopause – and spilled over into the mortuary realm". The *akhw*, via the freestanding busts, may also have been invoked for protection. Pinch (1993, 219) suggests, "It is possible that some of the fertility figurines from houses were offered to the male and female ancestors depicted in the busts and stelae in the hope that their spirits would help to ensure that children continued to be born into the family". In view of the high infant mortality rate (Baines and Lacovara 2002, 14; Meskell 2002, 69) and the risk of death during childbirth (Pinch 1983, 414), the busts in amuletic form (Andrews 1994, fig. 15b, fig. 69b; Kaiser 1990, pl. 63, fig. 5; Keith-Bennett 1981, 46, 52–53) may have had apotropaic qualities, similar to the Bes figures recommended for use during pregnancy in P. Leiden I 348 (Janssen 1975, 310–311; Pinch 1983, 412).

Placement of the busts within the house also provides an indication of their function. Meskell (2002, 125, table 4.1) divides the three main rooms of a typical Deir el-Medina house into distinct areas, the first being a place for women, possibly a shared area for menstruation (Wilfong 1999, 422, 432), in the same way that some households contained food processing areas which would presumably have been shared among several families (Meskell 1998, 234). Meskell believes the second room was dedicated to men, and subsequent rooms formed 'servile space' (Meskell 2002, 125). These distinctions are essentially based on the *lit clos*, Bruyère's (1939) term referring to an enclosed bed-like structure, versus the *divan* or bed

(Meskell 1998, 223, 229), given that ancestor busts, stelae and other 'cultic objects' and 'ritual fixtures' were found in both the first and second rooms (Figure 7). The function of the *lit clos* is uncertain; it could have had a variety of uses, from household shrine to post-natal recovery room (Meskell 1998, 225–226). The fact that many *lits clos* are decorated with images of Bes, Taweret, musicians and dancing girls – all of which are associated with birth and fertility – seems to support the latter interpretation (Kemp 1979, 47–52; Meskell 1998, 227).

The second room often contained niches and false doors that "may have facilitated contact with the spirits of ancestors" (Meskell 2002, 119). There seems to be no reason to suggest, as Meskell (2002, 122) does, that this room should be a largely male preserve. Indeed, the bed with flaring armrests, as found in the 'divan room' of Ipy's house (NE13; Meskell 1998, 231), and the columns usually found in the second room of houses at Deir el-Medina (Janssen 1975, 393) are reminiscent of ostraca depicting nursing women (*e.g.* Page 1983, fig. 79; Vandier D'Abbadie 1937, pl. 50, cat. nos. 2337, 2340; Figures 8 and 9). In the absence of any physical evidence for the assumed existence of a 'birth arbour' (Brunner-Traut 1955), it is possible that it was in this room that the new mother would receive visitors. The discovery of an entwined lotus and convolvulus plant motif painted on a plastered ceiling beam in the second room of an Amarna house (Kemp 1979, 51) lends some weight to this argument, as these plants are a prominent feature on the birth ostraca (*e.g.* Minault-Gout 2002, 113, cat. 53), and were used in *lit clos* scenes (*e.g.* house NE8 at Deir el-Medina; Andreu 2002a, 28; Figure 9). Convolvulus vines and flowers also decorate a number of fertility figurines attached to beds (Pinch 1983, 407). Childbirth may have taken place in the second room, where the larger space would have facilitated the birthing process for the mother and attendants. Evidence in the form of figurative

Figure 7. The second room of Sennedjem's house (SW6, to the right) at Deir el-Medina, with the central column base, bed and niches for stelae, 19th Dynasty. (© Nicola Harrington.)

Figure 8. Ostracon of nursing mother, with her attendant offering a mirror and kohl tube in the register below. Note the convolvulus vines wound around the column and hanging from the ceiling, New Kingdom, unprovenanced (after Winkes in Friedman 1994, 105).

Figure 9. Second room of a Deir el-Medina house, with central column base and entrance to the cellar with niche above (indicated by the arrow), 19th Dynasty. (© Nicola Harrington.)

and textual ostraca suggests that, at least in some cases, wooden purpose-built beds were erected (*cf.* model beds, *e.g.* Bruyère 1939, 138, fig. 57; Capel 1996a, 67), presumably within the house, and dismantled following the postpartum period (Meskell 1998, 225).

According to Meskell (2002, 121), "The fact that more men are named as dedicants and deified ancestors sits well with the location of these objects [busts, stelae and niches] in the divan [second] room, the area of greatest male potency". If we redress the balance by assuming that the majority of ancestor busts represented female relatives, this argument becomes much less persuasive. It must also be borne in mind that both stelae and busts are found in the first room as well, and whilst the second room may have been more focussed on ancestor and deity worship, it would not have been intended solely for that purpose, and would presumably have been used by both sexes, especially as the men were absent for an average of eight days of a 10-day week (Meskell 2002, 76). The above discussion of the *akhw* and the general layout of houses at Deir el-Medina were intended to place the busts within a religious and physical contextual framework. Busts were discovered in the first and second rooms of houses at the village, where they may have provided a means of communicating with the deceased, particularly in times of crisis, illness, birth and death. Busts found beyond the domestic environment may have had other uses and are indicative of ancient Egyptian attitudes to the past, and these are considered below.

Awareness of the past and attitudes to the dead

The apparently limited sense of the past at Deir el-Medina might help to explain the placement of the house-style busts beyond the domestic environment. The inhabitants of Deir el-Medina lived in the middle of a necropolis: the graves of their relatives were scattered over the eastern and western hills, and tomb chapels on the west directly overlooked the village below (Figure 10). The time, cost and effort expended on these monuments and their contents indicate veneration of the dead, in direct contrast with the tombs' desecration, usurpation and reuse, and the destruction of the mummified bodies themselves (Baines and Lacovara 2002, 6, 18, 24–25; Meskell 2002, 203). The tombs located closest to Deir el-Medina were gradually covered by middens and built over as the village expanded (Meskell 1994, 200). This apparently ambivalent view of the dead is also reflected in modern societies and is "symptomatic of how almost all the more remote deceased must fade from awareness, and from the responsibility of the living, if the burden of the dead is not to become intolerable" (Baines and Lacovara 2002, 17, 26–27).

From his study, Demarée (1983, 282) has concluded that the *ȝḫ iḳr n Rꜥ* stelae did not represent "members of the remote past" and states that, "It is not too much to say that they most probably were part of the living memory". Meskell (2002, 206) adds, "It is probably safe

Figure 10. View over the southern end of the artisan's village at Deir el-Medina, taken from the entrance of a 19th-dynasty tomb chapel. (© Nicola Harrington.)

to say that the dead were sustained through ongoing reflexive practices conducted by family members for a generation or two at most". The 'domestic' busts found in tombs and temples might be evidence that the dead of generations past were accorded some respect, but whilst a few may have been used in religious festivals (Meskell 2002, 111) or as votive objects perpetuating the memory of the dead, those that outlived their usefulness were discovered dumped amongst temple refuse with other domestic figurines (Keith-Bennett 1981, 47; Pinch 1983, 411).

Conclusions

In this paper, I have proposed that anthropoid busts can be divided into distinct categories according to size, appearance and, to a lesser extent, find context. Limestone busts less than 30 cm tall form the bulk of the corpus and may have been manufactured for use in the home, whereas larger busts with striated wigs may have been part of funerary equipment and involved in the passage of the deceased into the afterlife. Small busts and amulets probably had apotropaic qualities. The question that must always be asked of any artefact is, by whom and for whom were the objects made? It is possible that women constructed the busts, the *lits clos*, the murals or much of the female-oriented material deriving from Deir el-Medina and Amarna

Figure 11. Scene from the 18th-dynasty Tomb of Ramose (TT 55) at Sheikh Abd el-Qurna. (© Nicola Harrington.)

– though this is not a commonly held view among scholars (*e.g.* Meskell 2002, 116). The busts would presumably have had several functions, including consultation in times of crisis, and at dangerous transitional periods, such as birth and death. As Kemp states:

> It might be expected that childbirth would be surrounded by customs and observances wholly the prerogative of women; what is particularly noteworthy is the status accorded to this aspect of life by the community as a whole.
>
> (Kemp 1979, 53)

It has been argued here that anthropoid busts represented individual deceased family members in an idealised form, as they are portrayed in contemporary tomb scenes and stelae (Figure 11). If this is the case, most busts represent women; an interpretation supported by the fact that men did not wear tripartite wigs during life or in idealised scenes of the afterlife, and they were rarely depicted wearing earrings. The *akh*, a living entity, was represented in both the *akh iqr* stelae and the busts in *animate* form. The busts and stelae provided a point of contact between the living and the dead, where intercession could be sought on a personal level and where offerings could be made to pacify the *akhw*, who had the potential to afflict the living (Baines and Lacovara 2002, 21–23; Janssen and Janssen 1996, 57). As Baines (1991, 129) points out, "in general, the Egyptians had far more contact with the dead than they did with the gods".

In the absence of a comprehensive body of published material and illustrations, comparisons and general conclusions are limited, though on the basis of available evidence, it is probable that the busts were part of an ancestor cult in New Kingdom Egypt. They also indicate that women were accorded a certain amount of equality in the domestic sphere in both life and death.

University of Oxford

Acknowledgements

I am very grateful to Professor John Baines for providing detailed comments and criticism of the text. Thanks are also due to Professor John Tait and Dr. David Jeffreys. This paper is dedicated to the memory of Mrs. Barbara Adams.

References

Allen, J. P. 1989, The Natural Philosophy of Akhenaten, in W. K. Simpson (ed.), *Religion and Philosophy in Ancient Egypt*, 89–101. Yale University, New Haven.
Andreu, G. 2002a, Le Site de Deir el-Médineh, in G. Andreu (ed.), *Les artistes de pharaon*, 19–41. Reunion des Musées Nationaux, Paris
Andreu, G. 2002b, Figurine de Femme Nue, in G. Andreu (ed.), *Les artistes de pharaon*, 111–123. Reunion des Musées Nationaux, Paris.
Andreu, G. 2002c, Ostracon figuré: Tête de la déesse Hathor, in G. Andreu (ed.), *Les artistes de pharaon*, 234–281. Reunion des Musées Nationaux, Paris.
Andrews, C. 1994, *Amulets of Ancient Egypt*. British Museum Press, London.
Arnold, D. 1996a, The Workshop of the Sculptor Thutmose, in D. Arnold (ed.), *The Royal Women of Amarna*, 40–83. The Metropolitan Museum of Art, New York.

Arnold, D. 1996b, Aspects of the Royal Female Image During the Amarna Period, in D. Arnold (ed.), *The Royal Women of Amarna*, 84–119. The Metropolitan Museum of Art, New York.

Arnold, D. 1996c, Youth and Old Age: The post Amarna period, in D. Arnold (ed.), *The Royal Women of Amarna*, 120–127. The Metropolitan Museum of Art, New York.

Baines, J. 1991, Society, Morality, and Religious Practice, in B. E. Shafer (ed.), *Religion in Ancient Egypt*, 123–199. Routledge, London.

Baines, J. and Lacovara, P. 2002, Burial and the Dead in Ancient Egyptian Society: Respect, formalism, neglect, *Journal of Social Archaeology* 2, 5–36.

Bierbrier, M. B. 1982, *Tomb-builders of the Pharaohs*. British Museum Press, London.

Boreux, C. 1932, A propos de quelques bustes égyptiens, in S. R. K. Glanville (ed.), *Studies Presented to F. Ll. Griffith*, 395–401. Egypt Exploration Society, London.

Bothmer, B. V. 1987, Ancestral Bust, in E. Swan-Hall (ed.), *Antiquities from the Collection of Christos G. Bastis*, 24–29. Verlag Philipp von Zabern, Mainz.

Bourriau, J. 1982a, Flask, in E. Brovarski, S. K. Doll and R. E. Freed (eds.), *Egypt's Golden Age: The art of living in the New Kingdom 1558–1085 BC*, 101–106. Museum of Fine Arts, Boston.

Bourriau, J. 1982b, Chalices, in E. Brovarski, S. K. Doll and R. E. Freed (eds.), *Egypt's Golden Age: The art of living in the New Kingdom 1558–1085 BC*, 140–151. Museum of Fine Arts, Boston.

Brunner-Traut, E. 1955, Die Wochenlaube, *Mitteilungen des Instituts für Orientforschung* 3, 11–30.

Bruyère, B. 1939, *Rapport sur les fouilles de Deir el Médineh 1934–35, Troisième Partie*. Institut français d'archéologie orientale, Cairo.

Bryan, B. M. 1986, Evidence for Female Literacy from Theban Tombs of the New Kingdom, *Bulletin of the Egyptological Seminar* 6, 17–32.

Capel, A. K. 1996a, Female Figurine with Model Bed, in A. K. Capel and G. E. Markoe (eds.), *Mistress of the House, Mistress of Heaven: Women in ancient Egypt,* 49–102. Hudson Hills Press and Cincinnati Art Museum, New York.

Capel, A. K. 1996b, Votive stela with Taweret and Mut, in A. K. Capel and G. E. Markoe (eds.), *Mistress of the House, Mistress of Heaven: Women in ancient Egypt,* 121–144. Hudson Hills Press and Cincinnati Art Museum, New York.

Demarée, R. J. 1983, *The akh iqr n Re – Stelae: On ancestor worship in ancient Egypt*. Universiteit van Amsterdam, Leiden.

Demarée, R. J. 2002, Double buste de laraires, in G. Andreu (ed.), *Les artistes de pharaon*, 136–143. Reunion des Musées Nationaux, Paris.

Egyptian Antiquities Organisation 1978, *The Luxor Museum of Ancient Egyptian Art*. Egyptian Antiquities Organisation, Cairo.

Einaudi, S. 1998, Mannequin of Tutankhamun, in F. Tiradritti (ed.), *The Cairo Museum Masterpieces of Egyptian Art*, 230–231. Thames and Hudson, London.

Fazzini, R. A. 1996, Bust from a Statue of the Goddess Sekhmet, in A. K. Capel and G. E. Markoe (eds.), *Mistress of the House, Mistress of Heaven: Women in ancient Egypt*, 134–136. Hudson Hills Press and Cincinnati Art Museum, New York.

Fiore-Marochetti, E. 2002, Buste d'ancêtre féminine, in G. Andreu (ed.), *Les artistes de pharaon*, 136–143. Reunion des Musées Nationaux, Paris.

Friedman, F. 1985, On the Meaning of Some Anthropoid Busts from Deir el-Medina, *Journal of Egyptian Archaeology* 71, 82–97.

Friedman, F. 1986, *ȝḫ* in the Amarna Period, *Journal of the American Research Center in Egypt* 23, 99–106.

Friedman, F. 1994, Aspects of Domestic Life and Religion, in L. H. Lesko (ed.), *Pharaoh's Workers: The villagers of Deir el Medina*, 95–117. Cornell University Press, Ithaca and London.

Gardiner, A. 1957, *Egyptian Grammar: Being an introduction to the study of hieroglyphs*, (3rd edition). Griffith Institute, Ashmolean Museum, Oxford.

Habachi, L. 1976, The Royal Scribe Amenmose, Son of Penzerti and Mutemonet: His monuments in Egypt and abroad, in J. H. Johnson and E. F. Wente (eds.), *Studies in Honor of George R Hughes*, 83–103. Oriental Institute of the University of Chicago, Chicago.

Hayes, W. G. 1959, *The Scepter of Egypt, Part II: The Hyksos Period and the New Kingdom*. The Metropolitan Museum of Art, New York.

Holden, L. 1982, Ancestral Bust, in E. Brovarski, S. K. Doll and R. E. Freed (eds.), *Egypt's Golden Age: The art of living in the New Kingdom 1558–1085 BC*, 296–307. Museum of Fine Arts, Boston.

Hornung, E. 1999, *The Ancient Egyptian Books of the Afterlife*, (trans. D. Lorton). Cornell University Press, Ithaca and London.

Janssen, J. J. 1975, *Commodity Prices from the Ramesside Period*. E. J. Brill, Leiden.

Janssen, J. J. 1992, Literacy and Letters at Deir el-Medina, in R. J. Demarée and A. Egberts (eds.), *Village Voices*, 81–92. Centre of Non-Western Studies, Leiden.

Janssen, R. M. and Janssen, J. J. 1996, *Getting Old in Ancient Egypt*. The Rubicon Press, London.

Kaiser, W. 1990, Zur Büste als einer Darstellungsform ägyptischer Rundplastik, *Mitteilungen des Deutschen Archäologischen Instituts, Abteilung Kairo* 46, 269–285.

Kampp-Seyfried, F. 1998, Overcoming Death: The private tombs of Thebes, in R. Schulz and M. Seidel (eds.), *Egypt: The world of the pharaohs*, 249–263. Könemann, Köln.

Keith-Bennett, J. 1981, Anthropoid Busts Not from Deir el Medina Alone, *Bulletin of the Egyptological Seminar* 3, 43–72.

Kemp, B. J. 1979, Wall Paintings from the Workmen's Village at el-Amarna, *Journal of Egyptian Archaeology* 65, 47–53.

Lines, D. 2001, A Curious Middle Kingdom Stela in Birmingham, *Journal of Egyptian Archaeology* 87, 41–54.

Markoe, G. E. 1996a, Double Shabti of Bener-merut and Ikhem, in A. K. Capel and G. M. Markoe (eds.), *Mistress of the House, Mistress of Heaven: Women in ancient Egypt*, 49–102. Hudson Hills Press and Cincinnati Art Museum, New York.

Markoe, G. E. 1996b, Shabti of Kai-neferu, in A. K. Capel and G. M. Markoe (eds.), *Mistress of the House, Mistress of Heaven: Women in ancient Egypt*, 145–174. Hudson Hills Press and Cincinnati Art Museum, New York.

McDowell, A. 1992, Awareness of the Past at Deir el-Medina, in R. J. Demarée and A. Egberts (eds.), *Village Voices*, 93–109. Centre of Non-Western Studies, Leiden.

Meskell, L. 1994, Deir el Medina in hyperreality: Seeking the people of Pharaonic Egypt, *Journal of Mediterranean Archaeology* 7.2, 193–216.

Meskell, L. 1998, An Archaeology of Social Relations in an Egyptian Village, *Journal of Archaeological Method and Theory* 5.3, 209–243.

Meskell, L. 2002, *Private Life in New Kingdom Egypt*. Princeton University Press, Princeton and Oxford.

Minault-Gout, A. 2002, Ostracon figuré: Femme allaitant avec servante, in G. Andreu (ed.), *Les artistes de pharaon*, 111–123. Reunion des Musées Nationaux, Paris.

Murnane, W. J. 1999, The Return to Orthodoxy, in R. E. Freed, Y. J. Markowitz and S. H. D'Auria (eds.), *Pharaohs of the Sun: Akhenaten, Nefertiti, Tutankhamen*, 176–185. Thames and Hudson, London.

Page, A. 1983, *Ancient Egyptian Figured Ostraca*. Aris and Phillips, Warminster.

Petrie, W. M. F. 1974 [1894], *Tell el Amarna*. Aris and Phillips, Warminster.

Pinch, G. 1983, Childbirth and Female Figurines at Deir el-Medina and el-Amarna, *Orientalia* 52, 405–414.

Pinch, G. 1993, *Votive Offerings to Hathor*. Griffith Institute, Oxford.

Porter, B. and Moss, R. L. B. 1960, *Topographical Bibliography of Ancient Egyptian Hieroglyphic Texts, Reliefs and Paintings, I: The Theban necropolis, Part One: Private tombs*, (2nd edition). Griffith Institute, Ashmolean Museum, Oxford.

Robins, G. 1997, Women and Votive Stelae in the New Kingdom, in J. Phillips (ed.), *Ancient Egypt, the Aegean and the Near East: Studies in honour of Martha Rhoads Bell*, 445–454. Van Siclen Books, San Antonio.

Robins, G. 1999, Hair and the Construction of Identity in Ancient Egypt, *Journal of the American Research Center in Egypt* 36, 55–69.

Romero, J. 1999, Small Anthropoid Bust (cat. 263); Large Anthropoid Bust (cat. 264), in R. E. Freed, Y. J. Markowitz, and S. H. D'Auria (eds.), *Pharaohs of the Sun: Akhenaten, Nefertiti, Tutankhamun*, 273–282. Thames and Hudson, London.

Roveri, A. M. 1988, Ancestor Bust, in S. D'Auria, P. Lacovara and C. H. Roehrig (eds.), *Mummies and Magic: The funerary arts of ancient Egypt*, 132–161. Museum of Fine Arts, Boston.

Roveri, A. M., n. d., *Museo Egizio.* Barisone Editore, Turin.

Schulman, A. R. 1986, Some Observations on the *akh iqr n re* Stelae, *Bibliotheca Orientalis* 43.3/4, 302–348.

Shaw, I. and Nicholson, P. 1995, *British Museum Dictionary of Ancient Egypt*. British Museum Press, London.

Thomas, A. P. 1981, *Gurob, 1-2*. Aris and Phillips, Warminster.

Trapani, M. 1998, The Monument of Imeneminet (Naples, Inv. 1069): An essay of interpretation, in C. J. Eyre (ed.), *Proceedings of the 7th International Congress of Egyptologists*, 1170–1176. Peeters, Leuven.

Troy, L. 1997, Mut Enthroned, in J, Van Dijk (ed.), *Essays on Ancient Egypt in honour of H. Te Velde*, 301–315. Styx Publications, Groningen.

Vandier D'Abbadie, J. 1937, *Ostraca Figures de Deir el Médineh Nos. 2001–2722, 1–2*. Institut francais d'archéologie orientale, Cairo.

Vandier D'Abbadie, J. 1946, A propos des bustes de laraires, *Revue d'Égyptologie* 5, 133–135.

Wildung, D. and Schoske, S. 1984, *Nofret – die Schone Frau im Alten Ägypten*. Von Zabern, Cairo and Mainz.

Wilfong, T. G. 1999, Menstrual Synchrony and the "Place of Women" in Ancient Egypt (OIM 13512), in E. Teeter and J. A. Larson (eds.), *Gold of Praise: Studies on ancient Egypt in honour of Edward F. Wente*, 419–434. Oriental Institute of the University of Chicago, Chicago.

Iaau and the Question of the Origin of Evil According to Ancient Egyptian Sources

Mpay Kemboly

Introduction

This paper discusses Frandsen's (2000) article in which he proposes that Iaau is a primordial embodiment of evil which stands alongside Apopis and Seth, and whose existence challenges the idea that the creation of the world was perfect from the beginning, and that evil entered the world after creation. He bases this interpretation upon the contrast between the concept of *bwt* and that of *mꜣꜥt*, and upon the relationship between *bwt* and *ỉꜣꜣw*. According to his reading of particular spells from the Coffin Texts, Iaau transgresses a pivotal *bwt* which consists of not eating faeces and drinking urine, and so Iaau belongs to the reversed world – the counter-image of Maat. Thus, Iaau is an 'epitome of evil'. He is also a primeval being since "he lived in the body of the Unique One before creation" (Frandsen 2000, 15). He is the maker of the west wind. Frandsen (2000, 17) therefore states: "presupposing that Iaau embodies 'evil', creation itself contained this 'evil'. The four winds were the first product of creation, and of these, one was a bad wind. The world was not perfect in that not all creation was good".

I study anew the various texts upon which Frandsen bases his interpretation and confront these texts with evidence ranging from the Pyramid Texts to Graeco-Roman inscriptions (*c.*3050 B.C.E.–3rd century C.E.) to see whether his point of view is plausible. I set aside the question of whether creation was perfect or imperfect at its beginning. This question, in my view, should rather be dealt with in a broader study of creation accounts, hymns to the creator and creation, and the issue of justifying the creator in light of the problem of evil.

The discussion that follows is a summary of a long and detailed section from my doctoral thesis on ancient Egyptian perspectives on evil. Thus, parts of this present paper are not fully expounded here. I would like to note here that in this discussion, citation of Egyptian sources follows the abbreviations of *Lexikon der Ägyptologie* 7, columns 9–33 (Helck and Westendorf 1992). Pyramid Texts published by Sethe (1908-1910) are referred to by spell number. Coffin Texts are referred to by spell number, the volume number, and the page number from De Buck's (1935-1961) original edition. At times a coffin number, such as BIBo, YIC, or GIT, is added to the reference if one works on a particular version of the text. Citations of the Book of the Dead refer to Naville's 1886 edition.

CT spell 162: Context and genre

Just as Frandsen (2000, 14) first examines CT spell 162, which he considers to be "a source of paramount importance" as regards the delineation of the character of Iaau, so I start my discussion with the same spell. However, firstly, it is important to clarify its context and genre.

CT spell 162 belongs, in my understanding, to three categories. The deceased wants to cross the winding waterway to join the divine abode and enjoy a blissful hereafter. The deceased therefore needs to have power over the four winds of the sky (II 402c–405b). This spell, however, also pertains to a category of spells of which the aim is to enable the deceased to breathe, as well as to have water, food, and offerings at his/her disposal in the necropolis in order to come into being as an equipped spirit (II 389a, 398e–f BIBo). This spell equally belongs to the category of texts that celebrates the four winds. Each wind is addressed in the first part of the spell (II 389b–397d), but in the second part (II 399a–405b) all the four winds are called the 'bulls of the sky' (II 399a). They came into existence in the primordial times (II 399b–402b) and have been granted to the deceased by the four maidens so that he/she may live on/with them.

Before addressing the particular issue of the west wind, I should survey other Egyptian evidence concerning the four winds of the sky in general (see Kurth 1986) to see whether any of them is associated with evil. It is also important to bear in mind that the Egyptian word *ṯȝw* can be translated into English as 'wind' or 'breath'.

In the Pyramid Texts, a deity, who may be the sun god, is addressed:

> N has come to you, Old One.
> May you turn back to N like the east wind turns back after the west wind. May you come after N like the north wind comes after the south wind.
>
> (PT 340 §554a–c)

CT spell 355, which is similar to CT spell 297 and BD 57, bears the title: 'having power over the four winds, going forth to Djedu and to Iunu, and giving offerings in the horizon' (CT 355 V 1a–c). In my view, this spell belongs to three categories. The first category is that of spells which make a connection between the deceased, Osiris and Re, and between Djedu (Busiris), and Iunu (Heliopolis), the holy cities of Osiris and Re, respectively (see Willems 1996, 260; Yoyotte 1960, 28). CT spell 355 also pertains to the category of spells which establishes a relationship between air and offerings. This connection is possible, firstly, through the assimilation of Maat-Tefnut with the breath of life (*ṯȝw ʿnḫ*), which keeps the creator god alive (CT 80 II 32b–33a, 35b–h), as well as with offerings. Maat is called 'the mistress of offerings' (CT 689 VI 319g–j) and is the offering *par excellence*. Secondly, this connection is made possible through the association of Shu with breath and/or life (CT 75 I 354b, 355b, 356a–b; 80 II 39b–d), and with Osiris (CT 80 II 40c–41b). Thirdly, this connection is made possible through the association of Osiris with offerings in his role as the lord of sustenance and provider of offerings (P. Chester Beatty I recto 14, 10; 14, 12; 15, 10; Gardiner 1932, 57, 58) and the connection of Osiris with fertility, inundation, vegetation, and grain. Thus, this threefold relationship between air and offerings is made possible through the association of Shu, Maat-Tefnut, and Osiris with air/breath and offerings.

Finally, CT spell 355, just like CT spell 162, belongs to a category of spells, the aim of which is to provide the deceased with the means necessary for achieving an afterlife. Thus, CT spell 355 indicates that the deceased wishes to have his/her nose opened or to have his/her face perpetually to the wind so that he/she can breathe and come to life in the hereafter. Thus, the deceased says:

> If this sky comes with the north wind, I will sit in its south.
> If this sky comes with the south wind, I will sit in its north.
> If this sky comes with the west wind, I will sit in its east.
> If this sky comes with the east wind, I will sit in its west.
> I have pulled out a skin from my nostril, which is opened
> to the place which I wish to sit.
>
> (CT 355 V 3c–7b)

BD chapter 161 associates each of the four winds with a particular deity. Some texts attribute special powers to each of the four winds. For instance, CT spell 162 already states that the east wind makes a beautiful path for Re when he starts his daily journey (II 392b–393a), and the south wind brings rain and inundation (II 398a–b). The internal rooms of the Opet temple in Karnak, which date to Ptolemaic times (mid-2nd century B.C.E.), provide texts about the four winds (see De Wit 1957, 25–26):

(The southern wall): The good wind of the south: it is that which brings the Nile out of the cavern of the primeval ocean to inundate the earth with its all excellent (products), and to supply the offering-table with all good things for Osiris Wenen-nefer, the justified.

(The northern wall): The good wind of the north whose name is Kheb. The north wind of life, the breath that causes the fields to rest, makes excellent the flood on earth, and gives the breath of life to the nose of Osiris, [who is in the midst of Thebes].

(The eastern wall): The good wind of the east: it is Osiris (?) who is daily begotten within the netherworld. It lifts up your Ba to the sky together with the stars, Osiris-Wenen-nefer, the king of the gods.

(The western wall): The good wind of the west: it is that which brings about the flood of the Nile in the sky to make bright the land with plants, and bring into existence all the flowers for Osiris-Wenen-nefer, the king of the gods, and Isis the great, the god's mother and the lady of all the gods.

In addition, the four winds can all be embodied in a single deity such as Shu, Amun, or Khnum (*Esna* 377, 2; Sauneron 1962–1975, 3:347–348, 5:208–209). From a cosmological perspective the winds are endowed with special attributes related to the creation of the world. They separate the sky from the earth and form the egg from which the sun god emerges (Smith 2002, 194). From this perspective, one understands why the deceased wants to embody the four winds of the sky. He/she actually wishes to enact the creative powers of the winds and desires to ascend to heaven like the winds or by means of the winds (CT 297 IV 50a–l). CT spell 223 III 208c–209a reveals these major functions associated with the winds in the creation of the world: the creator god is the possessor of winds or breath which causes the formation of the primordial egg, and Shu embodies the air that separates the sky from the earth and represents the pillar between the sky and earth.

Just as in the case of CT spell 162, other texts treat each of the four winds, or the winds as a whole, as being of vital necessity (CT 630 VI 251g–h). CT spell 1130 VII 462e–463a states, for instance, that the four winds are one of the four good deeds that the 'Lord of All' made at the beginning. Thus, it emerges from this survey that none of the four winds of the sky is associated with evil.

The west wind and Ha

After discussing various sources related to the four winds in general, I now address the relationship that the west wind has with the god Ha. I examine the main passage from CT spell 162, and consider other evidence concerning Ha so as to discern whether Ha as a whole possesses negative attributes.

The passage of debate concerning the west wind is from CT spell 162; I propose the following reading:

> (395b) These winds have been given to me by these maidens.
>   (c) It is the west wind, the brother of Ha,
> (396a) and the offspring of Iaau,
>   (b) one who lived in one womb before two things came into being in this land.
>   (c) It is the breath of life, the west wind.
> (397a) It has been given to me so that I may live on/with it.
>
> (CT 162 II 395b–397a)

Spell II 395c yields two variants: 'It is the west wind which belongs to Ha' (YIC), and 'it is the west wind which belongs to the domain of Ha' (GIT). The west wind being the brother of Ha – a reading given by eight out of ten coffins – suggests that the west wind pertains to the domain of Ha, or even a manifestation of Ha. From his typical iconography, one may deduce that Ha is a deity associated with the desert. The dead person extols the western desert in these words:

> The place of plants is the western [desert?]
> I am the fledgling of [Ha?] in his desert.
> My position is made beside Osiris, among those who are.
> My place is his desert and my horizon is his western desert.
> I am among those who dwell in it, (those of) the northern one (?).
>
> (CT 695 VI 329c–g)

Some texts make clear the relationship of Ha to the western desert by referring to him as 'lord of the West' (CT 398 V 125a; 945 VII 161h), an epithet which is also ascribed to other deities, such as Osiris, and Hathor, lady of the West (BD 186). By virtue of this attribute, Ha preserves the dead against their enemies (CT 313 IV 90e–f), and thus he is propitious to the dead (CT 636 VI 259b–d; 755 VI 384o).

Ha is one of the gods with whom the deceased identifies his/her right foot so that his/her body might be fully divine (BD 125, 41). This identification process is known as apotheosis of bodily members; a ritual performance:

> where each and every member, from the top of the head to the tip of the toes, is identified with a divinity, although the catalogue of deities listed is not constant. The only important element is the confirmation, 'none of my members is without god', *i.e.* "I am divine, through and through!"
>
> (Hornung 1994, 136)

Ha is not related only to the western desert – the realm of the dead – but also to food. In CT spell 545 VI 142a–b, Ha occurs alongside Hu. This example, as well as the fact that Hu means both the creative utterance of the creator god and food, suggests that Ha may also have been associated with food (PT 204 §119b; Baines 1985, 146–164).

A survey of these texts suggests that the god Ha is mainly associated with the western desert. Like Osiris and Hathor, Ha is related to the blessed dead whom he receives in his desert, and he is also associated with Anubis (CT 755 VI 384p). In addition, Ha is associated with food through his connection with the fertile western desert (PT 204 §119b; CT 545 VI 142a–b). Therefore, Wildung (1977) asserts that Ha possesses some attributes that portray him as a god of fertility. He also states that the connection Ha has with the West makes him an embodiment of the night sun Atum.

As this investigation suggests, Ha does not have any negative associations; therefore, one cannot say at this stage that the west wind is evil. On the contrary, the west wind is associated with the West, the abode of Osiris and the glorious ones, and with the night sun. The west wind receives the *Bas* of the gods and the blessed dead when they come to rest in the West.

The west wind and Iaau

CT spell 162 II 396a does not just state that the west wind is the offspring of Ha, but also of Iaau, commonly written as 𓅱𓄿𓄿𓏲𓅭 or 𓅱𓄿𓄿𓏲𓅭𓏛. As in the case of Ha, I discuss evidence on Iaau, mainly the spells from the Coffin Texts that Frandsen has gathered, but I also examine other sources as mentioned above, so as to discover whether Iaau is explicitly associated with evil.

(a) CT spell 698: Iaau and the world reversed

The passage under discussion may be translated as follows:

> (332g) Your (Pedjet Shu's) tongue is your crotch,
>   (h) and your phallus is your mouth.
>   (i) Get back, Iaau, one who lives on his urine.
>
> (CT 698 VI 332g–i)

It is not clear whether the hostile being, to whom the spell is addressed, is Pedjet Shu, or Iaau, or an assimilation of both Pedjet Shu and Iaau. Whatever the possibility might be, Pedjet Shu and/or Iaau appear to be unfriendly to the dead (CT 698 VI 332e–f, j, r–s). Besides, the passage under debate, as it stands, seems to describe the present condition of Pedjet Shu and/or Iaau. This passage can also be interpreted as a curse placed on the enemy and may be rendered as: 'Your tongue shall be your crotch and your phallus shall be your mouth'. Since this reversed condition is associated with the theme of eating faeces and drinking urine, especially in funerary texts, Frandsen (2000, 18) states that:

> Iaau is a manifestation of the world reversed. Not only does he violate the most fundamental, pivotal and oldest *bwt* by living on faeces, but he is also the epitome of reversals with his tongue between his legs and his phallus in his mouth.

In other words, Iaau, according to Frandsen (2000, 12–13), belongs to the world of 'non-Maat', that is, to the world of *bwt* and *isft*.

This interpretation is supported by Zandee's (1960, 7–10, 72–78) reading of the scatophagous Egyptian, which establishes a relationship between eating faeces and drinking urine, and the reversed world. Kadish (1979, 210) questions this viewpoint. He proposes instead to interpret the scatophagous Egyptian by using Douglas' (1966) paradigm, which sees the body as an analogue for the individual and for the cosmos. From within this perspective, eating faeces or drinking urine would mean for any Egyptian, dead or alive, entering into the world of 'non-Maat' (Kadish 1979, 214–217). Egyptians want instead to dwell within the realm of Maat, that is, the integrated and ordered universe.

Like Kadish, Frandsen (forthcoming) contrasts "eating faeces and drinking urine" with Maat. Frandsen equates eating food, or to have an abundance of nutriment, with Maat, but he links eating excrement and drinking urine with the absence of Maat and with death, even with the second death. As a result, Frandsen (1999, 136–141) concludes that Iaau, who lives on urine, pertains to the domain of non-existence or a second death. Thus, Iaau is the embodiment of evil – that which is not Maat. Following from this, then, Frandsen asserts that the west wind, which is the offspring of Iaau, belongs to the realm of evil.

Taking into account what Kadish (1979, 210) has called the influence of Judaeo-Christian preconceptions of scholars, such as Zandee and Hornung, on their interpretations of ancient Egyptian concepts of the afterlife, I would not argue that walking upside down and its corollaries are considered to be the permanent state of the damned – the enemies of Osiris. Moreover, I question whether eating faeces and drinking urine are indeed prototypical symbols of evil and non-Maat and necessarily destine an individual to a second death. I accept, nevertheless, that everything may hold the possibility of danger and the risk of death in the context of the journey to the hereafter. Thus, I would instead regard walking upside down, eating faeces, and drinking urine as terrible ordeals. The real danger that threatens the deceased, however, is absolute and total annihilation, where the body and all the components of one's personality, such as the *ȝḫ*, *bȝ*, *kȝ*, *rn*, and *šwt*, are completely destroyed. Various sins and wrongdoings, such as those recorded in BD Chapters 30 and 125, cause the deceased to be thrown into the realm of non-existence, that is, to die a second time, to be dead forever. Surprisingly, 'eating faeces and drinking urine' are not mentioned in this catalogue (Assmann 1989, 76–85; Yoyotte 1961, 42–65). It follows that eating excrement and drinking urine, even though they represent a world reversed, are not automatically and necessarily the prototypical symbols of non-Maat (Frandsen, forthcoming). Therefore, Iaau, who lives on urine, is not the epitome of evil and cannot stand as an equal counter-part of Maat, and consequently cannot be placed alongside Apopis and Seth.

(b) CT spell 148: Iaau and cosmic order

Frandsen (2000, 18) finds a clear expression of "the hostile and 'evil' character of Iaau" in CT spell 148, which he considers to be related to the story of the birth of Horus. Before discussing in detail the passage relevant here, it is necessary to understand the context of the spell. As the title states (II 209c), the deceased desires to become a falcon in order to fly to the horizon and board the solar bark (II 220a–222a), thus passing from night to day (II 224b). The falcon is the very emblem of Horus, who is the son of Osiris and Isis (II 213b, 216d–217b, 225b), and the heir of Geb (II 212d). Thus, Horus the falcon represents the ruler of Egypt and the reigning pharaoh, the living Horus. This spell can also be placed in the context of the struggle between Horus and Seth for royal legitimacy over Egypt (II 209c–219b). After being recognised as the ruling monarch, Horus declares:

> (223b) My flight has reached the horizon.
>> I have surpassed the gods of the sky,
>> I have made my place more prominent than (that of) the primordial ones.
>> Iaau does not reach my first flight.
> (224a) My place is far from Seth, the enemy of my father Osiris.

(CT 148 II 223b–224a)

Here Iaau is represented as a bird, which may be associated with the primordial ones; Iaau flies high but cannot surpass the falcon (II 223e), neither does any god (II 223c–d). However, since Iaau is mentioned just before Seth within the context of the struggle for royal legitimacy over Egypt, one may associate or equate Iaau with Seth. Thus, Faulkner (1973, 126) renders II 223e as follows: "The Contender has not attained my first flight". If Iaau can thus be associated with Seth, I question whether Seth should be considered absolutely evil within the context of this royal dispute over Egypt to the extent suggested by Frandsen (2000, 18).

It is important to examine other evidence concerning the conflict between Horus and Seth in order to assess Frandsen's opinion: The New Kingdom story of Horus and Seth from P. Chester Beatty I recto (Gardiner 1932, 37–60a); the Ramesside or Late Period *Memphite Theology* (Breasted 1901); and the Ptolemaic *Myth of Horus* from the temple of Horus at Edfu (Chassinat 1931, 108–132, 213–223). In analysing this evidence one realises, however, that within the cycle of the royal struggle between Horus and Seth there are various allusions to the cycle of the conflict between Osiris and Seth to such an extent that the two cycles are blended or they interpenetrate in some sources. The same evidence frequently portrays Seth as the murderer of Osiris and consequently as the originator of evil in the world (Te Velde 1977). But this myth concerning the conflict between Osiris and Seth is, in my view, one of the complex factors that explains the presence of evil in the world and, with respect to cosmogony, can only be interpreted with extreme caution. As a result, the cycle of the conflict between Osiris and Seth – like the myth of Seth in the sky and in the solar bark, to some extent – should be set aside in this present discussion. I, therefore, focus on evidence concerning the very struggle for royal legitimacy over Egypt, which is not so much between Osiris and Seth, as between Horus and Seth.

The examination of evidence concerning this royal conflict has not yielded any reference to cosmogony as such. Furthermore, Horus and Seth are related to kingship, as is attested in the iconography of the *smꜣ tꜣwy* or 'uniting the two lands' motif (Te Velde 1980, 27). In addition, Iaau is not mentioned in any narrative of the cycle of Horus and Seth I have surveyed. Therefore, in my view, Frandsen's (2000, 19) assertion that, "Iaau and Seth are placed on an equal footing as the archenemies of cosmic order. Iaau was there when Horus was born and tried to prevent him from assuming his cosmic, as well (*sic*) 'social' role of the king", goes beyond the available evidence. The statement about Iaau (CT 148 II 222e–224a) is most likely a reference to what preceded and is simply a statement to the effect that Horus could outfly Iaau, the primordial deity-bird most renowned for his flight.

(c) CT spell 149: Iaau and aggressivity

Frandsen (2000, 23) argues that "the negative character of Iaau is supported by evidence from CT spell 149 which in five out of twelve cases follows immediately after spell 148". Like CT spell 148, the context of this present spell is drawn from the dispute between Horus and Seth. The deceased desires to be transformed into a falcon, to fly to the horizon, and to be vindicated against his/her enemy like Horus, who was vindicated before the tribunal of the 'Lord of All'. The deceased, having been vindicated, treats his/her enemy in a wild manner (II 236b–241a).

In the passage which mentions Iaau, he appears as a variant of a bird called 'Hau'. It reads: 'My wings against him are the Iaau-bird' (CT 149 II 238b). Iaau, like four other types of bird, appears alongside aggressive beasts and a 'gleaming knife'. One may conclude from this context that the deceased wishes to embody the strength of these aggressive animals and birds in order to destroy his/her vile enemy. Thus, Iaau is presented here as a violent and aggressive bird.

(d) CT spell 953: Iaau or something else?

Since the reading of Iaau and its interpretation are controversial and problematic in CT spell 953 VII 168j, in which a living or dead person addresses the tribunal that sits in front of the great one – either in this world or in the hereafter – I put it aside from this present discussion. Indeed, it has emerged from my analysis of this passage that if the Iaau-bird is meant here, it signifies either protection or an ominous destiny. Thus, the Iaau-bird has an ambivalent meaning. However, if the Iaau-bird is not meant here, but instead the passage refers to something else, such as growing old and dying, then CT spell 953 can be excluded from the discussion as Frandsen (2000, 27) himself suggests. Thus, this debate provides reasons for further analysing in detail the significance of Iaau.

(e) CT spell 170: Iaau and the 'old one'

This spell (CT 170 III 36c–39d), whose title is 'joining the two river-banks in the necropolis', contains a passage (III 36c) where the common spelling for the deity Iaau appears alongside two somewhat different spellings: ⟨hieroglyphs⟩ *iȝiw* and ⟨hieroglyphs⟩ *iȝw*. Six out of ten coffins produce this latter spelling, which I translate as 'the old one'. The text, as Frandsen (2000, 27) acknowledges, "does not lend itself to an easy interpretation, and this, in turn, makes it difficult to explain why it is addressed to Iaau". However, one gathers from the title and the context of the spell that the deceased wishes to cross a river so as to proceed to the realm of the gods. He/she addresses a deity called 'Iau' or 'the old one'.

But who might 'the old one' be? I have already pointed out in my interpretation of CT spell 148 that Iaau is represented as a primeval deity-bird. In addition, Atum can be conceived of as the old one – the evening manifestation of the sun god when he grows old and sets in the western horizon. The sun god is addressed as 'the old one' in many sources (*e.g.* PT 340 §554; *Esna* 196, 9–10; Sauneron 1962–1975, 3.7, 5.329–330). The P. Berlin hymn, for instance, praises Ptah who has acquired solar attributes as follows:

> Old one who is at the limit of eternity!
> Come you! Let us make jubilation for him.
> Let us give praise to his noble image
> in his all beautiful names.
> Old one who crosses eternity!
> Come you! Let us make jubilation for him.
> Let us give praise to his noble image
> in his all beautiful names.
>
> (P. Berlin 3048 IX, 5a–6a; Wolf 1929, 34–35)

Atum as the nocturnal form of the sun god is associated with Osiris. The tomb of queen Nefertari (Hornung 1999, 142) contains a representation of the unification of Re with Osiris in the form of a mummy whose head is that of a horned ram, where the accompanying text reads:

> It is Re who rests as/in Osiris.
> Osiris is the one who rests as/in Re.

Atum, like many other gods, protects the dead (PT 451 §840a–c; 452 §843a–b), and the deceased wishes to become Atum, the creator god, in order to share his destiny (CT 252 III 351d; 746 VI 375g).

Hence, CT spell 170 provides evidence which suggests that the primeval deity-bird Iaau may be associated with the sun god Atum, the old one, or that Iaau could be his substitute. In return, Atum is related to Osiris when he rests in the West, as evidenced above.

(f) CT spell 344: Iaau or Iaa?

The deceased, after being purified and embalmed, makes his way to the abode of Re and declares:

> The fair Iaa(u?) is announcing me in the bark of the one-who-came-into-being-by-himself.
>
> (CT 344 IV 341g)

Here *i3(w?)* appears with two somewhat different spellings, and . One may deduce that this passage apparently deals with a being other than Iaau. These two spellings are, however, also found in CT spell 617 VI 229a (B2L) and CT spell 1089 VII 369b. In CT spell 617 Iaa(u?) is related to the sun god, Thoth, and Osiris.

Despite the variety of spellings of Iaa(u?) that CT spell 617 VI 229a has yielded, it is worth noting that Iaa(u?), spelled with a plant determinative, is a thing or being with which the deceased can be identified: he is called 'this Ia(a)(u)' in the same manner as he can be named 'this Osiris'. This may explain why, on coffin B1Bo Iaau is written with a *djed*-like-pillar determinative (CT 1089 VII 369b; Frandsen 2000, 23). Iaau also appears here in a solar context and has no negative connotation since he can help the sun god to stay alive. Iaau's role is therefore similar to that of Shu and Tefnut, who keep their father alive, and to that of Horus who takes care of Osiris, and like Khnum 'the good protector of his father'.

It may be possible, therefore, to suggest that these two different spellings from CT spell 341 IV 344g refer to Iaau. By virtue of the association I have proposed between Iaau and the role of a god's son or god's daughter in taking care of his/her father, from my interpretation of CT spell 1089, one may understand why Iaau is called 'the fair one', 'the good one' or 'the perfect one' in CT spell 341 IV 344g (see Frandsen 2000, 21). In addition, just as in many spells where he appears, Iaau is also connected with the solar realm in CT spell 341; he is a member of the crew of the solar bark who introduces the deceased to Atum, 'the-one-who-came-into-being-by-himself' *par excellence* (CT 341).

Thus far, I have studied evidence gathered from the Coffin Texts dating to the First Intermediate Period and the Middle Kingdom (*c.*2160–1650 B.C.E.). What about other periods? PT 249 §264a–b provides an earlier reference for Iaau. Sethe (n.d., 264–265) and Faulkner (1969, 60–61) interpret Iaau as being two fighters, namely Horus and Seth. But Sethe (n.d., 264–265) also considers Iaau to be a pair of celestial gate-wardens or the two gates of the sky. It is clear that Iaau appears within a celestial setting and can be related to wind and air. Similar to the evidence in the Coffin Texts, Iaau is represented as a bird in sources from the Graeco-Roman Period (Chassinat 1929, 46, line 15). Wilson (1997, 30), for instance, in her study of texts in the Temple of Edfu, associates Iaau with the wind or air genie which takes the form of a bird.

The foregoing analysis shows that Iaau has a wide range of meanings. However, these can be placed into three broad groups. First, Iaau is a bird, often described as a bird of prey with the ability to fly as high and be as aggressive as the falcon (CT 148 and 149). Moreover, it has been suggested that Iaau can be viewed as a primordial bird most renowned for its flight, and therefore understood to be dissociated from Seth (CT 148). However, although the Iaau-bird may, in some instances, be associated with Seth and understood as a contender against Horus the falcon, the connotation of absolute evil does not seem to be associated with Seth within the context of his struggle against Horus for legitimacy over Egypt. As for the aggressive character of Iaau as a bird of prey, it is worth noting that even beneficent gods behave violently against their enemies to preserve their possessions. Thus, violence can be seen as a means of protection, and even as retribution (*e.g.* CT 149). The deceased desires, therefore, to embody the might of aggressive beings, such as Iaau, in a funerary setting (*e.g.* CT 148 and 149). Due to the focus of this paper, the question of the precise nature of the Iaau-bird must be put to one side. Nevertheless, Iaau seems to be a bird of prey similar to the falcon or, as Clark (1949–1950, 24, 28, 135, 139) suggests, it may be the *bnw*-phoenix or an eagle.

The second group of associations relating to Iaau often appears within the solar context. It is worth noting that Horus in his falcon form is a solar bird and represents the sun god himself as Re-Harakhty. The Iaau-bird, which can be associated with the falcon, is therefore a solar bird. Indeed, Iaau is a member of the solar bark crew (CT 341) and is closely related to Re, or to Thoth who is the deputy of Re, in being a plant or an efflux of the sun god's eye (CT 617). Since the term 'Iaau' might be related to the verb *i3wy*, meaning 'to grow old' (CT 953), Iaau can be associated with Atum, the old one, when he rests in the West (CT 170), where he is united with Osiris in the course of the night (BD 180). As does Horus, the nocturnal sun Atum takes care of Osiris and brings him to life momentarily. Other gods, like Khnum, 'the good protector of his father', play a similar protective role. Thus, Iaau can be called the 'fair one' through his association with the night sun Atum and through being a member of the solar crew who announces the deceased's arrival in the bark of the self-created god (CT 341).

Thirdly, Iaau is associated with the dead. Since Atum is associated with Osiris, Iaau is also a deity with whom the deceased would like to be identified. Indeed, as the deceased particularly wishes to enact the way the sun god came into being and share Osiris' destiny, he/she could accordingly be called 'this Iaau N' (CT 1089 VII 367a–370b). Moreover, Iaau, written with a plant determinative, can be associated with Osiris, who is viewed as a god of fertility, vegetation and grain, provider of offerings, and the lord of sustenance. In addition, although Iaau might, under certain circumstances, be associated with an ominous destiny (CT 953), which possibly consists of eating faeces and drinking urine (CT 698), he can also be propitious to the dead. For example, he is the ferryman who helped the dead cross to the abode of the gods (CT 170).

Iaau and Imy-Ia(a)u

The west wind does not only have Iaau as its progenitor but also Imy-Iau, ⸗ . CT spell 163, which according to Frandsen (2000, 31) adds 'nothing new to the discussion', may in fact provide further information concerning the relationships between Iaau, the west wind, and the West, and between these entities and Imy-Iau. I propose to translate a relevant passage from this spell as follows:

The west wind, the offspring of Imy-Iau,
which came forth between the thighs of the West,

and makes the slaughtering () among cattle.
Rejoice, rejoice (you) gods, with the breath of this N,
good and sweet of living. It shall be taken to this N
so that he might live on it.

(CT 163 II 405g–l)

This spell associates the west wind with the West, regarded as its progenitor. In my view, it also attributes a specific function, not to Imy-Iau, but to the west wind. This function is somewhat difficult to grasp, depending on how one reads 405i–k. The translation I have given above largely follows the way De Buck divided the text, as well as the translation proposed by Barguet (1986, 267–268). However, the passage can also be rendered differently: one may link *ḥtp* of 405j with the end of 405j. Thus, Faulkner (1973, 141) translated: "… who makes a butchery of the herds (reserved) for offering". He probably ascribes this function to Imy-Iau. Furthermore, the phrase 'good and sweet of living' seems to be attributed to the breath of the deceased. One may derive contrary meanings from these two readings: that the west wind is either destructive, since it kills herds; or that it is not, since this slaughtering is related to offerings. However, *ḥrwt/ḥryt* is believed to be "a generic term for sacrificial animals, but can have the more specialised use of 'slaughtered cattle'" (Wilson 1997, 746). This second interpretation brings to mind the association between the West, the domain of Osiris, and offerings. The fourth good deed that the 'Lord of All' made in the primordial time deals precisely with this association (CT 1130 VII 464d–e). Finally, the west wind is said to be the offspring of a deity called 'Imy-Iau'.

It is important to consider other evidence related to this deity in order to clarify his relationship to the west wind. For example, in CT spell 36 I 139a–40b, Imy-Iau appears alongside Ha, the lord of the western desert, where the deceased is introduced to Osiris. Imy-Iau seems to perform Horus' role as caretaker of Osiris. Imy-Iaau also appears in connection with the dead (PT 534 §§ 1265c, 1274a–b). Imy-Iau is written with the plural dot determinative in PT 534 § 1265c but without it in PT 534 § 1274a. The context suggests that it should be understood as plural, but it can also be taken as singular. Firstly, if one takes Imy-Iau as a plural, Imy-Iau may be interpreted as those who worship the sun god (Sethe 1962, 174–175). However, since *iꜣw* also means 'old one', Faulkner (1969, 201) wondered if Imy-Iau could not be translated as 'those who are among the old ones (?)'. The fact that they occur in connection with the *ḥꜣtyw* suggests that Imy-Iau were originally in the entourage of the dead king or the noble dead whom they protected. But through this connection with the *ḥꜣtyw*, Imy-Iau came to be associated with inimical beings who could threaten the dead. Secondly, if one understands Imy-Iau to be in the singular, Imy-Iau can be translated as 'the one who is among/with the old one', or 'the one who is the old one', or 'the one who is in adoration'. Although the context can support each translation, one gathers that Imy-Iau, whether considered to be plural or singular, is connected with Atum, the old one, with the sun god, and with the West, where the deceased king and the noble dead come to rest.

In addition, it is significant that Imy-Iau is not written with a ram's head determinative in the Pyramid Texts as it is in the Coffin Texts; and Imy-Iau occurs in the singular in Coffin Texts, just as it does in PT 534 § 1274a. One may, therefore, question whether or not the two *corpora texti* speak of the same being. Nevertheless, one may assume that Imy-Iau, when written in the singular at least in Pyramid and Coffin Texts, is considered to be a single being – as came to be the case in the Coffin Texts.

Imy-Iau is not the sole deity to be portrayed with a ram's head. For instance, *imy-shty*, which Derchain (1965, 138, n. 33) associates with Imy-Iau and views as a ram god, is represented with a ram's head determinative. Ram-headed gods also occur in representations of the four winds in other sources, especially from the Graeco-Roman Period. Each of the four winds corresponds to a cardinal direction and are represented by an animal, such as the falcon, the lion, the beetle, the snake, or a human figure. However, in such representations the most common animal is the ram (Gutbub 1977, 330–336).

The aim of the discussion which now follows is to consider the representation of the west wind in order to understand further the significance of Imy-Iau and its possible relationship to Iaau. An examination of representations gathered by Gutbub (1977, 330–336) shows some common features shared by the west and other winds: the ram motif; the ostrich feather; the human figure who represents the *ḥḥ*-gods who help Shu to lift and sustain the sky; and the ideograms which read 'the breath of life'. Nevertheless, the west wind is more commonly depicted as a ram-headed bird, which looks like a bird of prey, such as the falcon or eagle, and as a snake-headed human figure. As mentioned above, the ram is associated with Atum, Osiris and the West. The ram also symbolises the *bỉ* of the deceased and is one of the icons of Amun and Khnum, both of whom can also be associated with Shu. The ostrich feather is related to Shu and Maat-Tefnut, who are deities related to air and breath. In addition, the setting of Re in the West has connections with Horus as caretaker of Osiris. Thus, a perched falcon and the ostrich feather, 🪶, can be a symbol for the West. Furthermore, the falcon is one of the forms the deceased wishes to take in order to fly to the sky, board the solar bark, and thus become a god (*nṯr*), a word which can be determined with a perched falcon, 🦅. A snake-headed human figure, on evidence of Theban origin, can be understood as representing the west wind if one assumes that the snake refers to Meresger, a goddess who is often portrayed as a snake and represents the Theban necropolis.

The textual and pictorial evidence discussed above seems to suggest that Imy-Iau is linked to solar deities and the cardinal direction of the west. Imy-Iau, as a ram-headed bird, is associated with Atum, Osiris, the dead, and the West. He is the progenitor of the west wind (CT 163 II 405h) and appears with Ha, the lord of the western desert (CT 36 I 139a–140b). Thus, it appears that Imy-Iau holds characteristics similar to those ascribed to Iaau. The analysis above shows that Imy-Iau and Iaau can be equated with one another or can act as substitutes for each other.

This brief survey of sources concerning Ha, Iaau, and Imy-Iau does not seem to provide any decisive evidence which supports Frandsen's interpretation that Iaau embodies evil, nor the assertion that the west wind, as his offspring, is also evil. To paraphrase Gutbub (1977, 342), the crucial point is not so much the nature of the winds, as the significance they acquire through their association with each cardinal direction.

'One who lived in one womb before two things came into being in this land' (CT 162 II 396b)

This passage raises three difficulties. First, is this a statement about Iaau or the west wind? Second, how is one to translate 🪶🏺 *m ḫt wꜥt*? This passage could be interpreted as being in apposition to Iaau; that Iaau lived 'in one womb before two things came into being in this land', and thus showing Iaau is a primordial being. Some scholars translate *m ḥt wʿt* as 'being one womb/body' or as 'in the womb/body of the Sole One'. Hence, Iaau lived in the womb/body of the Sole One – the creator god – before two things came into existence in this land. The latter translation is the way Frandsen (2000, 16) interprets this passage.

This interpretation is plausible, but I have not yet encountered evidence which mentions a primeval deity who lived in/as the body/womb of the sole creator god. Iaau could be of primordial origin, without having lived 'in the womb of the Unique One', but simply through his association with Atum and the solar bird falcon or *bnw*-phoenix. Therefore, I suggest that CT spell 162 II 396b, whose syntax is similar to that of CT spell 163 II 405h, refers to the west wind since the entire spell concerns the four winds. Thus, I propose that it is the west wind which lived in/as one womb/body before two things came into being. Nevertheless, one may also suggest, on syntactical grounds, that II 396b is not concerned so much with the west wind as with a possible identification of, or unification between Ha and Iaau, two deities associated with the West, 'before two things came into being in this land'. But this interpretation remains conjectural at present.

The third question raised by the passage is, what does 'before two things came into being' mean? This translation is based upon the text written on five of ten coffins. The other coffins provide different versions, four of which offer a version which may be translated as: 'one who lived in/as one womb/body, forming a pair in this land', or 'one who lived in/as one womb/body, fraternising (?) in this land'. The version inscribed on coffin BIBo may be read as: 'one who lived in/as one womb/body (of?), the second in this land'. I do not know for certain what the expression *m ḥt wʿt* means (Bickel 1994, 115). In my view, however, the *t* of *wʿt* agrees with *ḥt*, which is feminine. Thus, it cannot be translated as 'the womb/body of the Sole One'.

One might question, as does Frandsen (2000, 16), why the west wind alone and none of the other winds can be united with the creator. The answer might simply be because of the importance attached to the West in the ancient Egyptian funerary religion. The West is the final destination of all deceased individuals, especially the resting place of the blessed dead and the gods, particularly of Osiris and Atum. In addition, the writing of the West has special ideograms – 𓋹 or 𓋹 – which visually associate it with the divine realm, the domain of Horus, Shu, and Maat. Moreover, the Iaau-bird, which can be associated with the falcon, represents the cardinal direction of the west, as does Imy-Iau through his association with the ram, the latter being connected with Atum resting in the West.

Conclusion

I have not found any decisive indication that evil is associated with winds. Nor have I found any firm evidence that supports the relationship that Frandsen asserts between evil and Iaau. He does so on the basis of the association he sets up between Iaau and the *bwt* consisting of not eating faeces and drinking urine, and between this *bwt* and the realm of non-Maat, that is, the reversed world and world of non-existence. However, this examination of textual and pictorial references to the four winds, and the west wind in particular, suggests that none are explicitly and/or absolutely associated with evil. I have not come across explicit evidence that Iaau, the progenitor of the west wind, was present in the womb of the creator god before creation, or that this entity embodied a form of primordial evil. Therefore, unlike Frandsen (2000, 17), I cannot state that "the four winds were the first product of creation, and of these one was a bad wind. The world was not perfect in that not all creation was good".

Campion Hall, University of Oxford

Acknowledgements

I am deeply grateful to Dr. Mark Smith, the supervisor of my doctoral thesis, for carefully reading the longer version of this study. I thank Dr. Paul Frandsen for giving me copies of his forthcoming publications and Professor John Baines for contacting him on my behalf. Special thanks to Fr. Richard Randolph, S. J., and Kathryn Piquette for reviewing my English.

References

Assmann, J. 1989, *Maât: L'Égypte pharaonique et l'idée de justice sociale*. Julliard, Paris.
Baines, J. 1985, *Fecundity Figures: Egyptian personification and the iconology of a genre*. Griffith Institute, Oxford.
Barguet, P. 1986, *Les textes des sarcophages égyptiens du Moyen-Empire*. Du Cerf, Paris.
Bickel, S. 1994, *La Cosmogonie égyptienne avant le Nouvel Empire*. Editions Universitaires, Fribourg.
Breasted, J. H. 1901, The Philosophy of a Memphite Priest, *Zeitschrift für Ägyptische Sprache und Altertumskunde* 39, 39–54.
Chassinat, E. 1929, *Le Temple d'Edfou, 4*. Institut français d'archéologie orientale, Cairo.
Chassinat, E. 1931, *Le Temple d'Edfou, 6*. Institut français d'archéologie orientale, Cairo.
Clark, R. T. R. 1949–1950, The Origin of the Phoenix: A study in Egyptian religious symbolism, *University of Birmingham Historical Journal* 2, 1–29, 105–140.
De Buck, A. 1935–1961, *The Egyptian Coffin Texts, 1–7*. University of Chicago Press, Chicago.
Derchain, P. 1965, *Le Papyrus Salt 825 (BM 10051): Rituel pour la conservation de la vie en Égypte*. Académie Royale de Belgique, Brussels.
De Wit, C. 1957, Les génies des quatres vents au temple d'Opet, *Chronique d'Égypte* 32, 25–39.
Douglas, M. 1966, *Purity and Danger: An analysis of concepts of pollution and taboo*. Routledge and Kegan Paul, London.
Faulkner, R. O. 1969, *The Ancient Egyptian Pyramid Texts*. Oxford University Press, Oxford.
Faulkner, R. O. 1973, *The Ancient Egyptian Coffin Texts, 1*. Aris and Phillips, Warminster.
Frandsen, P. J. 1999, On Fear of Death and the Three *Bwts* Connected with Hathor, in E. Teeter and J. A. Larson (ed.), *Gold of Praise: Studies on ancient Egypt in Honor of Edward F. Wente*, 131–148. University of Chicago Press, Chicago.
Frandsen, P. J. 2000, On the Origin of the Notion of Evil in Ancient Egypt, *Göttinger Miszellen* 179, 9–34.
Frandsen, P. J. (forthcoming), Bloodshed and Salvation, in S. J. Seidlmayer (ed.), *Religion in Context: Imaginary Concepts and Social Reality in Pharaonic Egypt*. Editions Universitaires, Fribourg.
Gardiner, A. H. 1932, *Late-Egyptian Stories*. Fondation Égyptologique Reine Elisabeth, Brussels.
Gutbub, A. 1977, Die Vier Winde im Tempel von Kom Ombo (Oberägypten). Bemerkungen zur Darstellung der Winde im Ägypten der griechisch-römischen Zeit, in O. Keel (ed.), *Jahwe-Visionen und Siegelkunst: Eine neue Deutung der Majestätsschilderungen in Jes 6, Ez 1 und 10 und Sach 4*, 328–353. Katholisches Bibelwerk, Stuttgart.
Helck, W. and Westendorf, W. 1992, *Lexikon der Ägyptologie, 7*. Otto Harrassowitz, Wiesbaden.

Hornung, E. 1994, Black Holes Viewed from Within: Hell in ancient Egyptian thought, *Diogenes* 165, 133–156.

Hornung, E. 1999, *The Ancient Egyptian Books of the Afterlife*. Cornell University Press, Ithaca and London.

Kadish, G. 1979, The Scatophagous Egyptian, *The Journal of the Society for the Study of Egyptian Antiquities* 4, 203–217.

Kurth, D. 1986, Wind, in W. Helck and W. Westendorf (eds.), *Lexikon der Ägyptologie, 6*, cols. 1266–1272. Otto Harrassowitz, Wiesbaden.

Naville, E. 1886, *Das Aegyptische Todtenbuch der XVIII. bis XX: Dynastie aus verschiedenen Urkunden, 1–2*. Asher and Co., Berlin.

Sauneron, S. 1962–1975, *Le Temple d'Esna, 2–6.1*. Institut français d'archéologie orientale, Cairo.

Sethe, K. 1908–1910, *Die altägyptischen Pyramidentexte*. Hinrich, Leipzig.

Sethe, K. 1962, *Übersetzungen und Kommentar zu den altägyptischen Pyramidentexte, 5*. J. J. Augustin, Hamburg.

Sethe, K. n.d., *Übersetzungen und Kommentar zu den altägyptischen Pyramidentexte, 1*. J. J. Augustin, Glückstadt and Hamburg.

Smith, M. 2002, *On the Primaeval Ocean*. Museum Tuscalanum and the Carlsberg Papyri, Copenhagen.

Te Velde, H. 1977, *Seth, God of Confusion: A study of his role in Egyptian mythology and religion*. E. J. Brill, Leiden.

Te Velde, H. 1980, Horus and Seth, in W. Helck and W. Westendorf (eds.), *Lexikon der Ägyptologie, 3*, cols. 25–27. Otto Harrassowitz, Wiesbaden.

Wildung, D. 1977, Ha, in W. Helck and W. Westendorf (eds.), *Lexikon der Ägyptologie, 2*, col. 923. Otto Harrassowitz, Wiesbaden.

Willems, H. 1996, *The Coffin of Heqata (Cairo JdE 36418): A case study of Egyptian funerary culture of the early Middle Kingdom*. Peeters, Leuven.

Wilson, P. 1997, *A Ptolemaic Lexikon: A lexicographical study of the texts in the Temple of Edfu*. Peeters, Leuven.

Wolf, W. 1929, Der Berliner Ptah-Hymnus (P 3048, II–XII), *Zeitschrift für Ägyptische Sprache und Altertumskunde* 64, 17–44.

Yoyotte, J. 1960, Les Pèlerinages dans l'Égypte ancienne, in Sources orientales 3, *Les Pèlerinages*, 17–74. Du Seuil, Paris.

Yoyotte, J. 1961, Le Jugement des morts dans l'Égypte ancienne, in Sources orientales 4, *Le Jugement des morts*, 15–80. Du Seuil, Paris.

Zandee, J. 1960, *Death as an Enemy According to Ancient Egyptian Conceptions*. E. J. Brill, Leiden.

Flower Arranging in Ancient Egypt? A new approach to archaeobotanical remains

Sally McAleely

Introduction

This paper describes in detail the construction of two archaeobotanical artefacts from ancient Egyptian burial contexts, introduces the research aims and methodology, and offers some preliminary findings. My research has been designed to record and analyse artefacts which have been deliberately manufactured using a process known today as 'flower arranging'. These 'arranged plant material' artefacts can be found in the archaeological record in a number of forms. Primary evidence includes the botanical remains themselves, and secondary evidence includes representational depictions in two- and three-dimensions using media such as monumental architecture, statuary, tomb paintings, mosaics, metalwork, jewellery and pottery, as well as textual references. I maintain that these artefacts constitute a hitherto unrecognised category of material culture, and as such can be analysed to provide social, cultural and technological insights. I suggest avenues for further research and ways in which the study of these botanical artefacts may contribute to our understanding of the past. This postgraduate project is a development of ideas promulgated in my BSc dissertation (McAleely 2001). The work presented here is part of a larger PhD project wherein I aim to use my analysis of material from ancient Egypt, together with that from a future ethnographic study, to make cross-cultural comparisons concerning the construction and use of these artefacts. Ultimately, I intend to use my data to study aspects of human cognitive development.

To date, I have studied and recorded 45 artefacts from two Egyptian collections which can be described as examples of ancient Egyptian flower arranging. The term 'flower arranging' may cause some confusion, because both flowers and other plant parts, such as leaves and berries, may be used in an arrangement, and I have therefore adopted the more general term 'arranged plant material' when referring to the artefacts. I define the term 'flower arranging' as selecting fresh plant material, removing it from its natural habitat and putting it in another location or context in order to make a statement. One or more flowers, either alone or with foliage, may be used, and the statement made varies depending on context.

A key component of flower arrangements is the mechanics. 'Mechanics' is a flower arranging term denoting the materials used to construct an arrangement. In a simple bouquet, the mechanics would be the 'string' that ties the plant material together. Mechanics hold the plant material in position and help maintain the strength and integrity of the design so that it can withstand handling and transport. To make an arrangement, tools and specialist equipment may be used, and sometimes accessories are added. For example, the floral collars found in the tomb of Tutankhamun (Carter 1927, pl. 36) included faience rings as accessories. The term 'garland' describes an arrangement made by joining together individual elements in a repetitive pattern and, rather than go into the semantics of terminology, I have used it in this paper to also denote artefacts described elsewhere as 'wreaths'.

Little research has been directed at understanding the construction and use of arranged plant material artefacts and their possible symbolic meanings, nor have they been analysed from the perspective of crafted material culture. As a modern example – the global cut flower industry is a multi-billion dollar business, and makes a significant contribution to national economies. For example, in 2002 Holland alone exported cut flowers worth over US$3 billion (Flower Council of Holland, 2003). Hughes (2001, 394) states that by 1998 Kenya exported cut flowers valued at US$80.9 million, and that other developing countries such as Colombia and Ecuador are encouraged to produce this high-value export crop to aid their economies. Despite their present day ubiquity and evidence for the symbolic use of flowers in many modern and past cultures, arranged plant material artefacts have received little attention in archaeology other than taxonomic identification. I maintain that the art of 'flower arranging' is evidence of deliberate human behaviour; implies botanical knowledge; and can give insights into craft technology, ideology, social differentiation, and the local environment.

In many modern cultures we use flowers for symbolic expression, "establishing, maintaining and even ending relationships with the dead as well as the living, with divinities as well as humans" (Goody 1993, 2), and there is evidence of a similar tradition in past cultures. An arrangement may say 'thank you' or 'happy birthday', or be used as a funerary offering or temple decoration. We assign meaning by 'reading' the context, and believe that currently only our own species, *Homo sapiens sapiens* has the cognitive skills to do this. According to Lowe (1998, 89), animals "do not conceptualise what they perceive and so cannot reflect upon past, future and merely possible situations". I believe we may be able to use evidence of symbolically placed arranged plant material as evidence for abstract thought, and it is this connection to which I hope to apply my data in order to explore human cognition. For example, there is some contentious evidence that Neanderthals buried their dead with flowers (Leroi-Gourhan 1975; Solecki 1972; Sommer 1999). My data will add new information to this debate, but further explanation of my ideas concerning cognition is beyond the remit of this paper.

For archaeologists, the main problem with arranged plant material is preservation. Because of their organic nature, botanical specimens rarely survive intact. However, ancient Egyptian ideology and climate, together with the enduring popularity of Egyptology, have conspired to ensure the survival of arranged plant material artefacts. The hot, dry sand surrounding Egyptian burials acted as a natural desiccant, and quite spectacular flower arrangements have been excavated from ancient Egyptian contexts. Perhaps the most well known are those discovered by Carter during his excavation of the 18th-dynasty tomb of Tutankhamun (Germer 1989; Hepper 1990; Newberry 1927).

Unfortunately, plant remains were often accorded little attention by early Egyptologists, and were deemed too mundane to have any inherent value. For example, like many of his contemporaries, Davis (1907) assigned little value to the arranged flowers that he discovered whilst excavating the tomb of Yuya and Tjuyu in the Valley of the Kings. Describing his first entry into the tomb, Davis writes:

> after descending about twenty feet, we found a shelf cut into one side of the wall and on it a large ceremonial wig made of flax and dyed black, also an armful of dried flowers which doubtless were offerings to the dead (as is done in our day and generation).
>
> (Davis 1907, xxvii)

He remarks upon the arranged flowers, but although a flax wig is later listed in the site report, Davis' 'armful of flowers' is consigned to this narrative aside and receives no further mention or analysis. There is even evidence that plant material was destroyed, during or soon after excavation (*e.g.* Winlock 1941, 17) and that, like Davis' (1907, xxvii) 'armful of flowers', some (many?) artefacts are not included in site reports. When arranged plant material is listed as a find in site reports, it is often poorly recorded and its analysis confined to enumeration and taxonomic identification. For example, Newberry (1890) discusses the funeral wreaths discovered by Petrie at Hawara. Other than commenting on how the colours of the flowers and leaves in one wreath complimented each other, his analysis concentrates on identifying and describing the native origins of the various plant species found during excavation. Early Egyptologists write of plant material crumbling to dust (see Hepper 1990, 9), and I believe that valuable information has been lost because these artefacts were considered too mundane to be noteworthy.

Method

In order to obtain uniform data, I developed a methodology for examining and recording individual artefacts. As the work progresses it may be necessary to adopt a sampling strategy, and also a method for including analysis of textual references and representational depictions, such as tomb inscriptions and paintings.

Each artefact was examined using a 70 mm hand lens and a x10 magnification hand lens, which allowed fine detail such as knots to be noted. A recording sheet was developed to ensure uniformity in data collection and particular attention was paid to the nature of the materials, the species used, and the manner of construction. Artefacts were measured, drawn, photographed, and their provenience has/will be researched and recorded.

Because of its fragile nature, the plant material could not be handled, and accurate measuring was therefore problematic. I devised a method which involves using a transparent sheet marked with a grid system of 1 cm and 1 mm squares. This can be laid directly onto glass mounts, or can be suspended over artefacts that are stored in open boxes by using supports of appropriate height. There is a problem with parallax, but this can be overcome by keeping the head and eyes in a fixed position relative to the artefact. Experimental work using a modern dried flower arrangement, which could be handled and deconstructed, showed that the method worked with a good degree of accuracy, provided that the artefact was viewed consistently through the transparent sheet. Curves were measured by the simple expedience of a length of household string.

Great care was taken when moving specimen boxes, and I was careful not to breathe directly onto any exposed specimens because introduced moisture from respiration could allow moulds to develop. The best preserved specimens that I have found to date are securely mounted under glass in sealed boxes, and are curated under controlled atmospheric conditions on fixed shelving protected from light. This helps prevent deterioration caused by agitation, light, moulds and insects.

A version of Leroi-Gourhan's (1975) *chaîne opératoire* was drawn up to describe the steps involved in manufacture and use of a 'flower arrangement' (Figure 1), and was used as a framework for analysis. Lemonnier (1986, 149), quoting Cresswell, describes the *chaîne opératoire* as "a series of operations which brings a primary material from its natural state to a fabricated state". I used this method for looking at the manufacturing process, because, firstly, it highlights ancillary factors such as cultivation, transport and labour, and secondly, allows insight into the cognitive implications of the technological process. For example, evidence

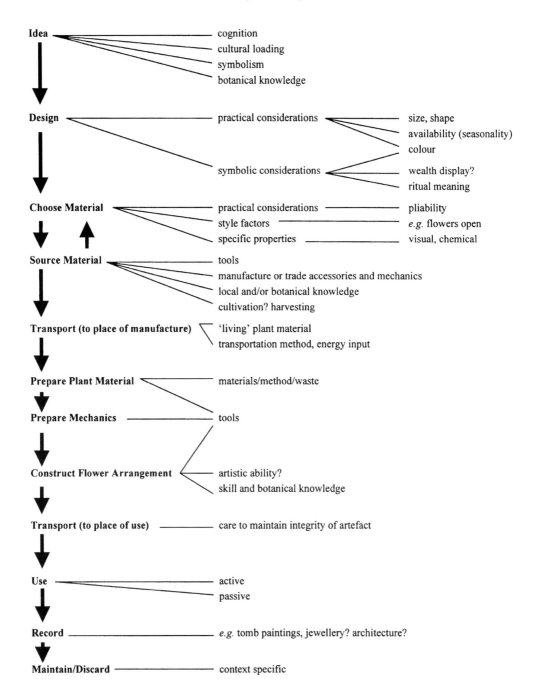

Figure 1. A 'chaîne opératoire' for the construction and use of a flower arrangement.

necessary for flower buds to open fully after picking, implies specific cognitive ability. The *chaîne opératoire* method has been used to study lithic technology and ceramics, but has not been used before in relation to plants. I intend to elaborate on this approach in a later paper.

Two garlands from ancient Egypt

(a) Garland 1

Figure 2 shows the remains of a garland mounted under glass. It is remarkably intact but has a number of damaged areas which give valuable insights into its construction. Affixed labels say that it originated from the German botanist Schweinfurth in 1884, and that it is from the coffin of a 21st-dynasty princess. Further research amongst historical documents concerning Schweinfurth's travels circa 1884 should shed more light on the context and provenience of this artefact.

The garland is composed of identical repeated elements, each consisting of a flowerhead (*Picris coronopifolia Asch.*) clasped in a folded leaf (*Salix safsaf Forsk.*). All elements have the same orientation, indicating that the garland was constructed so as to have a predetermined visual impact. The garland was built up by folding and binding leaves and whole flowers onto

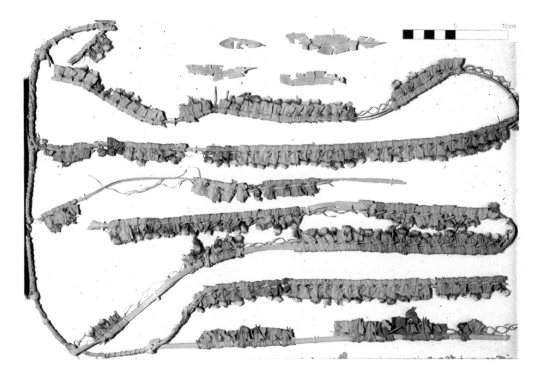

Figure 2. Garland 1 mounted under glass. The Economic Botany Collection, the Royal Botanic Gardens. Catalogue number 40746 (detail from a photograph by A. McRobb).

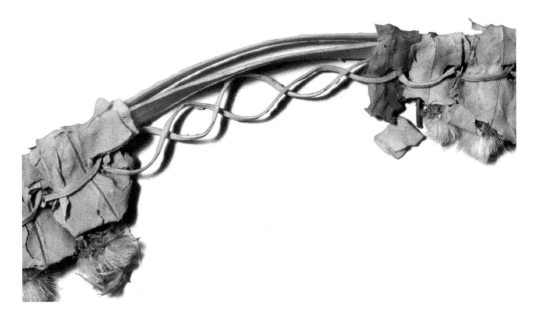

Figure 3. A damaged section of Garland 1. Missing elements allow the binding technique to be seen. Note also how the surviving elements partially overlap each other, and how the binding pierces the leaves. The Economic Botany Collection, the Royal Botanic Gardens. Catalogue number 40746 (detail from a photograph by A. McRobb).

a foundation consisting of a double layer of narrow strips of plant material, each strip being 3–5 mm wide. The foundation and binding (the 'mechanics') have not been botanically identified but are believed to be papyrus, *Cyperus papyrus L*. It was not possible to determine the length of the foundation strips, nor whether two individual strips or one strip folded in two was used. First, the stalk of a flowerhead, and then a folded leaf, were folded over the double foundation layer. This flower and leaf bundle forms one element of the design. Further elements were added to the foundation strips in a linear fashion, and each flower and leaf bundle was then bound firmly in place with plant material strips 0.8–1 mm wide. Two of these binding strips held each element in position, using a sewing or weaving technique (see Figure 3; note how leaves are pierced by the binding strips, indicating the use of a sewing technique). I have also seen this method used to construct other garlands from ancient Egyptian contexts, but where the binding encompasses rather than pierces the leaves. This latter method gives a much neater and more aesthetically pleasing result, and in my opinion would require more skill, so Garland 1 with its pierced leaves could indicate a degree of mass production. Experimental work with modern plant material is planned to help determine this and other questions, such as whether a piercing tool might be needed.

   Each bundle appears to be of a similar size (width 1.1 cm, plus or minus 0.2 cm), indicating that when harvested the leaves were selected at a similar stage of growth. This would demonstrate skill and botanical knowledge. There is a degree of overlap between the elements, with an average of 11 elements per 10 cm of garland. A damaged portion shows a binding strip firmly anchored in place by being wound twice around the foundation strip and tied with a knot. It should be possible to determine the length of the binding strips, and eventually make a quantitative assessment of the amount of papyrus used in the construction.

The remains of the garland are approximately 3 m long, appearing to consist of a number of loops. Each loop is made up of linearly arranged flower and leaf elements, and is knotted onto a supporting framework with the loose ends of each join bound in place (see Figure 4). This framework consists of three or four strips of papyrus, width indeterminate, bound together with narrower strips of papyrus, 1–1.2 mm wide. A total length of 287 cm of flower and leaf elements and 43.5 cm of supporting framework remain joined together to form one artefact. I

Figure 4. Section of Garland 1 showing knotted tie to the supporting framework. The Economic Botany Collection, the Royal Botanic Gardens. Catalogue number 40746 (detail from a photograph by A. McRobb).

counted 204 whole and partial flower and leaf elements, and 26 missing elements can be assumed from areas where the elements have been lost, but where the remaining binding material can be clearly seen. Thus, at least 230 individual flowerheads and leaves were selected and gathered to make this artefact. In addition, two different widths of binding material and one (or two?) different widths of foundation strips were prepared and used as the mechanics. Manipulating this amount of plant material quickly enough to prevent wilting would require planning and preparation, some skill and dexterity, and possibly a shelter to provide shade. I have not yet come to any conclusions as to how the garland was used or perhaps draped, although Germer (1989, 8) includes a sketch of a pectoral garland from Tutankhamun's burial, which shows one possibility. If further research shows that garlands were similarly constructed and used in the same manner over time, it could indicate evidence of contiguity, in this case between customs in the 18th and 21st Dynasties.

(b) Garland 2

A garland mounted under glass, labelled 'Petrie's collection 1888' (see Figure 5) is held in the Economic Botany Collection, the Royal Botanic Gardens, catalogue number 26721. The provenience and archaeological context of this garland is not known at present but may be determined with further research in the collection's archives.

This artefact (Figure 5) exemplifies a different construction method. Like Garland 1, it is made from individual elements bound to a plant material core, but these are arranged concentrically rather than linearly, giving a three-dimensional effect. Again, papyrus is used for the mechanics (the plant material foundation core and bindings), but the elements are joined together by a different technique using a circular binding method rather than a linear folding and weaving/sewing technique. Further study is needed to determine whether the elements are positioned in order to form a repeating visual pattern. Preliminary analysis indicates regularity to the design, which in turn indicates a planned visual effect. Each element consists of plant material bound to a central core of papyrus pith using papyrus strips, and the same technique is used to construct every element. However, unlike the previous garland which is composed of identical elements, Garland 2 is constructed from a number of different element types. Each type is composed of different plant species with varied use of plant parts, and is therefore visually distinct. Whole flowers, individual flower petals, and berries are used in different combinations of plant parts and species. Six plant species have been identified in the garland: flowers of *Lychnis coeli-rosa Desr.* and *Epilobium hirsutum L.*; petals and flowers of *Rosa richardii Rehd.*; petals of *Matthiola librator L.*; berries of *Solanum dulcamara L.*; and pith and strips of *Cyperus papyrus.*

One element type consisted of eight *Solanum dulcamara* berries strung together on strips of papyrus in two linear groups of four (see Figure 6). Each group was then individually bound to a central stem of papyrus pith. It appears that a plug of papyrus pith may have been inserted to support the berries, but this could not be determined without invasive techniques. Whole flowers of *Lychnis coeli-rosa* and possibly some flower petals (indeterminate) were then bound in a circle surrounding the papyrus core (see Figure 7), using a 2 mm-wide strip of papyrus (the lower binding in Figure 7). This was wound four times around the central papyrus pith and the flower stalks, and does not appear to be tied in place. A slightly wider strip of papyrus, approximately 2.5 mm wide (the upper binding in Figure 7), was then wound higher up, once or twice around the circle of flowers. I suggest that its function was to support the flowers in an

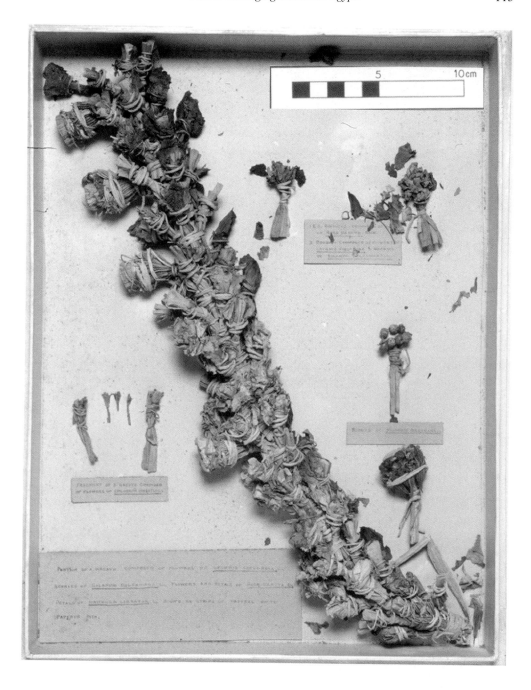

Figure 5. Garland 2 mounted under glass. The Economic Botany Collection, the Royal Botanic Gardens. Catalogue number 26721 (taken from a photograph by A. McRobb).

Figure 6. Early stage in construction of one element type found in Garland 2. Berries strung in two groups of four are bound onto a pith support. The Economic Botany Collection, the Royal Botanic Gardens. Catalogue number 26721 (detail from a photograph by A. McRobb).

Figure 7. Later stage in construction of the element from Garland 2. Flowerheads are added and bound into position. The Economic Botany Collection, the Royal Botanic Gardens. Catalogue number 26721 (detail from a photograph by A. McRobb).

upright position (hence its greater width), rather than to act as a binding material. Deconstruction would be necessary to accurately enumerate and measure the materials used in this element type, but six *Lychnis coeli-rosa* flowers were visible, arranged concentrically around the papyrus core. The indeterminate petals may have been from these *Lychnis coeli-rosa* flowerheads.

This element type was larger and more complex than the other element types and was the only one to include berries. It appeared to be spaced along the length of the garland in a vertical line at intervals of 5 cm (plus or minus 0.5 cm), indicating that, although three-dimensional, the finished artefact had a predetermined orientation. Other elements consisted of bound bunches of flowers and flower petals. All of the prepared elements were individually positioned and bound onto the central core, in a progressive overlapping manner, most likely working from top to bottom when orientated as in Figure 5. I counted 65 elements of varying constituents attached to the central core, with more (a similar number?) apparent on the underside of the mounted garland.

I could not determine precise details regarding construction of the central core of Garland 2, but it appeared to consist of a number of pith strips held together with papyrus binding to give a firm foundation. These binding strips were 1 mm wide and were more densely wound around the core at one end (the lower end in Figure 5). A strip of pith 0.6 cm wide and 9 cm long can be seen projecting from this bound end. The central core is substantial (*i.e.* thick) in comparison to the quantity of flowers used. This gives rigidity whilst maintaining flexibility, and suggests that the garland may have been designed to be held or placed in a specific manner, or even waved about, possibly using the projecting pith strip as a tie or handle.

In total the artefact is 39 cm long (plus the 9 cm pith strip) and appears to be oval in shape with an approximate circumference of 24 cm, although the garland may have originally been circular, and subsequently compressed to fit its current storage box. It was not possible to determine whether this example is a portion of a larger garland, or whether the remains represent the entire length of the original. It is therefore difficult to precisely quantify the materials used and the time (and hence the labour) needed for its construction, but I believe that useful estimates could be made.

Discussion

By identifying the species used, it should be possible to envisage these ancient Egyptian garlands in their original splendour, with the dull browns of the dried remains replaced with the vibrant colours and scents of the fresh material. I plan to produce a visual simulation using computer graphics. I have studied examples of arranged plant material ranging from poorly provenienced fragments to nearly complete artefacts, and have noted several different construction techniques. Preliminary analysis suggests that these objects reoccur over a wide geographical area and a long time span in ancient Egypt. I intend to report my findings regarding spatial and temporal distribution of arranged plant material artefacts in a later paper as my research progresses.

Whilst the method used to construct Garland 2 (Figure 5) is still used by flower arrangers (*e.g.* Vagg 1993, 74–77), I have not seen the linear technique used in Garland 1 (Figure 2) in modern flower arrangements, but it mirrors elements of a construction method known as 'twining' employed in basket making and in the construction of matting. Wendrich (2000, 256) illustrates this twining technique and states that it is one of nine different techniques employed in Egyptian basketry. She (Wendrich 2000, 257) mentions several examples of ancient Egyptian twined matting such as a twined matting fragment made of grass from the Predynastic Period, and twined grass matting used as a wall cover for the funerary chapel in the 1st-dynasty tomb 3505 at Saqqara. I have also noted a similar twining technique represented in Egyptian jewellery, for example in a gold necklace found in the coffin of Queen Tiye during excavations at Deir el-Bahri (Davis 1910, pl. 21). Davis (1910, 20) describes the necklace as being "in imitation of the plaited garlands of leaves and flowers with which mummies were surrounded". This find provides evidence that garlands were important cultural items, worthy of being copied in precious metal and worn as jewellery. It seems reasonable to assume that naturalistic jewellery imitated natural arrangements, thus making it possible to infer a pre-existing cultural tradition of arranging plant material to make garlands. I plan to explore the temporal and cross-cultural distribution of such techniques as my research progresses, and to look at parallels with basketry and textile technologies.

To facilitate construction the plant material would need to be pliable, thus indicating that it was fresh when used. In modern flower arranging, it is always necessary to gather an excess of material in order to select for factors such as correct leaf size, as well as to allow for spoilt material. For example, insect damage is often a problem, but I found little evidence of insect holes in the Egyptian garlands, indicating either careful selection or possible use of pesticide techniques and therefore deliberate cultivation. To my knowledge, the cultivation of flowers has not been researched despite evidence suggesting their extensive use in garlands and bouquets. There is also speculation regarding the use of flowers in ointments and to perfume oils (*e.g.* Vogelsang-Eastwood's (2000, 292) mention of a fragment of relief dating to the Ptolemaic Period which appears to depict the extraction of lily essence), and I think this adds to the case for deliberate cultivation. Hugonot (1989) and Wilkinson (1998) write about gardens in ancient Egypt, and work has been done concerning food crops; see for example Murray's (2000a) discussion of cereal production and processing during the Pharaonic Period, and her (Murray 2000b) chapter regarding fruits, vegetables, pulses and condiments in ancient Egypt. Nevertheless, with regard to archaeobotany in general, it is very much a question of 'where have all the flowers gone?'.

Our knowledge concerning past cultivation of non-food crops is very limited. For example, papyrus (*Cyperus papyrus L.*) had many non-food uses in ancient Egypt, but Leach and Tait (2000, 228) inform us that "the extent to which papyrus was cultivated for making a writing-ground or for other purposes in Pharaonic Egypt, as opposed to growing wild, is not known", and they (Leach and Tait 2000, 228) suggest that there "must have been some control over the way in which it was grown and harvested". I think that this must also have applied to the growing of flowers. By analogy with modern flower arranging and recourse to the *chaîne opératoire* (Figure 1), as my research progresses it should be possible to make a reliable estimate of the amount of plant material needed to construct the garlands. A quantitative assessment of the amount of plant material used in the non-food capacity of garland manufacture would provide evidence to support or disprove the notions of a craft industry and of deliberate cultivation of flowers, together with an indication of their economic contribution to life in ancient Egypt.

For maximum planned impact, flowers must be picked at the right stage of development, for example so that they are in full flower when the arrangement is used for its intended purpose. The more complicated the design, the more knowledge and effort is required to select and prepare the plant material and to ensure that it remains in a fresh condition. Once picked, the material would quickly deteriorate in the climate of ancient Egypt, and reference to the *chaîne opératoire* (Figure 1) indicates the necessity for either close proximity of areas reserved for growing plants and for artefact manufacture and use, or speed and care (and therefore planning) during transport and manufacture. Alternatively, conservation measures such as use of shade may have been employed. I believe that the finished, fresh plant material artefacts would have some weight, and might be subject to crushing. This raises the possibility of a need for protective structures to support the garlands in transit.

To construct arranged plant material artefacts, botanical knowledge regarding the physical properties of the flowers and leaves would be needed, together with skill and an understanding of design. If a sufficient number of artefacts can be reconstructed, it should be possible to observe design preferences, such as use of colour and scent, and whether there was preferential use of plants with known chemical (*e.g.* medicinal or psychotropic) effects, or which had a symbolic significance in Egyptian ritual. The seasonality of flowers can give unique chronological information and the co-seasonality of a number of species found in the same arrangement allows even finer tuning. For example, Hepper (1990, 10) notes how Newberry was able to conclude, from the seasonality of the flowers and fruits which made up the floral collar found on the innermost coffin of Tutankhamun, that the pharaoh "was buried at some time between the middle of March and the end of April". This has enabled scholars to date his death to within weeks, since the time taken to complete the ritual embalming and entombment process is known.

The survival of intact flower arrangements from ancient Egyptian contexts attests to the strength of the mechanics and to the skill with which they were made. They survived not only handling and use in ancient Egypt, but also the rigors of post-excavation conditions, including transport to their current housing, often involving several moves over time.

Flowers retain a semblance of life and continue metabolic activity after picking, but eventually fade and die. This could be interpreted as a visible transitional link between life and death and may explain why floral tributes are used in burials, often in close association with the physical corpse. Evidence such as Andrews' (1984, 64) report of a garland of Delphiniums (*Delphinium sp.*) which was placed on the chest of the mummy of Amenhotep I when it was rewrapped in the 21st Dynasty, indicates that the plant material was fresh when placed in ancient Egyptian burial contexts. Andrews (1984, 64) writes regarding this garland of delphiniums, "when the coffin was opened nearly three thousand years later, their pungent fragrance flooded the room and the body of a wasp … was found". This shows that the plant material was fresh when the mummy was reburied, because the delphiniums would not have otherwise retained their scent. Moreover, the wasp would probably only have been attracted to fresh flowers. It also shows that the people responsible for the reburial of Amenhotep I thought it important to make the symbolic gesture of placing a garland in close proximity to the mummy before it was sealed inside the coffin. I suggest that this symbolic placement of living arranged plant material was used to acknowledge the last personal, as opposed to ritualistic, human involvement with the body before it was separated from the living. This idea remains conjectural at this time, requiring further research, but perhaps the garlands found in Egyptian tombs are evidence of a 'human touch' which served to personalise ritual burial.

As well as generating information regarding Egyptian material culture, my research is aimed at using archaeobotanical remains to explore what is meant by 'the human touch' and how we might recognise such behaviours in the archaeological record. In particular, when and where the seemingly instinctive recognition of, and empathy for, a fellow human being is first evidenced in the archaeological record by the symbolic use of arranged plant material. Repeatedly, I find that excavators talk of the 'human touch' and are able to identify with the inherent symbolism of floral tributes. For examples see Davis (1907, xxvii as quoted above) who wrote almost 100 years ago, and Solecki (1972, xii) who attributed human-like characteristics to the Neanderthals by virtue of pollen evidence for flowers found associated with Neanderthal remains. Solecki (1972, xii) writes, "it is the fact that the Neanderthals of Shanidar Cave buried their dead with flowers which is of the highest significance to me. In my thinking, it swings the balance in favour of accepting the Neanderthals as our ancestors". Although there is much debate regarding the presence of flowers in this burial, Solecki nevertheless categorises floral offerings as a human trait. This personal identification with a burial tradition of floral offerings by Solecki (1972, xii) and Davis (1907, xxvii), and *ipso facto* the recognition of fellow humans in the beings who made the offerings, is interesting because, although we must be wary of making uniformitarian assumptions, arranged plant material cited as evidence of humanity is a common theme. I think that the idea of symbolically marking the point of last human contact before the dead are relinquished by an offering of living plant material also merits further consideration. Ultimately, I hope to use my Egyptian data as a case study to support my contention that the symbolic use of arranged plant material is a human trait which can be recognised in the archaeological record, and thus may provide a means for studying human cognition and what it means to be human.

Concluding remarks

I think that a key issue regarding 'flower arranging' for Egyptologists is, does the evidence indicate a hitherto unrecognised craft industry? At this stage in my research, I cannot give a definitive answer but I am accumulating sufficient evidence to suggest that this idea merits further consideration. Carter's (1927, 74) report concerning the arranged plant material found in the burial chamber of Tutankhamun states: "when the care and precision with which these are fashioned is recognized, there is a strong reason for belief that this particular occupation with the Ancient Egyptians, as in later days, must have been a specialized trade". Manniche (1999, 24) lists arranged plant material that Ramesses III contributed to the temple of Amun over a period of 1057 days, and which includes an average of nearly 2000 bouquets and 57 wreaths a day. This is a considerable amount of non-food plant material, particularly when tributes to other temples are taken into account, and I believe it adds to the evidence for craft specialisation and implies the cultivation of flowers.

With the proviso that I continue to search publications, I believe that much of the arranged plant material that I have located and examined is unpublished and poorly recorded. Most of the illustrations and photographs that do exist, such as Schweinfurth's sketches of garlands (in Germer 1988, 5), and Burton's photographs of plant material from the tomb of Tutankhamun (in Germer 1989, pls. 1–5), were originally published before the advent of modern reprographic techniques. It is difficult to use them to determine the precise construction and materials involved, and often there is no indication of scale, hence quantitative assessment is unsatisfactory. It is therefore all the more vital that Egyptologists ensure that these fragile plant material artefacts are adequately curated, and that their unique value to Egyptology and to archaeology in general is recognised. I hope that my work will provide a comprehensive record and analysis of these arranged plant material artefacts for future research.

Institute of Archaeology, UCL

Acknowledgements

I should like to thank my supervisors, Dr. Dorian Fuller and Prof. Ken Thomas for their continued support and encouragement. I am also grateful to Dr. Hew Prendergast, Dr. Mark Nesbitt and all the staff at the Centre for Economic Botany, the Royal Botanic Gardens, for their interest in my research and generous help whilst I studied the collection, as well as Dr. Stephen Quirke, Sally MacDonald and Hugh Kilmister of the Petrie Museum of Egyptian Archaeology, UCL, for assistance with the collection and discussion. The photographs were taken by Andrew McRobb, resident photographer at Kew, with the aid of a grant towards photographic costs from the Institute of Archaeology, UCL. Finally, my sincere thanks to the organisers of CRE 2003, especially Serena Love, Kathryn Piquette and Joanne Rowland, for their professionalism and kindness which helped calm my nerves before giving my first paper at the symposium.

References

Andrews, C. 1984, *Egyptian Mummies*. British Museum Publications, London.
Carter, H. 1927, *The Tomb of Tut.Ankh.Amen, 2*. Cassell and Co., London.
Davis, T. M. 1907, *The Tomb of Iouiya and Touiyou*. Archibald Constable and Co., London.
Davis, T. M. 1910, *The Tomb of Queen Tîyi*. Constable and Co., London.
Flower Council of Holland 2003, http://www.flowercouncil.org. Date accessed: March 2003.
Germer, R. 1988, *Katalog der Altägyptischen Pflanzenreste der Berliner Museen*. Otto Harrassowitz, Wiesbaden.
Germer, R. 1989, *Die Pflanzenmaterialien aus dem Grab des Tutanchamun*. Gerstenberg Verlag, Hildesheim.
Goody, J. 1993, *The Culture of Flowers*. Cambridge University Press, Cambridge.
Hepper, F. N. 1990, *Pharaoh's Flowers*. Cambridge University Press, Cambridge.
Hughes, A. 2001, Global Commodity Networks, Ethical Trade and Governmentality: Organizing business responsibility in the Kenyan cut flower industry, *Transactions of the Institute of British Geographers* 26.4, 390–406.
Hugonot, J. 1989, *Le jardin dans l'Égypte ancienne*. Peter Lang, Frankfurt am Main.
Leach, B. and Tait, J. 2000, Papyrus, in P. T. Nicholson and I. Shaw (eds.), *Ancient Egyptian Materials and Technology*, 227–253. Cambridge University Press, Cambridge.
Lemonnier, P. 1986, The Study of Material Culture Today: Toward an anthropology of technical systems, *Journal of Anthropological Archaeology* 5, 147–186.
Leroi-Gourhan, A. 1975, The Flowers Found with Shanidar IV, a Neanderthal Burial in Iraq, *Science* 190, 562–564.
Lowe, E. J. 1998, Personal Experience and Belief: The significance of external symbolic storage for the emergence of Modern Human cognition, in C. Renfrew and C. Scarre, (eds.), *Cognition and Material Culture: The archaeology of symbolic storage*, 89–96. Oxbow Books, Oxford.
Manniche, L. 1999, *An Ancient Egyptian Herbal*. British Museum Press, London.
McAleely, S. 2001, *Flower Arranging and Archaeology*. Unpublished BSc Dissertation, Institute of Archaeology, UCL.
Murray, M. A. 2000a, Cereal Production and Processing, in P. T. Nicholson and I. Shaw (eds.), *Ancient Egyptian Materials and Technology*, 506–536. Cambridge University Press, Cambridge.
Murray, M. A. 2000b, Fruits, Vegetables, Pulses and Condiments, in P. T. Nicholson and I. Shaw (eds.), *Ancient Egyptian Materials and Technology*, 609–655. Cambridge University Press, Cambridge.
Newberry, P. E. 1890, The Ancient Botany, in W. M. F. Petrie, *Kahun, Gurob and Hawara*, 46–50. Kegan Paul, Trench, Trübner and Co., London.

Newberry, P. E. 1927, Appendix III Report on the Floral Wreaths Found in the Coffins of Tut.Ankh.Amen in H. Carter, *The Tomb of Tut.Ankh.Amen, 2*, 189–196. Cassell and Co., London.

Solecki, R. 1972, *Shanidar: The humanity of Neanderthal man.* Penguin Press, London.

Sommer, J. 1999, The Shanidar IV 'Flower Burial': A re-evaluation of Neanderthal burial ritual,*Cambridge Archaeological Journal* 9.1, 127–137.

Vagg, D. 1993, *Complete Step-by-Step Flower Arranging Course*. Ebury Press, London.

Vogelsang-Eastwood, G. 2000, Textiles, in P. T. Nicholson, and I. Shaw (eds.), *Ancient Egyptian Materials and Technology*, 268–298. Cambridge University Press, Cambridge.

Wendrich, W. Z. 2000, Basketry, in P. T. Nicholson, and I. Shaw (eds.), *Ancient Egyptian Materials and Technology*, 254–267. Cambridge University Press, Cambridge.

Wilkinson, A. 1998, *The Garden in Ancient Egypt*. Rubicon Press, London.

Winlock, H. E. 1941, *Materials Used at the Embalming of King Tūt-'Ankh-Amūn*. The Metropolitan Museum of Art, New York.

A Kushite Temple in a Western Oasis?

Hironao Onishi

Introduction

Qasr el-Ghueita or 'Fortress of the Small Garden' (ancient Perwesekh or *Pr-wsḥt*; Figures 1 and 2) is located in the Kharga Oasis about 17 km south of the famous Hibis temple. Although the fortress, whose origin is likely to have been Roman (Vivian 2000, 82), has been cleared within its mud brick enclosure walls, it is said to be one of the most archaeologically unknown areas in the Kharga Oasis. According to Vivian (2000, 81–82), Qasr el-Ghueita was famous for its vineyards that supplied wine to the royal court in the Nile Valley. Inscriptions in the Theban tombs attest to the excellent quality of the grapes of Qasr el-Ghueita (Vivian 2000, 81). This clearly indicates that the site was inhabited long before the arrival of the Romans who supposedly built and occupied the fortress (Vivian 2000, 82).

Within the fortress walls stands a well preserved sandstone temple (Figure 3). Despite the uncertainty of its dating due to the lack of archaeological work in the area, the initial construction of the Qasr el-Ghueita temple has often been attributed to the 25th or 'Kushite' Dynasty. However, this seems to be based on a tentative suggestion made by Naumann (1939, 5) in the 1930s which was subsequently quoted by various scholars, notably Porter and Moss (1951, 291, 293), Cruz-Uribe (1999, 407), and, most recently, Wilkinson (2000, 237). In his article, Naumann (1939, 5) commented that the Qasr el-Ghueita temple seemed to be older than the Hibis temple – and therefore the oldest temple in the oasis – but the origin of its construction could not be determined because the cartouches in the sanctuary were erased. Nevertheless, Naumann suggested that the style, work and the shortness of these cartouche rings showed some similarities to other Kushite reliefs, but without presenting any other concrete evidence. By the 'shortness of the cartouche rings', he perhaps meant the relative shortness of Kushite kings' names. However, Naumann's suggestion that a temple of Kushite origin existed in the Kharga Oasis appears to have been justified by another intriguing suggestion that a Kushite chapel existed in the Baharia Oasis, located further north of Kharga (Figure 1). Fakhry (1939, 641; 1950, 73–80) claimed that inscribed blocks with cartouches, possibly naming Shabaqo, and blocks from a chapel of Taharqa were discovered reused in modern buildings in the area. This comment by Fakhry was referred to by Porter and Moss (1951, 311), and later cited by Kitchen (1986, 390) as evidence for a chapel of Taharqa in the Baharia Oasis. Although Fakhry's initial claim seems quite ambiguous, a block with the head of an unnamed king (Fakhry 1950, 75, fig. 55) does seem to show a similarity to other figures of Kushite kings elsewhere.

My personal visit to Qasr el-Ghueita in June 2002 was originally intended to look for conclusive evidence of the temple's Kushite origin. Regrettably, I was not able to locate the erased cartouches mentioned by Naumann (1939, 5) nor could I find traces of any cartouches in the raised reliefs on the rear wall of the sanctuary. Conclusive evidence regarding the earliest date for the temple's construction was not forthcoming. However, judging from the decoration preserved on the wall today, it does not appear to be the original and may have been restored or partially altered for the sake of conservation and tourism after the Naumann's visit in the 1930s. The trip, however, provided enough evidence to tentatively suggest that the Qasr el-Ghueita temple was *not* the work of the Kushites.

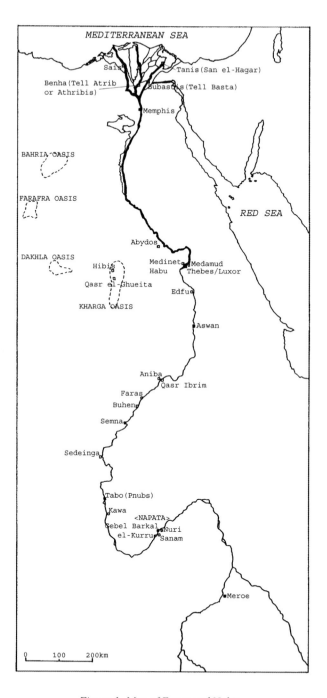

Figure 1. Map of Egypt and Nubia.

Figure 2. General view of Qasr el-Ghueita, from the north-east. (© Hironao Onishi.)

Figure 3. The stone-built temple inside the fortress, from the north-east. (© Hironao Onishi).

The temple of Qasr el-Ghueita

When it was built, the sandstone temple situated on the hilltop, overlooking a large part of the Kharga Oasis, would probably have been a dominant feature in the surrounding landscape. But it is now completely hidden from view within a massive mud brick structure of a later date with an enclosure wall preserved to a height of 8–10 m (Figure 4). According to 19th-century travellers such as Edmonstone (1822, 65–66), the mud brick buildings around the temple appeared to be the result of later occupation of the site by an Arab village. Some stone-built structures in front of the temple, within the enclosure wall, are possibly administrative buildings which suffered fire damage from the Blemmyes' attack in A.D. 450 (Cruz-Uribe 1999, 407). A similar secondary use of temple sites by Arabs at Kharga Oasis can be observed at a nearby Roman temple at Qasr el-Zaiyan (Cruz-Uribe 1999, 407; Vivian 2000, 82–83; Wilkinson 2000, 237–238), where, as at Qasr el-Ghueita, the sandstone temple is now surrounded by a series of later mud brick walls and buildings.

The Qasr el-Ghueita temple is believed to have been dedicated to the great Theban triad (Cruz-Uribe 1999, 407; Helck 1984; Porter and Moss 1951, 291–293; Wilkinson 1843, 369; Wilkinson 2000, 237): Amun, who is represented in his local form; Amun of Perwesekh (*Pr-wsḫt*), Mut, and Khonsu. Although they are somewhat damaged, painted figures of Amun and Khonsu can be seen on the side walls of the sanctuary with some of the original colour still preserved. These wall paintings will be discussed in more detail below.

The temple is rectangular in plan (25.53 m in length by 10.56 m in width, as measured by Naumann (1939, 4); Figure 5), oriented almost exactly along an east-west axis, facing east. The temple axis leads to an uninscribed stone gateway which stands at a distance of 12.55 m from the front of the temple proper.

The interior of the temple can be divided into four main sections: a forecourt, which seems to have been added later; a columned hall with a row of two composite columns with plain campaniform capitals situated in front (which appear to be common in Ptolemaic and Roman temples; Phillips 2002, 22); and behind these, another row of two composite columns, this time with lotus capitals; a vestibule with a stairway to the roof at the southern end; and a tripartite sanctuary (or possibly a single sanctuary in the middle with a storeroom to each side of it). The general plan of the temple seems to follow the layout of a traditional Egyptian temple. However, the architectural features described so far seem to indicate that the temple was built after the 25th Dynasty, based on the presence of the gateway in front of the temple and the use of composite columns in the hall. According to Phillips (2002, 22), the composite column was developed during the 26th 'Saite' Dynasty, or, more probably, the 27th Dynasty from the campaniform papyrus column, which had been popular in the New Kingdom (for types of Egyptian temple columns, see Phillips 2002, 5–26 and Wilkinson 2000, 66–67).

Most of the walls, doorjambs, and columns in the forecourt, the columned hall, and the vestibule are embellished with reliefs and accompanying hieroglyphic inscriptions. At the rearmost part of the temple, Edmonstone (1822, 65–66) reported that the sanctuary was the only inscribed of the three rooms at the back of the temple. During my visit to the temple, I was able to confirm that the door jambs of the sanctuary are inscribed with incised hieroglyphic inscriptions, while the walls of the sanctuary bear paintings but no reliefs. I was also able to confirm that the chamber to the south of the sanctuary is indeed uninscribed. Unfortunately, it was not possible to see whether or not the chamber to the north of the sanctuary was inscribed since the chamber was being used as a locked storage area and therefore inaccessible.

Figure 4. The main entrance to the fortress and the mud brick enclosure wall, from the south-east. (© Hironao Onishi.)

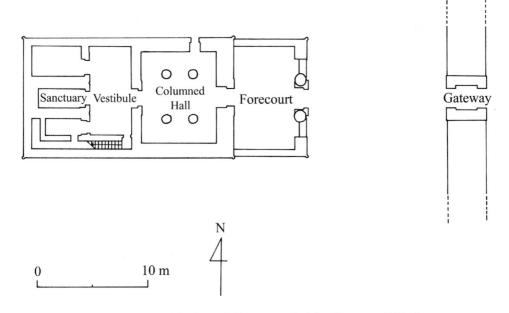

Figure 5. Plan of the Qasr el-Ghueita temple (after Naumann 1939, 4).

Figure 6. The rear wall of the sanctuary with an altar-like pedestal in the foreground. (© Hironao Onishi.)

As for the sanctuary, it contains a small altar-like pedestal and the rear wall of the sanctuary
(Figure 6) bears rather crude raised reliefs of a familiar offering scene (a king standing and making offerings before a seated god in front of an offering table) with an accompanying hieroglyphic inscription mentioning *Imn n Pr-wsḫt* 'Amun of Perwesekh'. If one compares these reliefs to those in Kushite monuments elsewhere, one notices that, in many cases, sunk relief was favoured for monuments in both Egypt and Nubia. That the reliefs in this temple are raised may suggest that it was not constructed by the Kushites.

However, there are also wall paintings preserved on both of the side walls, *i.e.* the north and south walls of the sanctuary, which means that there is a difference in the method of decoration employed on the walls within a single room. That is to say, there are paintings on the side walls of the sanctuary, while raised reliefs are employed on the rear wall. Despite their poor state of preservation, it appears that both side walls were originally adorned with brightly painted scenes, some of which still retain their original colours. The figures of Amun and Khonsu, mentioned above, are on the north wall which is the better preserved of the two. Amun (Figure 7) is depicted with his distinctive, tall double-plume on his head and, judging from a raised hand holding a flail to the left of his head, perhaps takes the form of Min-Amun. His body is painted blue and he is oriented to face east (*i.e.* towards the doorway of the sanctuary). In front of the figure of Amun is a figure of the falcon-headed moon-god Khonsu with the moon-disc on his head (Figure 8). His body is also painted blue and he faces the same direction as his father. A figure of the goddess Mut would probably have been present in front of the figure of Khonsu, as suggested by the remains of faint traces. A figure of a king may have faced the three divinities, but sadly no trace can be detected. Except for a small section containing one name in a cartouche on the north wall close to the doorway (which will be discussed shortly) the accompanying hieroglyphic inscriptions are too damaged to be of any help as far as the history of the temple is concerned.

Returning to the two different decoration methods seen in the sanctuary, these may be indicative of two different episodes of decoration. If either of these is indeed secondary, it is probably the rear wall, since one would normally expect the back wall to be the main focal point of the temple cult, especially when an altar is placed in front of it. Therefore, anyone wishing to redesign or redecorate part of the chamber as his/her own would have likely chosen the rear wall as the subject of alteration. The raised relief in the sanctuary looks quite similar to those reliefs in many other parts of the temple. As for the issue of who may have been responsible for the alteration of the rear wall in the sanctuary, the stylistic similarity between the raised relief here and elsewhere suggests that it could have been anyone whose name appears in the raised reliefs in the temple.

This speculation leads us to consider who was responsible for the wall paintings on the north and south walls of the sanctuary. Who might have started building the nucleus of the Qasr el-Ghueita temple? It may be possible to suggest here that the Persian king Darius I (*c.*522–486 B.C.) of the 27th Dynasty may have been the original builder, as he also seems to have been responsible for the construction/decoration of at least a large part of the Hibis temple in the same oasis (Cruz-Uribe 1986, 157; Vivian 2000, 77; Winlock 1941, 4).

The strongest evidence to support this suggestion comes from the north 'painted' wall of the sanctuary near the doorway, where a cartouche containing Darius I's *nomen,* though it is somewhat damaged (Figures 9 and 10), is still quite clearly visible in the horizontal row of hieroglyphic inscription located below the two aforementioned divine figures (Amun and Khonsu). The closest variation of the hieroglyphic renderings of Darius I's *nomen* to the Qasr el-Ghueita cartouche seems to be E6 in Von Beckerath (1999, 221). Fakhry (1975, 909) was the first to note the presence of this cartouche on the painted wall of the sanctuary during brief excavations which he carried out in 1972. Since then, the name of Darius I has been mentioned quite often as one of the kings who conducted building work at the Qasr el-Ghueita temple, (Cruz-Uribe 1999, 407; Vivian 2000, 82; Wilkinson 2000, 237). However, Fakhry's discovery is not mentioned specifically by any of these later investigators,

Figure 7. Figure of Amun on the north wall of the sanctuary. (© Hironao Onishi.)

hence it is not clear whether or not these recent references originate from Fakhry's work. Perhaps the details of Fakhry's unpublished excavations were largely overlooked and later scholars may have seen the cartouche themselves when they visited the temple. However, despite the presence of the cartouche of Darius I, which is the earliest known datable evidence from the temple, Fakhry (1975, 909) attributes the original temple to the 26th Dynasty without providing us with any explanation for his conclusion. Nevertheless, the contribution that Fakhry made towards the investigation into the origin of the Qasr el-Ghueita temple should be recognised.

Figure 8. Figure of Khonsu on the north wall of the sanctuary. (© Hironao Onishi.)

Figure 9. The cartouche of Darius I on the north wall of the sanctuary. (© Hironao Onishi.)

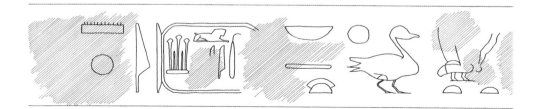

Figure 10. Line drawing of the cartouche on the north wall of the sanctuary.

As for the cartouche of Daruis I, the surviving part of the hieroglyphic text on the north wall reads: '--- King of Upper and Lower Egypt, son of Re, Lord of the Two Lands, the one who appears in glory, Darius, (beloved of) Amun-Re (of Hibis?) ---' (a possible transliteration being: --- (*nsw-bity*) *s3 R^c nb t3(wy) ḫ^c (Drywš)| (mry) 'Imn-R^c (n Hbt?)* ---).

A name in the cartouche on the left (south) doorjamb of the sanctuary may also belong to the same king, but due to poor preservation it cannot be identified with certainty. Both doorjambs of the sanctuary are covered with columns of incised hieroglyphic inscriptions. However, the carving style of the inscriptions on the doorjambs of the sanctuary appears to be unique in its crudeness and is quite clearly different from all other inscriptions in the temple.

On the doorjambs of the doorway between the columned hall and the vestibule, I was able to locate three cartouches of Ptolemy III (Euergetes I, *c.*246–221 B.C.), one on the right (north) and two on the left (south). The cartouche of his sister-wife Berenike II is also visible on the right (north) doorjamb with her titles, '--- Lady of the Two lands, wife and sister of son of Re, Ptolemy (III) ---' (a possible transliteration being: --- *nb(t) t3wy (Brnyk3t)| ḥmt snt n s3 Rˁ Ptwrmys ˁnḫ-ḏt mry-Ptḥ ---*).

On the whole, the name of Ptolemy III (Euergetes I) is the most conspicuous in the temple. It is also found on the doorway to the sanctuary (at least three times), on the walls of the four-columned hall (three sets of *prenomen/nomen* cartouches on the north wall and at least two sets on the south wall), and perhaps on the left (south) doorjamb of the doorway to the forecourt, *i.e.* the main entrance to the temple proper.

A possible history of temple construction at Qasr el-Ghueita

The names in cartouches found in the Qasr el-Ghueita temple allow us to propose a possible history, though a very brief one, of the temple's construction. As far as the present evidence suggests, Darius I of the 27th 'Persian' Dynasty was probably the one who began building the Qasr el-Ghueita temple, as evidenced by his name on one of the painted walls of the sanctuary. The painted walls are also likely to be the only remaining part from the original building that the workmen of Darius I were able to complete. There is no reason to doubt Darius I's strong connection to the Kharga Oasis due to his extensive activities at the Hibis temple (Cruz-Uribe 1986, 157; Vivian 2000, 77; Winlock 1941, 4), only 17 km north of Qasr el-Ghueita. It would not be surprising if Darius I indeed tried to build another temple in the same area. If this is the case, the construction of another temple at Qasr el-Ghueita, in an elevated position overlooking a large part of the Kharga Oasis, may suggest that the oasis played an important role around the time of Darius I, perhaps as a junction of trade routes or as a defensive post against hostile Western Desert nomads.

The unfinished Qasr el-Ghueita temple of Darius I, then, might have been left untouched until Ptolemy III came onto the scene. We will probably never know how much of the original plan of the building was completed during the reign of Darius I, but he may have been able to finish the building work of the temple as far as the columned-hall area and the gateway (which has survived by being integrated into the mud-brick enclosure wall of the fortress). If this was the case, he could only have embellished the interior of the sanctuary and its door jambs, which may explain why the other parts were left undecorated. Judging from the large number and location of the names of Ptolemy III found in the temple, one may assume that it was he who altered the rear wall of the sanctuary (from an original wall painting of Darius I to the raised relief which is still in place), added a forecourt to the temple, and completed the temple by decorating the walls and columns with the same kind of reliefs. Earlier writers (Naumann 1939, 5; Wilkinson 1843, 369) also document the names of Ptolemy IV (Philopator, *c.*221–205 B.C.) and Ptolemy X (Soter II/Lathyrus, *c.*116–107 B.C. and 88–80 B.C.). The names of these two Ptolemaic kings were also mentioned by Porter and Moss (1951, 291–293) and Cruz-Uribe (1999, 407). However, I was not able to locate any of these names during my visit to the Qasr el-Ghueita temple, perhaps due to the fault of my inexperience in distinguishing between the similar cartouches of the three Ptolemaic kings in question (Ptolemies III, IV, and X; *cf.* Von Beckerath 1999, 234–247). Nevertheless, the latter two Ptolemaic kings are likely to have carried out relatively minor works at the temple and left their names for their activities.

Suggestions for future research at Qast el-Ghueita

As a result of my research trip to Qasr el-Ghueita, the long-unchallenged suggestion that the Qasr el-Ghueita temple is of a 25th-dynasty 'Kushite' origin seems less tenable than before. However, we should not eliminate a Kushite king completely, especially the renowned builder Taharqa, from the list of possible founders of the Qasr el-Ghueita temple until we find more concrete evidence against the possibility. Perhaps the matter could be settled by a systematic archaeological survey in the area in the future. Like the epigraphic survey carried out at the Hibis temple by Cruz-Uribe (1986; 1987) during the 1980s, any kind of future archaeological work at Qasr el-Ghueita is very likely to provide crucial evidence for the origin of this relatively unknown temple.

I hope that the present reader would allow this writer to draw attention to Cruz-Uribe's (1986; 1987) survey of the Hibis temple, which, I believe, underlines the necessity and importance of future work at Qasr el-Ghueita. After carrying out an epigraphic survey of the temple and the recording of a small blockyard within the temple perimeter, Cruz-Uribe (1986, 164–165; 1987, 225–230) was able to suggest that the Hibis temple was of the 26th or 'Saite' Dynasty in origin, perhaps founded by Psamtik II (c.595–589 B.C.), and therefore older than previously believed. If, as Cruz-Uribe (1987, 230) suggests, Psamtik II was the founder of the Hibis temple, it is perhaps even possible that the foundation of the Hibis temple dates back to the reign of Taharqa (c.690–664 B.C.) because Psamtik II is commonly known to have usurped many of Taharqa's monuments by adding simple alterations to them (Yoyote 1951, 222–223), *e.g.* the so-called Edifice of Taharqa by the Sacred Lake at Karnak (Parker *et al.* 1979). Indeed, there are some interesting similarities between the Hibis temple and Taharqa monuments, including the Qasr el-Ghueita temple as a possible candidate. For example, Cruz-Uribe (1986, 166) noted that a 'confusion' of offering scenes in Room K1 of the Hibis temple could be related to the scenes depicted on the walls of the Edifice of Taharqa. Similarly, the presence of the god Min-Amun on the wall of Room K of the Hibis temple may be connected to the same god's probable presence in the sanctuary of the Qasr el-Ghueita temple (see above).

Thus, these few examples from the nearby Hibis temple show that there is still much detailed research to be done at the Qasr el-Ghueita temple. Once it is carried out, we will probably be able to obtain more information concerning the origin of the temple, which might be as old as the Hibis temple, *i.e.* 'Saite', or perhaps even older, as has often been suggested before (Cruz-Uribe 1999, 407; Naumann 1939, 5; Porter and Moss 1951, 291, 293; Wilkinson 2000, 237), and which I believe remains a possibility.

University of Cambridge

Acknowledgements

The trip to Qasr el-Ghueita was made possible by a generous grant given by the Thomas Mulvey Fund, the Faculty of Oriental Studies, University of Cambridge.

References

Cruz-Uribe, E. 1986, The Hibis Temple Project 1984–1985 Field Season, Preliminary Report, *Journal of the American Research Center in Egypt* 23, 157–166.

Cruz-Uribe, E. 1987, The Hibis Temple Project: Preliminary report, 1985–1986 and summer 1986 field seasons, *Varia Aegyptiaca* 3.3, 215–230.

Cruz-Uribe, E. 1999, Kharga Oasis, Late Period and Graeco-Roman Sites, in K. A. Bard (ed.), *Encyclopedia of the Archaeology of Ancient Egypt*, 406–408. Routledge, London.

Edmonstone, A. 1822, *A Journey to Two of the Oases of Upper Egypt.* J. Murray, London.

Fakhry, A. 1939, Bahria and Farafra Oases: Second preliminary report on the new discoveries, *Annales du Service des Antiquités de l'Égypte* 39, 627–642.

Fakhry, A. 1950, *Bahria Oasis.* Government Press, Cairo.

Fakhry, A. 1975, Charga Oase, in W. Helck and E. Otto (eds.), *Lexicon der Ägyptologie, 1*, cols. 907–910. Otto Harrassowitz, Wiesbaden.

Helck, W. 1984, Qasr Gueida, in W. Helck and E. Otto (eds.), *Lexicon der Ägyptologie, 5*, col. 43. Otto Harrassowitz, Wiesbaden.

Kitchen, K. A. 1986, *The Third Intermediate Period in Egypt (1100–650 B.C.).* Aris and Phillips, Warminster.

Naumann, R. 1939, Bauwerke der Oase Khargeh, *Mitteilungen des Deutschen Instituts für Ägyptische Altertumskunde in Kairo* 8, 1–16.

Parker, R. A., Leclant, J. and Goyon, J.-C. 1979, *The Edifice of Taharqa*, (trans. C. Crozier-Brelot). Lund Humphries, London.

Phillips, J. P. 2002, *The Columns of Egypt.* Peartree, Manchester.

Porter, B. and Moss, R. L. B. 1951, *Topographical Bibliography, 7: Nubia, the Deserts and Outside Egypt.* Claredon Press, Oxford.

Vivian, C. 2000, *The Western Desert of Egypt: An explorer's handbook.* The American University in Cairo Press, Cairo.

Von Beckerath, J. 1999, *Handbuch der ägyptischen Königsnamen.* Von Zabern, Mainz.

Wilkinson, J. G. 1843, *Modern Egypt and Thebes, 2.* J. Murray, London.

Wilkinson, R. H. 2000, *The Complete Temples of Ancient Egypt.* Thames and Hudson, London.

Winlock, H. E. 1941, *The Temple of Hibis in El Khargeh Oasis, Part 1: The excavations.* Metropolitan Museum of Art, New York.

Yoyote, J. 1951, Le martelage des noms royaux éthiopiens par Psammétique II, *Revue d'Égyptologie* 8, 215–239.

Bifacial Technology, Socioeconomic Competition, and Early Farming and Herding in the Fayum

Noriyuki Shirai

Introduction

While the beginning of cattle domestication occurred very early in Egypt (*c.*9000 B.P. or 8000 cal. B.C. following Hassan 2002, 12), the adoption of foreign domesticates, such as wheat/barley and sheep/goat, occurred at a considerably later date (after 7000 B.P. or 5800 cal. B.C.). Previous studies often focus on the reasons for the late adoption of foreign domesticates, citing adaptation to local climatic and environmental changes in the Early Holocene (*c.*9000–6000 cal. B.C.), as well as to the availability of domesticates in neighbouring regions during the same period. However, despite attempts to reconstruct climatic and environmental changes in the Eastern Mediterranean and North Africa (*e.g.* Close 1996; Hassan 1986a; Rossignol-Strick 2002), much of this previous research is characterised by a climatic and environmental determinism, and neglects to explain human motivations behind efforts to cultivate wheat/barley or herd sheep/goat in Egypt. Other research has centred on evolutionary changes in the cognitive abilities of modern humans and how such developments may have been related to the development of early farming and herding (Mithen 1996). Although the contributions of archaeobotany and zooarchaeology have been significant in this area (Barakat 2002; Gautier 2002), it has been observed that the study of material culture, especially lithic artefacts, has not contributed to these debates concerning the beginning of farming and herding in Egypt (Hassan 1986a, 73).

In surveying the past research on this topic, my attention has been drawn to a general model which suggests that in complex hunter-gather societies, socioeconomic competition between ambitious individuals who increasingly gained control of rich, wild food resources would have eventually led to the beginning of food production (Hayden 1990; 1995). This model not only suggests an explanation for the human motivation to attempt farming and herding, but can also be tested using archaeological material. In addition, this model assumes that only in regions where wild food resources were rich and invulnerable, could farming and herding have emerged independently, or been adopted from outside. This assumption seems to fit the resource-rich situation in northern Egypt where two major Neolithic sites, the Fayum and Merimde Beni Salama, were located. I have undertaken the examination of archaeological data from the former site in order to test this model for socioeconomic competition and to examine the possible implications for the beginning of farming and herding in Egypt. In particular, this paper will focus on Fayum Neolithic bifacial stone tools. I consider the social significance of this technology and attempt to link its appearance to broader social changes and changes in subsistence practises.

Within current archaeology there is a growing interest in the anthropology of technology; ideas obtained from anthropology have illuminated the study of cognitive and behavioural processes of tool making and their social contexts (Lemonnier 1992; Pfaffenberger 1992). In Egyptian archaeology, however, the understanding of ancient technology from an anthropological point of view has been a neglected area of study. Therefore, in the following I will also attempt to demonstrate how the study of the beginning of farming and herding in the Fayum may benefit from anthropological understandings.

The Fayum Neolithic

The Fayum Neolithic dates between 5200 cal. B.C. and 4500 cal. B.C. (Hassan 1988, 141; Midant-Reynes 2000, 105) and is regarded as the period when the first manifestation of a farming and herding culture appears in Egypt. It is possible that archaeological evidence for earlier Neolithic cultures could be buried under the accumulated alluvium in both the Nile Valley and the Delta (Midant-Reynes 2000, 106, 108; Wetterstrom 1993, 201*ff*). If this were the case, the Fayum Neolithic culture could be understood as a later marginal adaptation. For the moment, however, arguments concerning the beginning of wheat/barley farming and sheep/goat herding in Egypt must rely on the Fayum data. Since I am principally concerned with the initial adoption of wheat/barley farming and sheep/goat herding in Egypt, this paper will centre on the Fayum data.

Previous research in the Fayum has revealed that there was a long hiatus of human habitation, probably due to acute aridity, between the Epipalaeolithic (*c.*7100–6030 cal. B.C. following Hassan 1986b, 488; 1988, 143) and the Neolithic Periods. This is based on the lack of evidence for cultural continuity between these periods (Wendorf and Schild 1976, 225; Wenke *et al.* 1988, 38). Thus, domesticates seem to appear suddenly in the Fayum at the beginning of the Neolithic Period. Given that it has not been possible to demonstrate a gradual change in subsistence practises or patterns in material culture, the Neolithic culture of the Fayum is often thought to have derived from outside the area (Wenke *et al.* 1988, 38, 47).

While there is little doubt that major domesticates like wheat/barley and sheep/goat came from the Levant, the origins of Fayum Neolithic material culture are still ambiguous. As for parallels with typical Fayum Neolithic stone tools, small leaf-shaped arrowheads and tanged arrowheads are attested in the Egyptian Western Desert (*e.g.* Barich *et al.* 1996, fig. 2; Caton-Thompson 1952, pl. 100; Kuper 1996, fig. 3; McDonald 1996, fig. 2), as well as the Levant, although in earlier periods (Gopher 1994). Thus, it is not an easy task to determine the origin of these lithic traditions. Interestingly, concave-based points are not attested in the Levant but have been found in the Egyptian Western Desert, though in limited numbers (*e.g.* Caton-Thompson 1952, pl. 111; McDonald 1996, fig. 2a). A form which is particular to the Fayum Neolithic culture are sickle blades which were made from leaf-shaped points. In contrast, contemporary Levantine Neolithic sickle blades were essentially denticulated backed blades (Gopher and Gophna 1993, figs. 2, 7–8). Although Levantine subsistence practises are attested in the Fayum, given these differences in lithic traditions it is unlikely that Levantine toolmakers colonised the Fayum directly, bringing their domesticates with them. The autonomous development of Neolithic stone tool making somewhere in the Nile Valley or the Egyptian Western Desert, and the adoption of domesticates by the inhabitants of Egypt is thus inferred.

Even if the inhabitants of the Neolithic Fayum came from elsewhere in Egypt, the reasons for and the processes of the incorporation of farming and herding into local subsistence require explanation. It is clear that hunting and fishing were still dominant subsistence activities during the Fayum Neolithic as these activities are well attested archaeologically. Both the Epipalaeolithic and Neolithic peoples exploited the same species of fish and migratory waterfowl in similar relative abundances, using similar strategies during the same time of year (Brewer 1989a; 1989b). The question must then be raised as to why domesticates were adopted by the Neolithic inhabitants of the Fayum, in spite of a seemingly successful way of life based on hunting and fishing. Since the prior Epipalaeolithic inhabitants did not practise farming and herding, although the environmental circumstances were similar, the explanation that the Neolithic inhabitants must have had a wider resource base than their predecessors, and were therefore better adapted to the unpredictable environment of the Fayum (*e.g.* Brewer 1989b, 171; Wetterstrom 1993, 225*ff*) does not seem to be satisfactory. It must be noted that the cultivation of wheat and barley was already well established in the southern Levant no later than 6500 cal. B.C., and herding of domesticated sheep and goats was also established in the Egyptian Western Desert, as well as along the Red Sea coast, no later than 7000 B.P. or 5800 cal. B.C. (Close 2002; Hendrickx and Vermeersch 2000). They may have been available to the inhabitants of the Fayum at that time. Therefore, reasons other than adaptation must be sought for the adoption of domesticates.

Fayum Neolithic bifacial stone tools

Antiquarians and scholars alike have collected Neolithic stone tools at several locations around Lake Qarun in the Fayum, including Kom K, Kom W, Qasr el-Sagha and FS-1 (Figure 1). These

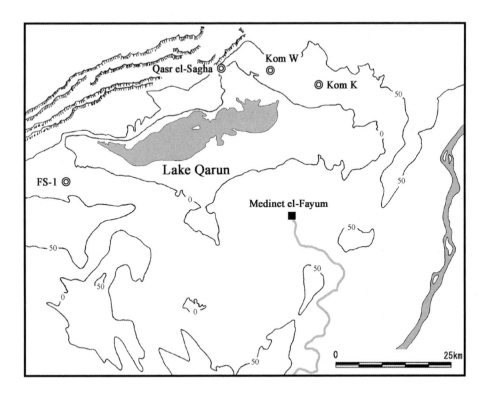

Figure 1. Map of the Fayum showing the locations of major Neolithic sites.

Fayum Neolithic stone tools were divided into two types: bifacially-retouched formal tools and less-retouched flake tools. At most locations, however, bifacial tools have only been selectively collected and published (Caton-Thompson and Gardner 1934; Dagnan-Ginter *et al.* 1984; Ginter *et al.* 1980; Kozlowski 1983; Kozlowski and Ginter 1989; Mussi *et al.* 1984; Puglisi 1967; Seton-Karr 1904; 1905; Wendorf and Schild 1976; Wenke 1984; Wenke and

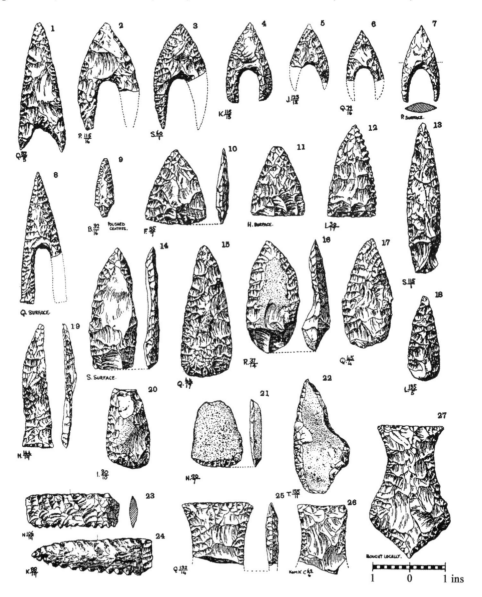

Figure 2. Bifacial tools (except for nos. 21 and 22) collected at Kom W (Caton-Thompson and Gardner, 1934, pl. 11). (© Blackwell Publishing.)

Casini 1989; Wenke *et al.* 1983; 1988). It has been difficult to understand the assemblages and densities of stone tools at specific locations. Additionally, these published assemblages cannot be regarded as representative of the lithic traditions of the entire Fayum region. Consequently, little attempt has been made to construct a typology of Neolithic sites (such as the distinction between residential and task sites) in the Fayum based on the assemblage and density of stone tools. Caton-Thompson and Gardner (1934), the excavators of many Neolithic sites on the northern shore of Lake Qarun, had reported a predominance of bifacial stone tools in their Fayum Neolithic inventory (Figure 2). However, other researchers have recently undertaken excavations in Qasr el-Sagha, as well as surface surveys at Kom W, sites which also previously explored by Caton-Thompson and Gardner, and revealed that Caton-Thompson and Gardner had overlooked the presence of crude flake tools at Kom W.

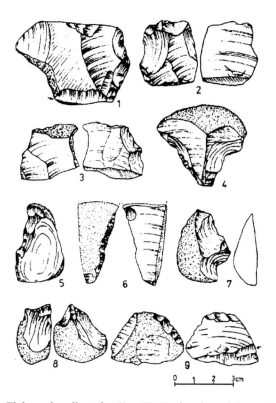

Figure 3. Flake tools collected at Kom W. (Kozlowski and Ginter 1989, 175, fig. 7.)

Therefore, it became apparent that previously accepted images of the regional lithic tradition of the Fayum Neolithic were distorted by selective collecting. On the basis of the Qasr el-Sagha lithic assemblage (Figure 3), it has been argued that 90 percent of the Fayum Neolithic stone tool assemblage must have been composed of flake tools, such as notches, denticulates and sidescrapers. Thus, bifacial tools were quite minor components, even though bifacial tools certainly existed at most Neolithic sites of the Fayum (Kozlowski and Ginter 1989: 172*ff.*; Midant-Reynes 2000, 101).

Despite increased understandings of the cultural history of the Fayum Neolithic and the origins of Fayum Neolithic material culture, previous studies have treated bifacial tools exclusively as cultural markers (*e.g.* Holmes 1989). In an effort to achieve a more holistic understanding of the evidence, I attempt to show that bifacial tools were signifiers of other important aspects of Fayum Neolithic culture. I begin my examination with the question of why such a limited percentage of stone tools in the Neolithic Period were made using bifacial technology. Bifacial technology involves making thin tools with sharp cutting edges. Replication and experimental studies demonstrate that the manufacture of bifacial stone tools is labour-intensive and time-consuming, and that bifacial stone tools are not robust, fracturing easily when used as projectile points (Whittaker 1994).

It may be said that bifacial technology does not make sense in the light of the costs versus the benefits. Nevertheless, during the Fayum Neolithic, bifacial technology was employed mainly to make arrowheads, spearheads, sickle blades and axes, all of which are related to hunting, fishing, harvesting and probably hoe-cultivation. Moreover, recent analysis of faunal remains found in the Fayum reveals that, with regard to the variety of fish and wild animals exploited and the seasons of exploitation, there was no difference between Neolithic and Epipalaeolithic subsistence practises (Brewer 1989a; 1989b). In contrast, stone tools employed in hunting and fishing show dramatic morphological elaboration, particularly with the introduction of bifacial technology during the Neolithic Period. From this one can conclude that technological change in stone tool manufacture does not seem to be associated with changes in hunting and fishing methods. Therefore, I suggest that the objective of bifacial technology was not necessarily to increase efficiency in hunting and fishing.

Moreover, it should also be noted that bifacial stone tools were not only collected on the surface of sites where hunting, fishing, harvesting and hoe-cultivation probably took place, but were also found in excavations of large settlement sites, such as Kom K and Kom W. Most of these tools seem to be in good condition, though few comprehensive analyses of use-wear or breakage patterns have been conducted to date. It may be possible that these bifacial stone tools were curated tools, prepared at residential locations prior to use, transported from location to location, and resharpened and used repeatedly. The rest of the Fayum Neolithic stone tool assemblage consisted of expedient tools made at the time of need; used and then discarded upon completion of the task (Bamforth 1986; Binford 1979; Nash 1996; Nelson 1991).

However, it has been argued that the curation of stone tools was closely related to mobility and the raw materials procurement strategies of toolmakers (*e.g.* Andrefsky 1994; 1998). Thus, it is insufficient to discuss curation without considering settlement patterns and how they relate to the distribution of lithic raw materials and food resources. Both mobility and the raw materials procurement strategies of toolmakers have yet to be well studied in the case of the Fayum Neolithic. Nonetheless, since most of Fayum Neolithic stone tools were made from local flint pebbles which were abundant and readily available (Caton-Thompson and Gardner 1934, 87), it is difficult to regard the curational practise as a form of economising behaviour due to the scarcity of lithic raw materials (*cf.* Bamforth 1986; Odell 1996).

Although it is easy to describe the difference between bifacial tools and flake tools, in terms of the curation-expediency dichotomy, the reason why curated technology was applied to hunting, fishing, harvesting and cultivating tools in the Fayum Neolithic may have not always been adaptational. Therefore, it should not be assumed that Fayum Neolithic bifacial stone tools were merely utilitarian, but, as I elaborate below, that their manufacture involved additional meanings.

Social meanings of technology

While archaeology has been preoccupied with Systems Theory which emphasises that optimal technological organisation is an adaptation to environmental conditions (Nelson 1991, 58–61), recent studies of prehistoric technology have been inspired by anthropology, as well as by sociology. Anthropologists advocate that technological activities were a fundamental medium through which social relationships, power structures, world views and other social production were represented and defined. Sociology focuses on the role of agents in the continuity and transformation of social structures which enabled and constrained individual actions. Consequently, a number of archaeologists have begun to highlight human agency in technological activities and to discuss how technology was structured within culturally and historically specific contexts of dynamic social interaction and meaning-making. Thus, it is important that the goal of technological studies is not only to describe prehistoric activities, but also to understand these activities in relation to social processes involving individuals and groups (*e.g.* Dobres and Hoffman 1994, 211–235; Hegmon 1998, 264–271; Sinclair 1990).

It is generally accepted by archaeologists that variations in material culture can carry information about the identity of individuals or groups, and that the variations, referred to as 'style', often mark the division of age and/or gender groups, social stratification within a group or social boundaries between groups. Additionally, style does not simply carry information about personal or group identity but also functions as an active tool used in social strategies, such as impressing other people and promoting reciprocal relationships. Therefore, in addition to taking into consideration the shape or decoration of the artefacts, a crucial question deals with the circumstances under which artefacts were made and used in such social strategies (Lemonnier 1992, 91–103).

An interesting ethnographic example of stylistic behaviour derives from the Kalahari Bushmen who greatly enjoy discussing their arrows and evaluating the makers. Skilled arrow makers are admired as 'professionals' by member of the community and express pride in their abilities. They tend to be much more enthusiastic than other community members in discussing the details of their craft – not in terms of the making of specific shapes, but in terms of precision and quality. Interestingly, the skilled arrow makers are not necessarily the best hunters. The reason why they are very much concerned with arrow making is that arrow makers either receive a large portion of meat procured by bow hunters or are responsible for the distribution of the meat. The arrows are widely exchanged in order to fill the need of meat sharing and to solidify socioeconomic ties (Wiessner 1983).

In another ethnographic example relating to the social significance of technology, it is reported that when the Inuit hunters carve 'tourist art', they try to embody boldness, perseverance and exactitude in their carvings. The choice of a complicated design means boldness, while the care which carvers take in rendering the carvings stresses exactitude and the hardness of the material emphasises perseverance. The reason why they engage in such craft activities is that demonstrating these qualities is considered to be important for the success of an Inuit hunter, and indeed, the Inuit hunters attain personal status through possession of these qualities (Sinclair 1990, 77; 1995, 58; 2000, 205).

This Inuit example of the relationship between practical activities and social qualities has already been considered in the interpretation of bifacial technology in Palaeolithic Europe. Based on the fact that elaborated, Solutrean bifacial stone tools are exclusively associated with hunting and butchering, it is argued that personal qualities, such as carefulness, perseverance and exactitude, were important for both successful hunting and successful bifacial tool making so that a correspondence may have been created between similar skills exercised in different activities. Consequently, those tools became not only utilitarian objects, but also symbolic items which communicated meanings about both the nature of tasks for which they were used and the persons who undertook the tasks (Sinclair 1995; 2000).

If the Fayum data is considered in the light of ethnographic examples of social meanings attributed to artefacts, it is possible to suggest that Fayum Neolithic bifacial stone tools embodied similar personal characteristics and skills, such as carefulness, perseverance and exactitude. Indeed, all of these attributes are essential for successfully undertaking subsistence activities, including the making of the tools used in these activities. Therefore, it may be argued that such characteristics and skills would have been recognised socially as favourable for the survival of individuals and groups, and that individuals who were engaged in subsistence activities in the Fayum Neolithic may have acquired personal status by emphasising their skills of making good quality stone tools. Given the apparent success of flake tool technology as discussed above, Fayum Neolithic toolmakers would not have needed to take the trouble to make such elaborate tools for use in everyday tasks. However, it can be argued that the cost of making and maintaining bifacial stone tools met the benefit of increasing one's status. For instance, if the Bushmen example is taken into consideration, the elaboration of bifacial stone tools in the Fayum Neolithic may reflect competitive aestheticism among individuals in obtaining prestige as excellent toolmakers, rather than the pursuit of a purely functional improvement. In this sense, Fayum Neolithic bifacial technology may be regarded as a prestige technology, as well as practical technology (*cf.* Hayden 1998).

Socioeconomic competition: A possible explanation for the emergence of farming and herding

The coincidence of the emergence of bifacial technology with the advent of wheat/barley farming and sheep/goat herding in the Fayum may imply a relationship between them. If Fayum Neolithic bifacial stone tools reflect competitive aestheticism in the quest for higher social status, I suggest that the first step toward the adoption of farming and herding as part of subsistence activities may also have been motivated by such competition in the quest for increased status among individuals.

According to the socioeconomic competition model mentioned above, socioeconomic equality and reciprocity tend to be dominant in regions where wild food resources are poor. Conversely, socioeconomic competition using food resources is likely to occur in regions where wild food resources are abundant. In such regions, ambitious individuals acquire control of food resources, creating reciprocal relationships with others, and eventually generate debt relationships with members of the community. Any ethic of sharing and equality is weakened and status quests through food provisioning do not need to be repressed. Ambitious individuals may distribute food generously and competitively on occasions such as feasts, thereby raising their status. Recipients become indebted to providers such that they become subordinate to the providers (Hayden 1990; 1995).

Although this model for the emergence of socioeconomic competition does not make clear *who* could become an ambitious food provider, it is plausible that these might be exceptionally skilled toolmakers, or persons who used their exceptional ability to please others who were ambitious. Provided that the circumstances became favourable for the abandonment of the ethic of socioeconomic equality, and novel food resources became available, ambitious food providers would have had various motives for attempting farming and herding. This, in turn, could provide a large amount of novel food, in order to impress other people and to wage competition. Recipients of food would have been obliged to undertake additional work because they were indebted to ambitious providers.

In north-eastern Africa, dramatic increases in rainfall occurred after a period of worldwide cooling known as the Younger Dryas (*c.*11000–9500 cal. B.C. following Rohling *et al.* 2002, 40–42; Rossignol-Strick 2002, 158) and resulted in the emergence of a complex hunting, gathering and cattle herding culture at sites such as Nabta Playa in the Egyptian Western Desert (Wendorf and Schild 1998; 2002). The subsequent return of extreme aridity known as the Great Mid-Holocene Arid Phase (*c.*8000/7500–7000/6500 B.P. or 6900/6300–5800/5400 cal. B.C. following Muzzolini 1993, 234) or successive short-term arid phases (7900–7700 B.P., 7260 B.P. and 7000 B.P., or, 6800–6500 cal. B.C., 6100 cal. B.C., and 5800 cal. B.C. following Hassan 1986a, 65; 1997, 216; 2002, 16), are assumed to have not only brought the culture to an end but also forced Epipalaeolithic inhabitants of the Fayum to leave the region.

In the Neolithic Period, the Fayum became rich in wild food resources and therefore inhabitable once again. As for the introduction of domesticates, because the Fayum was located at the intersection of one route from the Egyptian Western Desert and another from the Levant, domesticates became available from both regions after the Younger Dryas. However, geographical and climatic factors alone do not explain why domesticates were introduced into the Fayum. It has been argued that a chance coincidence of events, in which complex hunter-gatherer societies encountered rare climatic change, played a definitive role in the beginning of farming and herding (Layton 1999; Sherratt 1997). I develop this argument and consider that climatic changes stimulated socioeconomic competition for food resources which in turn led to the adoption of wheat/barley farming and sheep/goat herding in Egypt.

Most scholars concur with the assertion that a baseline of richness in food resources is essential for the concentration of population which is associated with increasing social complexity. However, controversy remains over whether constant rich conditions or occasional stressful conditions provided the primary stimulus for socioeconomic competition, and the emergence of ambitious food providers. Based on the assumption that there must have been periods when overall resource richness was occasionally diminished by climatic or other events, some argue that such periods were never times of emerging socioeconomic competition. Others are of the opinion that such periods were precisely the times that inequality increased, and as a consequence certain members of society were able to stimulate the reorganisation of labour (Arnold 1993, 82–89; 1996, 96–101).

I suggest that while the Early Holocene wet phase following the Younger Dryas probably fostered socioeconomic competition among Epipalaeolithic peoples, the Mid-Holocene arid phases were possibly the time when ambitious and competitive persons may have had the opportunity to reorganise subsistence and toolmaking strategies. Although tentative at this stage of research, Fayum Neolithic bifacial technology may be interpreted as material evidence for the reorganisation of subsistence resulting from incipient socioeconomic competition.

Conclusions

As for future research on this subject, it is necessary to demonstrate the historical contingency of the emergence of socioeconomic competition in the Fayum context while considering additional archaeological data concerning demographic changes in and around the Fayum. It remains possible that these processes occurred at an earlier date among social groups elsewhere in Egypt which, led by ambitious persons, came to the Fayum with domesticates. Indeed, further study of the processes which led to the emergence of skilled toolmakers – as possibly represented in the development of Fayum Neolithic bifacial technology, and the emergence of ambitious food providers – is necessary in order to support the interpretation proposed above. It may not always be possible to discover the intentions of Neolithic toolmakers. Nevertheless, the consideration of the social implications of the development of bifacial technology may be able to offer further perspectives on the beginning of farming and herding in the Fayum.

Faculty of Archaeology, Leiden University

Acknowledgements

I am grateful to Annette and Ben Albers, Professor John Bintliff, Dr. Annelou van Gijn, Dr. Gerrit van der Kooij, Professor Leendert Louwe Kooijmans, Professor Avraham Ronen, and Professor Willeke Wendrich, who encouraged me and commented at length on an earlier version of this paper. I am indebted to Dr. Janusz Kozlowski, who gave me permission to reproduce an illustration of flake stone tools obtained from Kom W, originally published in his article. I would also like to thank Lindsay Doyle of Blackwell Publishing for giving me permission to reproduce an illustration of bifacial stone tools collected at Kom W, originally published by the Royal Anthropological Institute of Great Britain and Ireland. Lastly, I wish to thank the anonymous referee for comments and criticism on this paper, and Kathryn Piquette and Serena Love for their meticulous editorial work.

References

Andrefsky, W., Jr. 1994, Raw-material Availability and the Organization of Technology, *American Antiquity* 59, 21–34.

Andrefsky, W., Jr. 1998, *Lithics: Macroscopic approaches to analysis.* Cambridge University Press, Cambridge.

Arnold, J. 1993, Labor and the Rise of Complex Hunter-Gatherers, *Journal of Anthropological Archaeology* 12, 75–119.

Arnold, J. 1996, The Archaeology of Complex Hunter-Gatherers, *Journal of Archaeological Method and Theory* 3, 77–126.

Bamforth, D. 1986, Technological Efficiency and Tool Curation, *American Antiquity* 51, 38–50.

Barakat, H. 2002, Regional Pathways to Agriculture in Northeast Africa, in F. Hassan (ed.), *Droughts, Food and Culture: Ecological change and food security in Africa's later prehistory*, 111–122. Kluwer Academic/Plenum Publishers, New York.

Barich, B., Hassan, F. and Stoppiello, A. 1996, Farafra Oasis Between the Sahara and the Nile, in L. Krzyzaniak, K. Kroeper and M. Kobusiewicz (eds.), *Interregional Contacts in the Later Prehistory of Northeastern Africa*, 71–79. Poznan Archaeological Museum, Poznan.

Binford, L. 1979, Organization and Formation Processes: Looking at curated technologies, *Journal of Anthropological Research* 35, 255–273.

Brewer, D. 1989a, A Model for Resource Exploitation in the Prehistoric Fayum, in L. Krzyzaniak and M. Kobusiewicz (eds.), *Late Prehistory of the Nile Basin and the Sahara*, 127–137. Poznan Archaeological Museum, Poznan.

Brewer, D. 1989b, *Fishermen, Hunters and Herders: Zooarchaeology in the Fayum, Egypt (ca.8200–5000 bp).* British Archaeological Reports, Oxford.

Caton-Thompson, G. 1952, *The Kharga Oasis in Prehistory*, The Ashlone Press, London.

Caton-Thompson, G. and Gardner, E. 1934, *The Desert Fayum.* The Royal Anthropological Institute of Great Britain and Ireland, London.

Close, A. 1996, Plus Ça Change: The Pleistocene-Holocene transition in Northeast Africa, in L. Straus, B. Eriksen, J. Erlandson and D. Yesner (eds.), *Humans at the End of the Ice Age: The archaeology of the Pleistocene-Holocene transition*, 43–60. Plenum Press, New York.

Close, A. 2002, Sinai, Sahara, Sahel: The introduction of domestic caprines to Africa, in Jennerstrasse 8 (eds.), *Tides of the Desert: Contributions to the archaeology and environmental history of Africa in honour of Rudolph Kuper*, 459–469. Heinrich Barth Institut, Köln.

Dagnan-Ginter, A., Ginter, B., Kozlowski, J., Pawlikowski, M. and Sliwa, J. 1984, Excavations in the Region of Qasr el-Sagha, 1981: Contribution to the Neolithic period, Middle Kingdom settlement and chronological sequences in the northern Fayum desert, *Mitteilungen des Deutschen Archäologischen Instituts, Abteilung Kairo* 40, 33–102.

Dobres, M-A. and C. Hoffman, 1994, Social Agency and the Dynamics of Prehistoric Technology, *Journal of Archaeological Method and Theory* 1, 211–258.

Gautier, A. 2002, The Evidence for the Earliest Livestock in North Africa: Or adventures with large bovids, ovicaprids, dogs and pigs, in F. Hassan (ed.), *Droughts, Food and Culture: Ecological change and food security in Africa's later prehistory*, 195–207. Kluwer Academic/Plenum Publishers, New York.

Ginter, B., Heflik, W., Kozlowski, J., and Sliwa, J. 1980, Excavations in the Region of Qasr el-Sagha, 1979: Contribution to the Holocene geology, the Predynastic and Dynastic settlement in the northern Fayum desert, *Mitteilungen des Deutschen Archäologischen Instituts, Abteilung Kairo* 36, 105–169.

Gopher, A. 1994, *Arrowheads of the Neolithic Levant: A seriation analysis.* Eisenbrauns, Winona Lake.

Gopher, A. and Gophna, R. 1993, Cultures of the Eighth and Seventh Millennia BP in the Southern Levant: A review for the 1990s, *Journal of World Prehistory* 7, 297–353.

Hassan, F. 1986a, Desert Environment and Origins of Agriculture in Egypt, *Norwegian Archaeological Review* 19, 63–76.

Hassan, F. 1986b, Holocene Lakes and Prehistoric Settlements of the Western Faiyum, Egypt, *Journal of Archaeological Science* 13, 483–501.

Hassan, F. 1988, The Predynastic of Egypt, *Journal of World Prehistory* 2, 135–185.

Hassan, F. 1997, Holocene Palaeoclimates of Africa, *African Archaeological Review* 14, 213–230.

Hassan, F. 2002, Palaeoclimate, Food and Culture Change in Africa: An overview, in F. Hassan (ed.), *Droughts, Food and Culture: Ecological change and food security in Africa's later prehistory*, 11–26. Kluwer Academic/Plenum Publishers, New York.

Hayden, B. 1990, Nimrods, Piscators, Pluckers and Planters: The emergence of food production, *Journal of Anthropological Archaeology* 9, 31–69.

Hayden, B. 1995, Pathways to Power: Principles for creating socioeconomic inequalities, in T. D. Price and G. M. Feinman (eds.), *Foundations of Social Inequality*, 15–86. Plenum, New York.

Hayden, B. 1998, Practical and Prestige Technologies: The evolution of material systems, *Journal of Archaeological Method and Theory* 5, 1–55.

Hegmon, M. 1998, Technology, Style, and Social Practices: Archaeological approaches, in M. Stark (ed.), *The Archaeology of Social Boundaries*, 264–279. Smithsonian Institution Press, Washington.

Hendrickx, S. and Vermeersch, P. 2000, Prehistory from the Palaeolithic to the Badarian Culture (*c.*700,000–4,000 BC), in I. Shaw (ed.), *The Oxford History of Ancient Egypt*, 17–43. Oxford University Press, Oxford.

Holmes, D. 1989, *The Predynastic Lithic Industries of Upper Egypt: A comparative study of the lithic traditions of Badari, Nagada and Hierakonpolis*. British Archaeological Reports, Oxford.

Kozlowski, J. (ed.), 1983, *Qasr el-Sagha 1980*. Panstwowe Wydawnictwo Naukowe, Warszawa.

Kozlowski, J. and Ginter, B. 1989, The Fayum Neolithic in the Light of New Discoveries, in L. Krzyzaniak and M. Kobusiewicz (eds.), *Late Prehistory of the Nile Basin and the Sahara*, 157–179. Poznan Archaeological Museum, Poznan.

Kuper, R. 1996, Between the Oases and the Nile – Djara: Rohlfs' cave in the Western Desert, in L. Krzyzaniak, K. Kroeper and M. Kobusiewicz (eds.), *Interregional Contacts in the Later Prehistory of Northeastern Africa*, 81–91. Poznan Archaeological Museum, Poznan.

Layton, R. 1999, The Human Evolutionary Time-scale and the Transition Between Hunting and Gathering, and Farming, in J. Bintliff (ed.), *Structure and Contingency: Evolutionary processes in life and human society*, 102–117. Leicester University Press, London.

Lemonnier, P. 1992, *Elements for an Anthropology of Technology*. University of Michigan, Ann Arbor.

McDonald, M. 1996, Relations Between Dakhleh Oasis and the Nile Valley in the Mid-Holocene: A discussion, in L. Krzyzaniak, K. Kroeper and M. Kobusiewicz (eds.), *Interregional Contacts in the Later Prehistory of Northeastern Africa*, 93–99. Poznan Archaeological Museum, Poznan.

Midant-Reynes, B. 2000, *The Prehistory of Egypt*. Blackwell, Oxford.

Mithen, S. 1996, *The Prehistory of Mind: A search for the origins of art, religion and science*. Thames and Hudson, London.

Mussi, M., Caneva I. and Zarattini, A. 1984, More on the Terminal Palaeolithic of the Fayum Depression, in L. Krzyzaniak and M. Kobusiewicz (eds.), *Origin and Early Development of Food-Producing Cultures in North-Eastern Africa*, 185–191. Poznan Archaeological Museum, Poznan.

Muzzolini, A. 1993, The Emergence of a Food-producing Economy in the Sahara, in T. Shaw, P. Sinclair, B. Andah and A. Okpoko (eds.), *The Archaeology of Africa: Food, metals and towns*, 227–239. Routledge, London.

Nash, S. 1996, Is Curation a Useful Heuristic? in G. Odell (ed.), *Stone Tools: Theoretical insights into human prehistory*, 81–99. Plenum Press, New York.

Nelson, M. 1991, The Study of Technological Organization, *Archaeological Method and Theory* 3, 57–100.

Odell, G. 1996, Economizing Behavior and the Concept of Curation, in G. Odell (ed.), *Stone Tools: Theoretical insights into human prehistory*, 51–80. Plenum Press, New York.

Pfaffenberger, B. 1992, Social Anthropology of Technology, *Annual Review of Anthropology* 21, 491–516.

Puglisi, S. 1967, Missione per Ricerche Preistoriche in Egitto, *Origini* 1, 301–312

Rohling, E., Casford, J., Abu-Zied, R., Cooke, S., Mercone, D., Thompson, J., Croudace, I., Jorissen, F., Brinkhuis, H., Kallmeyer J. and Wefer, G. 2002, Rapid Holocene Climate Changes in the Eastern Mediterranean, in F. Hassan (ed.), *Droughts, Food and Culture: Ecological change and food security in Africa's later prehistory*, 35–46. Kluwer Academic/Plenum Publishers, New York.

Rossignol-Strick, M. 2002, Holocene Climatic Changes in the Eastern Mediterranean and the Spread of Food Production from Southwest Asia to Egypt, in F. Hassan (ed.), *Droughts, Food and Culture: Ecological change and food security in Africa's later prehistory*, 157–169. Kluwer Academic/Plenum Publishers, New York.

Seton-Karr, H. 1904, Fayoum Flint Implements, *Annales du Service des Antiquites de l'Égypte* 5, 145–186.

Seton-Karr, H. 1905, Discovery of a Neolithic Settlement in the Western Desert North of the Fayoum, *Annales du Service des Antiquites de l'Égypte* 6, 185–187.

Sherratt, A. 1997, Climatic Cycles and Behavioural Revolutions: The emergence of modern humans and the beginning of farming, *Antiquity* 71, 271–287.

Sinclair, A. 1990, Technology as Phenotype? An extended look at Time, Energy and Stone Tools, *Archaeological Review from Cambridge* 9.1, 71–81.

Sinclair, A. 1995, The Technique as a Symbol in Late Glacial Europe, *World Archaeology* 27.1, 50–62.

Sinclair, A. 2000, Constellations of Knowledge: Human agency and material affordance in lithic technology, in M-A. Dobres and J. Robb (eds.), *Agency in Archaeology*, 196–212. Routledge, London.

Wendorf, F. and Schild, R. 1976, *Prehistory of the Nile Valley*. Academic Press, New York.

Wendorf, F. and Schild, R. 1998, Nabta Playa and its Role in Northeastern African Prehistory, *Journal of Anthropological Archaeology* 17, 97–123.

Wendorf, F. and Schild, R. 2002, Implications of Incipient Social Complexity in the Late Neolithic in the Egyptian Sahara, in R. Friedman (ed.), *Egypt and Nubia: Gifts of the desert*, 13–20. The British Museum Press, London.

Wenke, R. 1984, Early Agriculture in the Southern Fayum Depression: Some test survey results and research implications, in L. Krzyzaniak and M. Kobusiewicz (eds.), *Origin and Early Development of Food-Producing Cultures in North-Eastern Africa*. 193–198. Poznan Archaeological Museum, Poznan.

Wenke, R. and Casini, M. 1989, The Epipaleolithic-Neolithic Transition in Egypt's Fayum Depression, in L. Krzyzaniak and M. Kobusiewicz (eds.), *Late Prehistory of the Nile Basin and the Sahara*, 140–155. Poznan Archaeological Museum, Poznan.

Wenke, R., Buck, P., Hanley, J., Lane, M., Long, J. and Redding, R. 1983, The Fayyum Archaeological Project: Preliminary report of the 1981 season, *Newsletter of the American Research Center in Egypt* 122, 25–40.

Wenke, R., Long, J. and Buck, P. 1988, Epipaleolithic and Neolithic Subsistence and Settlement in the Fayyum Oasis of Egypt, *Journal of Field Archaeology* 15, 29–51.

Wetterstrom, W. 1993, Foraging and Farming in Egypt: The transition from hunting and gathering to horticulture in the Nile Valley, in T. Shaw, P. Sinclair, B. Andah and A. Okpoko (eds.), *The Archaeology of Africa: Food, metals and towns*, 165–226. Routledge, London.

Whittaker, J. 1994, *Flintknapping: Making and understanding stone tools*. University of Texas Press, Austin.

Wiessner, P. 1983, Style and Social Information in Kalahari San Projectile Points, *American Antiquity* 48, 253–276.

Royal Funerary Cults During the Old Kingdom

Yayoi Shirai

Introduction

The Old Kingdom (*c.*2687–2191 B.C.) is the period in which socioeconomic development and expansion of ancient Egypt can clearly be seen in long-term state projects, such as pyramid construction and royal funerary cults (Trigger 1984, 106). It has been thought that royal funerary cults were not only the most important Old Kingdom religious practice, but given the vast number of resources and people involved, they also played a key social and economic role during this period (Kemp 1983, 85–96; Malek 2000, 105–108; Trigger 1984, 106). Texts are an important source for the study of Old Kingdom funerary cults, however, they refer to only a limited number of the royal cults established and maintained during this period. For example, royal decrees provide evidence for the presence of cults for two 4th-dynasty kings, Snefru (Borchardt 1905; Goedicke 1967, 55–57; Sethe 1933, 209–213) and Menkaure (Goedicke 1967, 16–21, 148–154; Reisner 1931, 277–281; Sethe 1933, 273–278). The Abusir Papyri make mention of cults for two 5th-dynasty kings, Neferirkare (Posener-Kriéger 1976, 1979; Posener-Kriéger *et al.* 1968) and Neferefre (Verner 1994; 2002). Except for these textually documented cults, most other royal funerary cults have not been examined and discussed.

In this paper, I attempt to elucidate the presence and development of Old Kingdom royal funerary cults through an analysis of various aspects of the tombs of funerary priests who served in the royal cults. The analysis of the date and location of tombs, and titles of the tomb owners, enables us to comprehend each royal funerary cult diachronically, as well as synchronically, and also to explore how royal cults related to the individuals who served them.

In order to understand the development of royal funerary cults, two questions will be posed. Firstly, were funerary cults established for every king and, if so, how long were they maintained? This question serves to investigate not only the nature of royal funerary cults, but also to verify the theoretical assumption that a new funerary cult was set up for every succeeding king (Roth 1987, 133). Secondly, is there any relationship between the spatial distribution of the pyramid of a given king and the tombs of his funerary priests? This question is helpful in examining the role of royal funerary cults as social institutions and understanding the status of royal funerary priests as a social group.

I should mention here that I use the phrase 'royal funerary cult' to refer to the cults of a king, whether established and maintained during his lifetime, and/or after his death. While the issue of royal cults existing during the lifetime of a king deserves further consideration, for the purpose of this brief study I follow the position of Baer (1960, 45–46), whose method for determining whether or not a royal cult was practiced during a king's lifetime is based on a detailed chronological analysis of priestly titles.

For the present study I have selected 197 firmly dated and located tombs from the Memphite area which were the tombs of funerary priests associated with various Old Kingdom royal pyramids and kings (Baer 1960, 245–295). Regarding the dates of these tombs, Baer's dating is one of the most comprehensive among previous studies. Although Cherpion (1989) proposed dates for these tombs more recently, her methodology relies on the problematic assumption that the presence of a royal name in a tomb is a principal indicator for the upper and lower dates of that tomb (Kanawati 1992). However, Baer's dating methods has been revised and developed by Harpur (1987, 33–42), therefore it is upon her method that I mainly rely. The general chronological framework used in this paper is presented in Figure 1.

Period		King	Date of Reign	Length of Reign
4th Dynasty				
	*	Snefru	*c.*2649–2609 B.C.	(40 years)
	*	Khufu	*c.*2609–2584 B.C.	(25 years)
	*	Djedefre	*c.*2584–2576 B.C.	(8 years)
	*	Khafre	*c.*2576–2551 B.C.	(25 years)
	*	Menkaure	*c.*2551–2523 B.C.	(28 years)
	*	Shepseskaf	*c.*2523–2519 B.C.	(4 years)
		[Two unknown kings]	*c.*2519–2513 B.C.	(6 years)
5th Dynasty				
	*	Userkaf	*c.*2513–2506 B.C.	(7 years)
	*	Sahure	*c.*2506–2492 B.C.	(14 years)
	*	Neferirkare	*c.*2492–2482 B.C.	(10 years)
		Shepseskare	*c.*2482–2475 B.C.	(7 years)
	*	Neferefre	*c.*2475–2474 B.C.	(1 year)
	*	Niuserre	*c.*2474–2444 B.C.	(30 years)
	*	Menkauhor	*c.*2444–2436 B.C.	(8 years)
	*	Djedkare	*c.*2436–2404 B.C.	(32 years)
	*	Unas	*c.*2404–2374 B.C.	(30 years)
6th Dynasty				
	*	Teti	*c.*2374–2354 B.C.	(20 years)
		Userkare	?	(?)
	*	Pepi I	*c.*2354–2310 B.C.	(44 years)
	*	Merenre	*c.*2310–2300 B.C.	(10 years)
	*	Pepi II	*c.*2300–2206 B.C.	(94 years)
		[Antyemsaf] II	*c.*2206 B.C.	(less than 1 year)
		Nitokerty (Nitocris)	*c.*2205–2200 B.C.	(5 years)
		Neferka the child	[*c.*2200–2199 B.C.]	(1 year)
		Nefer	*c.*2199–2197 B.C.	(2 years)
		Aba	*c.*2197–2193 B.C.	(4 years)
		[...]	*c.*2193–2191 B.C.	(2 years)
		[...]	*c.*2191 B.C.	(less than 1 year)

*Figure 1. Chronological table of kings from the 4th to the 6th Dynasties (after Redford 2001). * indicates kings whose funerary cult are attested. The estimated length of a reign is given after the absolute date of each reign.*

Presence and duration of royal funerary cults

The first issue to be considered is the presence and duration of each royal funerary cult. Based on the analysis of the 197 tombs, mentioned above, including the titles of royal funerary priests and the dates of their tombs, one is able to infer which royal funerary cults existed during the Old Kingdom and how long they lasted. The priest's titles generally include the name of an office and the name of a king or his pyramid. For example, the cult of Khufu is attested in the priestly title *ḥm-nṯr ḫwfw* 'Prophet of Khufu' (Porter and Moss 1974, 200). The cult of Niuserre is known from the title *wʿb mn-swt-njusrrʿ* 'Wab-priest of the pyramid of Niuserre' (Hassan 1936, 211). In addition to these two titles, 55 other titles relate to the royal funerary cults (Baer 1960, 250–252). Following the chronology of kings from the 4th to the 6th Dynasties (Figure 1), the results of this first stage of analysis are shown in Figure 2.

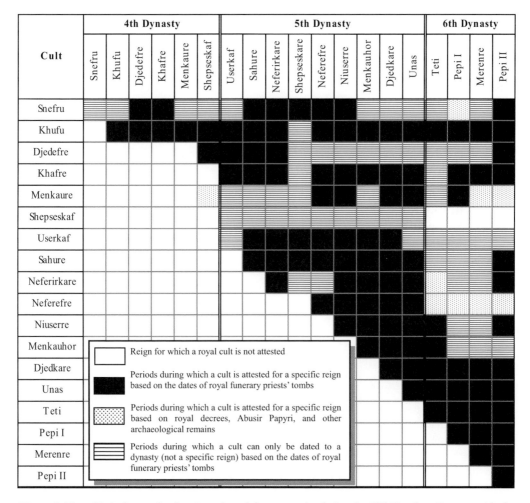

Figure 2. The table indicates the duration of royal funerary cults during the Old Kingdom. Rows provide the names of 18 kings whose funerary cults are attested. Columns indicate the duration of each royal funerary cult.

This shows that, for instance, the funerary cult of Khufu was maintained from sometime in his reign and continued into the reign of Pepi II. However, based on the fact that tombs of the funerary priests of Shepseskaf are no longer attested in the 6th Dynasty, his funerary cult seems to have ended during the 5th Dynasty. The time span in which a royal funerary cult is attested through the analysis of priestly titles is also indicated in Figure 2. However, periods within the time span of some cults cannot be determined with the same level of accuracy and this is indicated in the table in three ways. Firstly, if the tomb of a royal funerary priest can be dated with certainty to the reign of one king, then this reign is indicated in the blackened areas of the table. Secondly, if a tomb cannot be dated more precisely than to a single dynasty, then this dynasty is marked by horizontal lines. Thirdly, where textual and archaeological evidence supplement the data obtained from priestly titles, this is indicated by the dotted areas of the table.

Textual sources employed in this analysis include royal decrees issued by the 5th- and 6th-dynasty kings. These include a decree of Pepi I for the cult of Snefru (Borchardt 1905; Goedicke 1967, 55–57; Sethe 1933, 209–213), and the decrees of Shepseskaf, Merenre, Pepi I and Pepi II for the cult of Menkaure (Goedicke 1967, 16–21, 148–154; Reisner 1931, 277–281; Sethe 1933, 273–278). In addition, the papyri from the temple of Neferirkare at Abusir document cults for the reigns of Djedkare, Teti and Pepi II (Verner 1994, 163). The papyri (Verner 2002, 131) and archaeological finds such as stone vessels (pers. comm. Petra Vlčková) from the temple of Neferefre prove that the cult of this king lasted through the reign of Pepi II.

In total, my analysis of the titles, texts and dates suggests that funerary cults existed for 18 kings who reigned from the 4th to the 6th Dynasties (see Figures 1 and 2). These include the funerary cults of Snefru, Khufu, Djedefre, Khafre, Menkaure, Shepseskaf, Userkaf, Sahure, Neferirkare, Neferefre, Niuserre, Menkauhor, Djedkare, Unas, Teti, Pepi I, Merenre and Pepi II. The results also indicate a coincidence where the 4th-6th dynasty kings who are well attested historically and archaeologically are the same kings whose funerary cults are well attested. In contrast, kings who are poorly attested archaeologically and textually, such as the 4th-dynasty kings Shepseskare and Userkare, and other kings following Pepi II (Figure 1), are also those kings whose funerary cults are poorly attested.

With regard to second main issue of the duration of the royal funerary cults, a pattern emerges whereby the funerary cults can be divided into three groups based on aspects of their duration. The first group of royal funerary cults, Group I, is characterized by a relatively short duration (Figure 3). This group includes the funerary cults of Shepseskaf and possibly those of Userkaf and Menkauhor – if the cults of the latter two kings ended in the early part of the 6th Dynasty.

Group II is characterized by royal funerary cults which experienced a relatively long duration, but have periods in which their presence can only be dated to a dynasty (indicated by horizontal lines) rather than a specific reign (Figure 4). The lack of chronological precision is due to the fact that the dates of some priests' tombs are somewhat imprecise. Group II contains the funerary cults of Snefru, Djedefre, Khafre, Menkaure, Sahure, Neferirkare and Niuserre, those kings who reigned in the first half of the 5th Dynasty. The royal funerary cults which form Group III are well attested throughout their duration (Figure 5) and include the cults of Khufu, Neferefre, Djedkare and the kings who succeeded him up until the reign of Pepi II.

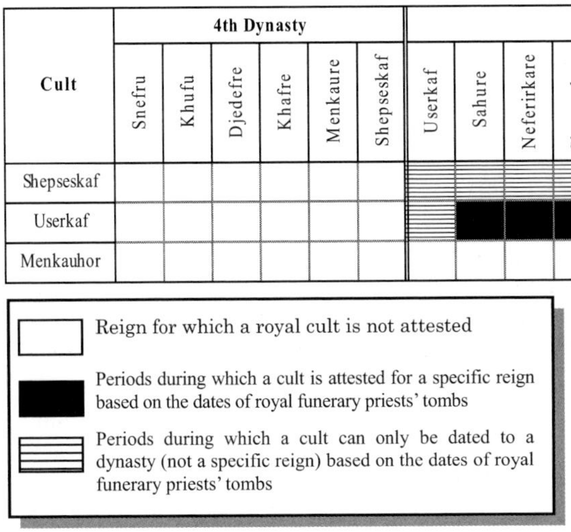

Figure 3 table

Cult	4th Dynasty						5th Dynasty									6th Dynasty			
	Snefru	Khufu	Djedefre	Khafre	Menkaure	Shepseskaf	Userkaf	Sahure	Neferirkare	Shepseskare	Neferefre	Niuserre	Menkauhor	Djedkare	Unas	Teti	Pepi I	Merenre	Pepi II
Shepseskaf																			
Userkaf																			
Menkauhor																			

Legend:
- □ Reign for which a royal cult is not attested
- ■ Periods during which a cult is attested for a specific reign based on the dates of royal funerary priests' tombs
- ▤ Periods during which a cult can only be dated to a dynasty (not a specific reign) based on the dates of royal funerary priests' tombs

Figure 3. The duration of royal funerary cults which comprise Group I. Rows provide the names of the three kings whose funerary cults are attested. Columns indicate the duration of the royal funerary cults.

Figure 4 table

Cult	4th Dynasty						5th Dynasty									6th Dynasty			
	Snefru	Khufu	Djedefre	Khafre	Menkaure	Shepseskaf	Userkaf	Sahure	Neferirkare	Shepseskare	Neferefre	Niuserre	Menkauhor	Djedkare	Unas	Teti	Pepi I	Merenre	Pepi II
Snefru																			
Djedefre																			
Khafre																			
Menkaure																			
Sahure																			
Neferirkare																			
Niuserre																			

Legend:
- □ Reign for which a royal cult is not attested
- ■ Periods during which a cult is attested for a specific reign based on the dates of royal funerary priests' tombs
- ▒ Periods during which a cult is attested for a specific reign based on royal decrees, Abusir Papyri, and other archaeological remains
- ▤ Periods during which a cult can only be dated to a dynasty (not a specific reign) based on the dates of royal funerary priests' tombs

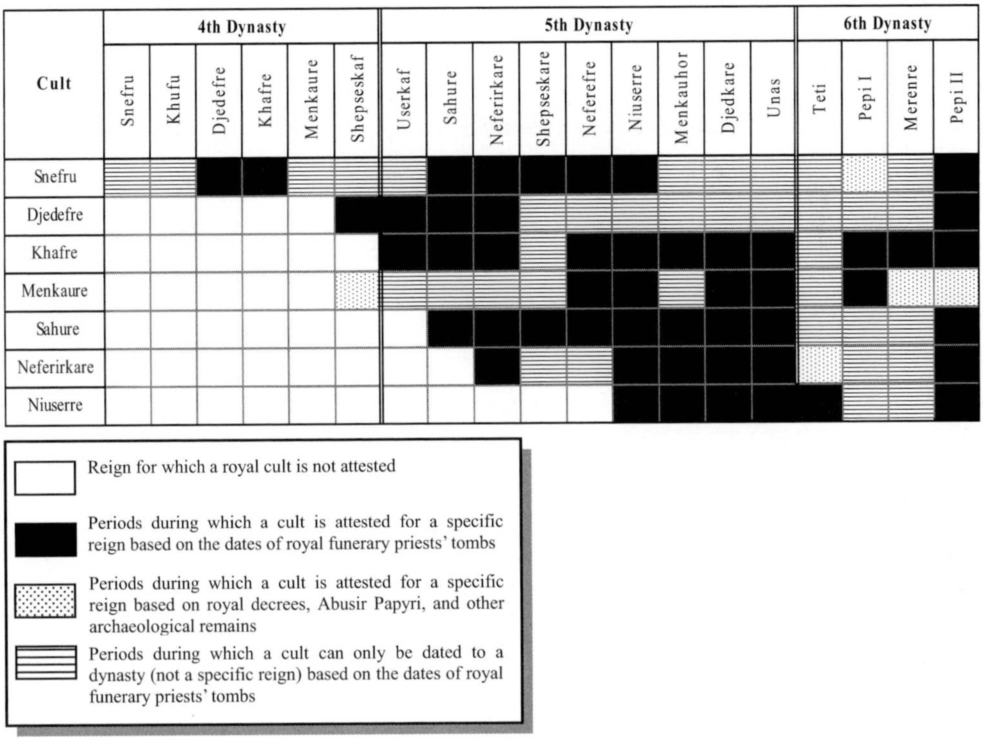

Figure 4. The duration of royal funerary cults which comprise Group II. Rows provide the names of the seven kings whose funerary cults are attested. Columns indicate the duration of the royal funerary cults.

These patterns in the duration of the royal funerary cults raise various questions, several of which I consider here. For example, why did the duration of Old Kingdom royal funerary cults differ from each other in these ways? And, how do we understand the periods where funerary cults are well attested? With regard to the issue of duration, I propose that two main factors were related to the differences observed: the length of a king's reign and the level of support for the cult by successors. It would make sense that the longer a king ruled, the more time he had to establish his funerary endowment, and to assemble the staff and economic resources. Conversely, a king who ruled for a short time might not be able to sufficiently endow his funerary cult. Indeed, the results presented here show that the short-lived royal funerary cults (Group I, Figure 3) generally correspond to those kings whose reigns were short. Even if a king was, however, able to sufficiently prepare for his funerary cult during his lifetime, it stands to reason that the cult would decline over the course of time.

Group II (indicated by horizontal lines in Figure 4) possibly illustrates this kind of decline for the funerary cults of seven kings who ruled early in the Old Kingdom (c.2613–c.2421 B.C.). For the funerary cult of Snefru, for example, there is a period spanning from the later part of the 5th Dynasty to the reign of Merenre (with the exception of the reign of Pepi I) where the

Cult	4th Dynasty						5th Dynasty									6th Dynasty			
	Snefru	Khufu	Djedefre	Khafre	Menkaure	Shepseskaf	Userkaf	Sahure	Neferirkare	Shepseskare	Neferefre	Niuserre	Menkauhor	Djedkare	Unas	Teti	Pepi I	Merenre	Pepi II
Khufu		■	■	■	■	■	■	■	■	▤	■	■	■	■	■	■	■	■	■
Neferefre											■	■	■	■	■	▒	▒	▒	▒
Djedkare														■	■	■	■	■	■
Unas															■	■	■	■	■
Teti																■	■	■	■
Pepi I																	■	■	■
Merenre																		■	■
Pepi II																			■

☐	Reign for which a royal cult is not attested
■	Periods during which a cult is attested for a specific reign based on the dates of royal funerary priests' tombs
▒	Periods during which a cult is attested for a specific reign based on royal decrees, Abusir Papyri, and other archaeological remains
▤	Periods during which a cult can only be dated to a dynasty (not a specific reign) based on the dates of royal funerary priests' tombs

Figure 5. The duration of royal funerary cults which comprise Group III. Rows provide the names of the eight kings whose funerary cults are attested. Columns indicate the duration of the royal funerary cults.

cult is less precisely documented. For the cult of Djedefre, the poorly documented period extends from the reign of Shepeskare to Merenre. The other royal funerary cults in Group II are, likewise, only generally attested during the reigns of Pepi I, and less so for Merenre.

This brings us to another question raised by the patterns related to a cult's duration – that of its reappearance following a gap or poorly attested period. This is particularly apparent during the reign of Pepi II (dotted pattern in Figure 4) where funerary cults for the kings who ruled during the early part of the Old Kingdom, *i.e.* Snefru, Djedefre, Khafre, Menkaure, Sahure, Neferirkare, and Niuserre, are simultaneously attested in precisely datable evidence. I suggest that this reappearance of royal cults in the archaeological and textual evidence may be understood as renewed patronage by the ruling king of his predecessors' declining cults through the provision of staff and other economic support. This hypothesis may be supported by the fact that royal decrees, issued mainly by the 6th-dynasty kings (Borchardt 1905; Goedicke 1967, 55–57, 148–154; Reisner 1931, 277–281; Sethe 1933, 209–213, 273–278), were only for temple functionaries who had served the funerary cults of Snefru and Menkaure, which again are included in Group II. These royal decrees mention exemptions from specified kinds of taxes and labor, thus affording economic privileges to temple functionaries serving the funerary cults of these past kings (Roth 1987, 134). It appears, therefore, plausible that the royal funerary cults in Group II became re-established or attained renewed status during the 6th Dynasty.

Concerning the funerary cults which form Group III (Figure 5) – those which are well attested throughout their duration (Djedkare, Unas, Teti, Pepi I, Merenre, and Pepi II) – it appears that the closer in time a royal cult was to the reigning king, the greater the likelihood that the cult would receive support from that reigning king. However, the cult of Neferefre may be an exception in that his cult continued to be maintained up until the reign of Pepi II, despite the fact that Neferefre appears to have reigned for one or two years at most (Verner 2002, 120). It is hoped that the report on the excavation of the cult temple of Neferefre will be published in the near future and perhaps shed further light on the nature of his cult. The funerary cult of Khufu is also exceptional in that it is the only one which was continuously maintained for at least 300 years. Its extraordinary length may be due to Khufu's ability to establish an abundant funerary endowment during his lifetime, or, if not in addition to, continuing support from his successors.

The spatial relationship between the king's pyramid and the tombs of his funerary priests

The second main aspect of the analysis presented here centers on the spatial relationship between the pyramid of a king and the tombs of his funerary priests. Recent research has demonstrated that various aspects of society, including social relationships, were represented in the way tombs were situated within the necropolis. Roth's (1995, 1) analysis of individuals who held the title of *ḥnty-š pr-ꜥꜣ* 'Palace Attendant' reveals that their tombs were clustered in the same general area of the Western Cemetery at Giza. Silverman (2000, 267–271) has similarly remarked on the social aspects of tomb distribution with regard to his recent rediscovery at Saqqara of the tombs of two 12th-dynasty priests, Ihy and Hetep. These priests carried out their duties in the funerary cult of Teti, the first king of the 6th Dynasty, whose cult temple was located near his pyramid at Saqqara. Both priests built their tombs near the axial corridor of Teti's funerary temple. According to Silverman (2000, 267), they chose not to be buried near the tomb of the reigning king, Amenemhat I, at Lisht, but in Saqqara at a site adjacent to the burial of Teti whose cult they served in life. Both studies seem to suggest that the profession of some individuals influenced where they chose to build their tombs.

Using this previous research as a model, I analyzed the spatial distribution of the 197 tombs of funerary priests in the Memphite necropolis, the results of which are presented in Figure 6. The rows of this table indicate the names of 18 kings – all of whose funerary cults are attested during the Old Kingdom. For each cult, the number of the tombs of funerary priests who served that cult is given. The columns of the table indicate six main areas of the Memphite necropolis, ranging from Abu Rowash in the north to Dahshur in the south. These six areas are further divided into 17 sub-areas on the basis of tomb clustering in relation to the location of

Cult Name	Total Tombs	Abu Rowash	Giza					Abusir	Central Saqqara				Saqqara South			Dahshur		
			Khufu East	Khufu West	Khufu South	Khafre East	Menkaure Southeast		Teti North	Djoser North	Djoser East	Djoser West	Unas East	Around Merenre	Around Pepi II	Around Khendjer	North	South
† Snefru	6		1														3	2
† Khufu	57		7	44	1	4			1									
† Djedefre	4	3		1														
† Khafre	21	1	1	3		14												2
† Menkaure	11		1	2		7	1											
Shepseskaf	1		1															
† Userkaf	11									5	6							
‡ Sahure	15			3		1		1	2	4	3	1						
‡ Neferirkare	13			1				1	2	5	1	3						
‡ Neferefre	4									2	2							
‡ Niuserre	19			3		2			1	7	1	4		1				
‡ Menkauhor	8			1						2	2	3						
‡ Djedkare	9									2	1	6						
† Unas	16			1						3			12					
† Teti	18								14	3			1					
‡ Pepi I	18		2	1					5			1	5		3	1		
† Merenre	2													2				
† Pepi II	5														5			

Figure 6. Enumerates the location of royal funerary priests' tombs in the Memphite necropolis. Rows provide names of 18 kings whose funerary cults are attested. For each cult the number of affiliated funerary priests' tombs is given. Columns indicate six main areas of the Memphite necropolis and 17 sub-areas. † indicates that the tombs of funerary priests who served that king's cult fit the first distribution pattern. ‡ indicates the same for funerary priests' tombs which fit the second distribution pattern.

royal pyramids. For example, six tombs of Snefru's funerary priests occur in three different areas (Figure 6): one tomb in the Western Cemetery at Giza ('Khufu West'), three tombs at 'Dahshur North', and two tombs at 'Dahshur South' (Figure 6).

All tomb locations were analyzed according to this general framework. Except for the tombs of priests who served the cults of Shepseskaf and Pepi I, the patterns of clustering can be grouped into two types. The tombs of the priests who served 16 of the kings cluster in specific areas. The six tombs of Snefru's funerary priests cluster primarily in the two cemeteries at Dahshur in which two pyramids of Snefru lie. Virtually all the tombs of Khufu's funerary priests (56 of 57 tombs) cluster in the cemeteries at Giza. The majority of the tombs (44 of 56) are located in the Western Cemetery (see 'Khufu West', Figure 6). The 11 tombs of Userkaf's funerary priests also cluster around his pyramid (five tombs at 'Djoser North', six tombs at 'Djoser East').

In the first pattern the funerary priest's tombs cluster around the royal pyramid of the king they served. This pattern can be observed in the location of the tombs of priests who served the cults of Snefru, Khufu, Djedefre, Khafre, Menkaure, Userkaf, Unas, Teti, Merenre and Pepi II (see royal names marked † in Figure 6). The second pattern is characterized by funerary priests' tombs which are *not* clustered around the pyramid of the king they served. This pattern occurs for the tombs of priests who served the cults of Sahure, Neferirkare, Neferefre, Menkauhor, Djedkare and Pepi I (see royal names marked ‡ in Figure 6). For example, the tombs of Sahure's funerary priests are mainly situated in 'Central Saqqara', despite the pyramid of Sahure being located at Abusir.

As for the first clustering pattern, these tomb locations seem to compare with the findings of Silverman (2000, 267–271). The pattern exhibited by the tombs of Khufu's funerary priests is remarkable with regard to the number and concentration within one cemetery (Figure 6). Close examination of the dates of the tombs for Khufu's funerary priests reveals not only significant spatial patterns, but also temporal patterns. Chronological analysis of the data (Figure 7) clearly shows that the tombs of Khufu's funerary priests were constructed continuously at Giza, especially in the Western Cemetery ('Khufu West' in Figure 6) from the 4th to the 6th Dynasties. It should be noted that from the reign of Shepseskaf (*c.*2503–2494 B.C.) to the reign of Pepi II (*c.*2278–2184 B.C.) royal cemeteries were not located at Giza, but at Abusir and Saqqara. Nevertheless, during the 5th and 6th Dynasties,

| Period | Abu Rowash | Giza | | | | | Abusir | Central Saqqara | | | | | Saqqara South | | | Dahshur | |
		Khufu East	Khufu West	Khufu South	Khafre East	Menkaure Southeast		Teti North	Djoser North	Djoser East	Djoser West	Unas East	Around Merenre	Around Pepi II	Around Khendjer	North	South
4th Dynasty		2	2		1												
5th Dynasty		3	22		1				1								
6th Dynasty		2	20	1	2												
Total		7	44	1	4				1								

Figure 7. Indicates the date and number of tombs of Khufu's funerary priests. Rows show three different dynasties during which the tombs of Khufu's funerary priests were built. Columns indicate six main areas of the Memphite necropolis and 17 sub-areas.

51 out of 57 tombs were built at Giza, mainly in Western Cemetery where 44 tombs of these tombs are located (Figure 7). Consequently, it is plausible that tomb building for Khufu's funerary priests had been ongoing throughout the reign of Pepi II with careful attention given to tomb location in relation to the pyramid of Khufu.

As for the second pattern (*i.e.* those tombs which do not cluster around the pyramid where the tomb owner served), this can be observed for funerary priests who served the cults of Sahure, Neferirkare, Neferefre, Niuserre, and Pepi I. These tombs tend to be situated within the area of 'Central Saqqara' (see Figure 6). Following Roth's interpretation (1995, 1), this clustering pattern implies that, to some degree at least, profession influenced the relative location of a funerary priest's tomb. The picture is still incomplete, however, since there is evidence that many of the tombs of funerary priests affiliated with the cults of the 5th-dynasty kings are still buried under the sands of Abusir, a site which is known to have served as a royal cemetery during the 5th Dynasty (Verner 2002, 41–64). Indeed, that these tombs follow the second pattern of clustering, being mainly situated in 'Central Saqqara' (Figure 6) suggests that this cemetery was related to the southern extension of the principal cemetery at Abusir. It is hoped that this hypothesis can be tested through further excavations at Abusir, perhaps through the work of the Czech Institute of Egyptology, Charles University.

While it has been possible to identify these two different clustering patterns in tomb distribution, it is still unclear why the tombs of the priests of Menkauhor and Djedkare are situated to the west of Djoser's Step Pyramid (Figure 6), especially since the pyramid of the latter is located at 'Saqqara South' and the pyramid of the former has not yet been found. As for understanding the location of the tombs of these kings' priests, Roth (1988, 214) points out that, based on the fact that some tombs in this area, such as that of Ptahhetep, could be dated back to the reign of Menkauhor, the pyramid of this king may be situated to the west of the Step Pyramid. There is also reason to believe that the funerary priests' tombs assigned to Djedkare could be backdated to the reign of Menkauhor. If Roth's hypothesis is correct, the reason behind the location of these tombs could be similar to those tombs which follow the first pattern of clustering.

In addition to the patterns of tomb clustering discussed thus far, I should note that there are certain 'deviations' which cannot yet be explained. For instance, why is one tomb of a royal funerary priest who served the cult of Snefru located in the Western Cemetery at Giza? And why is another tomb of a priest who served the cult of Khufu situated on the northern side of the Djoser's pyramid? Presumably these exceptions (Figure 6) indicate that burial location was not always influenced by an individual's occupation. Certainly there are other factors which also influenced Old Kingdom burial practices; however, it is not possible to explore these issues here.

Despite some exceptions, the general pattern of spatial proximity between the pyramid of a king and the tombs of the royal funerary priests who served that king's cult emphasises the importance of funerary cults as Old Kingdom social and economic institutions (Helck 1975, 64–68). As members of a royal cult, priests performed various duties in the pyramid temples. In return for their services they received food offerings after they had been presented to the diseased king. This process is generally referred to as the 'circulation' of royal food offerings (Altenmüller 1982; Bárta 1968, 302; Helck 1982; Malek 2000, 105). It is plausible that the royal funerary priests expected to continue to partake of the royal funerary offerings, even in death. Perhaps it was for the benefit of their own funerary cults that they built their own tombs in the vicinity of the royal pyramid. Thus, the spatial proximity of tombs may reflect the social and economic relationship between the diseased king and his funerary priests.

Similar patterns which support this interpretation can be observed in the distribution of the tombs of private persons and priests who maintained their funerary cults. At Giza we have several examples which fit the first pattern of tomb distribution. For example, the funerary priest, Kakherniswt, built his tomb adjacent to the tomb of Rawer, his employer (Hassan 1936, 65). Likewise, in the Western Cemetery at Giza, the tombs of three generations of funerary priests lie directly west of the tombs of Senedjemib and his family whose cult they served (Brovarski 2001, 3). Additionally, other priests and servitors of this family also built tombs in the immediate area – to the south and west of the complex (Brovarski 2001, 3, fig. 2). Junker (1938, 123–124) also discusses the relationship between members of a funerary endowment and tomb location, noting an example where a princess Iabtet and her priest, Kai, have adjacent tombs. Inscriptions in the tomb of Kai explain that he and his family served the funerary endowment of the princess.

Conclusion

In an attempt to understand the development of royal funerary cults during the Old Kingdom, two central questions were explored in this analysis of the tombs of royal funerary priests. These questions concerned the existence and duration of royal funerary cults, as well as the spatial relationship between royal pyramids and the tombs of affiliated funerary priests. It was revealed that funerary cults existed for 18 kings from the 4th to the 6th Dynasties. The duration of the cults appears to have been effected by two principal factors: the length of a king's reign and the level of endowment provided by later kings. While not all distribution patterns for the tombs of Old Kingdom funerary priests can be explained, the majority of examples demonstrate that the location of tombs was predominately influenced by the tomb owner's participation in a royal funerary endowment.

In contextualizing these observations and interpretations, it is important to consider how they relate to broader social processes taking place during the Old Kingdom. The establishment and/or renewal of the royal funerary endowments, especially during the 6th Dynasty, fulfilled to some degree the need for social and economic stability and cohesion among certain upper class groups. During the 6th Dynasty the central government experienced a decline in power. Various factors seem to have contributed to this shift including an increase in the power of local administrators of provincial towns in Middle and Upper Egypt; the development of hereditary succession to office, and the weakening of the kingship due to complacency which seems to have developed in the court during the long reign of Pepi II (Malek 2000, 116–117; Martin-Pardey 1976, 148–152). The government seems to have taken several steps in an attempt to reverse the decline of central power. I suggest that the revival of some royal funerary cults can be explained if we understand these institutions to have functioned as devices for strengthening and legitimizing the position of the reigning king through ancestor worship. Similarly, the building of royal *k3*-chapels, such as those of Teti (El-Sawi 1979, 75–76) and Pepi I at Tell Basta (Habachi 1957, 11–43) could be interpreted as an attempt to reassert royal authority and power in provincial towns. Likewise, the previously mentioned royal decrees issued by the 6th-dynasty kings (Borchardt 1905; Goedicke 1967, 55–57, 148–154; Reisner, 1931, 277–281; Sethe 1933, 209–213, 273–278) may also be viewed as attempts by the powers in Memphis to secure favor.

The posited renewal of some royal funerary cults during the 6th Dynasty would have influenced the social standing of the royal funerary priests. In fact, we know from the royal decrees (Goedicke 1967, 16–21, 55–57, 148–154) that functionaries of the temples of Snefru and Menkaure occupied privileged positions and were under royal protection. In the written evidence for priesthoods at provincial temples at Abydos and El-Kab, a rise in the social status of the priestly class can be observed at both temples from the mid-5th Dynasty onwards (Goedicke 1979, 128–129; Vandekerckhove and Müller-Wollermann 2001, 338). Goedicke (1979, 130) refers to the probability that this rise in the social status of priests, in fact, caused the development of local centers in the provinces, and subsequently a decentralization and decline in the power of the royal administration. In considering the situation of Memphis, it seems reasonable to suppose that abuse of these special privileges granted to royal funerary priests caused the rise of power of the priesthood, and a simultaneous decay of the state economy. However, the data for the tomb locations of the royal funerary priests reveal little about the precise circumstances at Memphis.

Nevertheless, the results of the analysis presented here demonstrate the interdependence between funerary priests and the royal funerary endowments and the importance both held for past, as well as reigning kings, particularly at the end of the 6th Dynasty. By looking at archaeological and textual evidence together, it is possible to construct a more complete picture of the development and changing status of royal funerary cults and the fundamental role they played in the social and economic life in Old Kingdom Egypt.

Freie Universität Berlin

Acknowledgements

I am grateful to Professor Dr. Stephan J. Seidlmayer who inspired me through discussions in his class and encouraged me to present a developed version of my MA thesis in English. I am indebted to Professor Dr. Miroslav Verner and Petra Vlčková for giving me invaluable information about the funerary cult of Neferefre. I would like to thank Paul Ford for correcting my English draft of this paper. I also owe a particular debt to Annette and Ben Albers for helpful advice in its preparation. Finally, I wish to acknowledge my indebtedness to the editors, Kathryn Piquette and Serena Love, for their painstaking work.

References

Altenmüller, H. 1982, Opferumlauf, in W. Helck and Westendorf, W. (eds.), *Lexikon der Ägyptologie, 4*, cols. 596–597. Otto Harrassowitz, Wiesbaden.

Baer, K. 1960, *Rank and Title in the Old Kingdom: The structure of the Egyptian administration in the Fifth and Sixth Dynasties*. University of Chicago Press, Chicago.

Bárta, W. 1968, *Aufbau und Bedeutung der altägyptischen Opferformel*. J. J. Augustin, Glückstadt.

Borchardt, L. 1905, Ein Königserlaß aus Dahschur, *Zeitschrift für Ägyptische Sprache und Altertumskunde* 42, 1–11.

Brovarski, E. 2001, *Giza Mastabas, 7: The Senedjemib Complex, Part I: The mastabas of Senedjemib Inti (G2370), Khnumenti (G2374), and Senedjemib Mehi (G2378)*. Museum of Fine Arts, Boston, Boston.

Cherpion, N. 1989, *Mastabas et Hypogées d'Ancien Empire: Le problème de la datation.* Connaissance de l'Égypte Ancienne, Brussels.

El-Sawi, A. 1979, *Excavations at Tell Basta.* Charles University, Prague.

Goedicke, H. 1967, *Königliche Dokumente aus dem Alten Reich.* Otto Harrassowitz, Wiesbaden.

Goedicke, H. 1979, Cult Temple and "State" During the Old Kingdom in Egypt, in E. Lipinski (ed.), *State and Temple Economy in the Near East*, 113–131. Peeters, Leuven.

Habachi, L. 1957, *Tell Basta.* 'Institut français d'archéologie Orientale, Cairo.

Harpur, Y. M. 1987, *Decoration in Egyptian Tombs of the Old Kingdom: Studies in orientation and scene content.* Kegan Paul, London.

Hassan, S. 1936, *Excavations at Giza: 1930–1931, 2.* Government Press, Cairo.

Helck, W. 1975, *Wirtschaftsgeschichte des Alten Ägypten im 3. und 2. Jahrtausend vor Chr.* E. J. Brill, Leiden.

Helck, W. 1982, Opferstiftung, in W. Helck and Westendorf, W. (eds.), *Lexikon der Ägyptologie, 4,* cols. 590–594. Otto Harrassowitz, Wiesbaden.

Junker, H. 1938, *Giza, III: Grabungen auf dem Friedhof des Alten Reiches bei den Pyramiden von Giza.* Hölder-Pichler-Tempsky, Vienna.

Kanawati, N. 1992, Review: Mastabas et Hypogées d'Ancien Empire: Le problème de la datation. by Nadine Cherpion, *Journal of Egyptian Archaeology* 78, 324–326.

Kemp. B. J. 1983, Old Kingdom, Middle Kingdom and Second Intermediate Period *c.*2686–1552, in B. G. Trigger, B. J. Kemp, D. O'Connor and A. B. Lloyd (eds.), *Ancient Egypt: A social history*, 71–182. Cambridge University Press, Cambridge.

Malek, J. 2000, The Old Kingdom (*c.*2686–2125 B.C.), in I. Shaw (ed.), *The Oxford History of Ancient Egypt*, 89–117. Oxford University Press, Oxford.

Martin-Pardey, E. 1976, *Untersuchungen zur ägyptischen Provinzialverwaltung bis zum Ende des Alten Reiches.* Gebrüder Gerstenberg, Hildesheim.

Porter, B. and Moss, R. L. B. 1974 [1931], *Topographical Bibliography of Ancient Egyptian Hieroglyphic Texts, Reliefs, and Paintings, 3: Memphis: Abu Rawash to Abusir*, (2nd edition, revised and augmented by J. Málek). Clarendon Press, Oxford.

Posener-Kriéger, P. 1976, *Les archives du temple funéraire de Néferirkarê-Kakaï (les papyrus d'Abousir): Traduction et commentaire.* 2 vols. Institut français d'archéologie orientale, Cairo.

Posener-Kriéger, P. 1979, Les Papyrus d'Abousir et l'économie des temples funéraires de l'Ancien Empire, in E. Lipiński (ed.), *State and Temple Economy in the Ancient Near East, 1,* 133–151. Peeters, Leuven.

Posener-Kriéger, P. and De Cenival, J. 1968, *Hieratic Papyri in the British Museum, Fifth Series: The Abu Sir Papyri.* Trustees of the British Museum, London.

Redford, D. B. (ed.), 2001, *The Oxford Encyclopedia of Ancient Egypt.* 3 vols. Oxford University Press, Oxford.

Reisner, G. A. 1931, *Mycerinus: The temples of the third pyramid at Giza.* Harvard University Press, Cambridge, Massachusetts.

Roth, A. M. 1987, The Organization and Functioning of the Royal Mortuary Cults of the Old Kingdom in Egypt, in M. Gibson and R. G. Biggs (eds.), *The Organization of Power: Aspects of bureaucracy in the Ancient Near East,* 133–140. University of Chicago Press, Chicago.

Roth, A. M. 1988, The Organization of Royal Cemeteries at Saqqara in the Old Kingdom, *Journal of the American Research Center in Egypt* 25, 201–214.

Roth, A. M. 1995, *Giza Mastabas, 6: A Cemetery of Palace Attendants: Including G 2084–2099, G 2230+2231, and G 2240.* Museum of Fine Arts, Boston.

Sethe, K. 1933, *Urkunden des Alten Reiches, 2.* J. C. Hinrichs, Leipzig.

Silverman, D. P. 2000, Middle Kingdom Tombs in the Teti Pyramid Cemetery, in M. Bárta and J. Krejčí (eds.), *Abusir and Saqqara in the Year 2000*, 259–282. Academy of Sciences of the Czech Republic Oriental Institute, Prague.

Trigger, B. G. 1984, The Mainlines of Socio-economic Development in Dynastic Egypt to the End of the Old Kingdom, in L. Krzyżaniak and M. Kobusiewicz (eds.), *Origin and Early Development of Food-Producing Cultures in North-Eastern Africa*, 101–108. Polish Academy of Sciences and Poznan Archaeological Museum, Poznan.

Vandekerckhove, H. and Müller-Wollermann, R. 2001, *Elkab, VI: Die Felsinschriften des Wadi Hilal, 1: Text*. Brepols, Turnhout.

Verner, M. 1994, *Forgotten Pharaohs, Lost Pyramids*: *Abusir.* Academia Škodaexport, Prague.

Verner, M. 2002, *Abusir: The realm of Osiris.* American University in Cairo Press, Cairo.

Abusir South at the End of the Old Kingdom

Petra Vlčková

Introduction

The archaeological activities of the Czech (former Czechoslovak) Institute of Egyptology have been linked primarily with Abusir since its founding (Bárta 2002; Verner 2002, 232–236; Verner *et al.* 1990). The site lies on the west bank of the Nile, some 30 km southwest of Cairo. Before the Institute's excavations, this site was generally known as the burial place of several kings from the 5th Dynasty, namely Sahure, Neferirkare, Neferefre and Niuserre, and members of the royal family and the kings' high officials. Initially, the excavations concentrated mainly on the pyramid field in Abusir North and the mastaba tombs in this area.

For almost a half century (1950s to 1990s), the area of Abusir South had been overlooked by most archaeologists. The first Czech archaeological excavations in Abusir South took place during the fall of 1991. This work followed up on activities of the Inspectorate of the Saqqara Zone from 1989, which dealt with the rescue of several blocks from the tomb chapel of 'the overseer of the army', Kaaper, after it was badly looted by modern robbers (Bárta 2001, 143; Verner 1993). In 1991, the Institute initiated a long-term project focusing on a comprehensive archaeological examination of the Abusir South area. This project has since become one of the main scientific posts of the Institute (beside the investigation of the royal necropolis of the 5th Dynasty, and the shaft tombs cemetery from the Late Period).

Abusir South can be easily determined geographically (Figure 1). The shallow wadi that separates the Abusir pyramid plateau from the non-royal necropolis forms its northern limit. The southern area extends to the Wadi Abusiri. This wadi separates Abusir from both the non-royal necropolis of Saqqara North and the Late Period (715–332 B.C.) sacred animal necropolis at the bottom of the cliffs. The edge of the cultivation and the location of the former Lake of Abusir represent its eastern border. To the west, the cemetery extends towards the low slope of Lion's Hill (Bárta 2001, x). The focus of our interest at Abusir South is a large *kom* situated in the southern part of the area just opposite the Late Period animal galleries at North Saqqara.

This area represents the 'missing link' between Abusir North and the Saqqara regions in terms of the development of the non-royal funerary architecture with regard to typological and spatial distribution. Abusir South played a crucial role at the end of the 3rd and beginning of the 4th Dynasties as it was the last place of building activity within the area of the Abusir-Saqqara necropolis, and therefore relates closely to the shift towards increased development at Giza. Moreover, several officials buried at Abusir South are attested both in the Abusir papyrus archives and in other Saqqara tombs, thereby increasing our understanding of the relationship between Abusir North and Saqqara.

The spatial distribution of non-royal tombs in Abusir South during the Old Kingdom

The earliest known examples of non-royal funerary architecture at Abusir South are dated to the end of the 3rd and beginning of the 4th Dynasties. During this period, Abusir South was an extension of the North Saqqara cemeteries, and large mastabas were constructed in dominant positions alongside the northern border of Wadi Abusiri (*e.g.* anonymous mastaba MM 2002 (unpublished), and the mastaba of Ity (Bárta 2001, 1–16)).

Following the reign of Snefru, there is a time-gap for the rest of the 4th Dynasty when tomb-building ceased in the Abusir-Saqqara area and the majority of building activities was moved northwards to the Giza region. At the beginning of the 5th Dynasty, the building activities in the Abusir-Saqqara necropolis resumed. Among the first 5th-dynasty tombs built in the Abusir-Saqqara necropolis was that of Kaaper, which was built just next to the western wall of the tomb of Ity (Bárta 2001, 143–145). During the later part of the 5th Dynasty, the area was used for building an extensive necropolis of mud brick family tombs (Verner 1994).

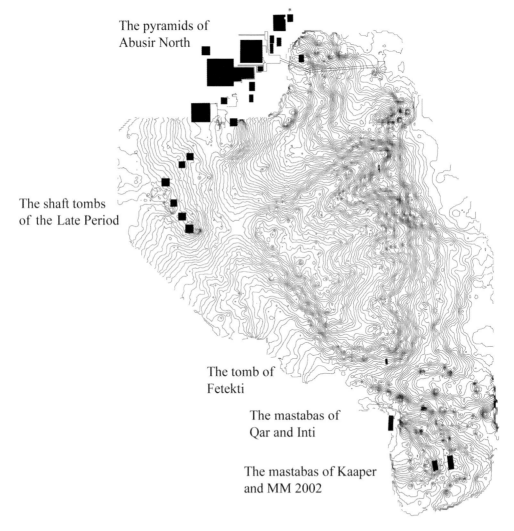

Figure 1. Topographic plan of Abusir indicating the archaeological monuments. (Plan courtesy of Ing. V. Brůna, Geoinformatics Laboratory of the University of J. E. Purkyně, Usti.)

Although our current understanding of the cemetery's development is limited pending further archaeological exploration of the locality, the core of the family mastaba cemetery is situated in the lower, northern part of the Abusir South area. The owners of these tombs were mainly priests of the royal funerary cults and lower ranking officials at the royal court (Bárta 2001, 55–142). Some of the tomb owners (Hetepi, Fetekty and Renpetneferet) are attested in the Abusir papyrus archives found in the mortuary temples of Neferirkare (Posener-Kriéger 1976, 224, 303, 308, 486, 491) and Neferefre (unpublished).

The funerary complex of a family of high-ranking officials, including the vizier Qar and his son and judge, Inti, stands out from these simple family tombs in terms of the social rank of the tomb owners, architectural elaboration, and the tomb equipment. The mastabas of this high-ranking family are situated on the northern edge of the central *kom* of Abusir South.

The funerary complex of Qar and Inti

From the 1995 season onwards, excavations concentrated on the tomb complex of the vizier Qar and his family (Figure 2). The archaeological excavations have revealed at least three generations of the male members of a family which served as high-ranking officials during the first half of the 6th Dynasty. And thus we enter the politically unstable period that is so well documented in the whole Saqqara necropolis and especially in the Teti Pyramid Cemetery (Kanawati 2003). This social and political unrest is illustrated in the funerary evidence by the phenomenon of *damnatio memoriae*, *i.e.* the erasure of figures, names and titles of officials (including the tomb owners, their family members, and even servants) from the wall decoration, and even the dismantling of whole tombs. Based on the analysis of the contemporary archaeological and historical evidence, Kanawati (2003, 147–182) reconstructs events that occurred during the reigns of Teti and his son Pepi I, including the assassination of Teti, the trial of an allegedly disloyal queen, and the plot of the vizier, Rawer. After the Pepi I re-seized power, it appears that the officials who were identified as having taken part in the conspiracies were punished in various ways, including through acts of *damnatio memoriae*.

Qar's tomb appears to have been an important monument in this part of the necropolis (Bárta and Callender 1996, Verner 1996, 80–85). The mastaba is prominently situated just above the southern edge of a shallow wadi that formed the ancient access road to this part of cemetery. The tomb's importance is also suggested by the numerous libation basins of lower-ranking officials which were found in the area of the open court (Figure 2, area OC), lying to the north of the entrance to the tomb. It seems that lower-ranking officials hoped to benefit from offerings granted to the vizier Qar and placed their offering basins near the entrance to his tomb chapel.

Based on the titles inscribed on the first false door in his undecorated chapel (Figure 2, room I), Qar held the office of judge (*r N̲ḫn n z3b*) and was also involved in the administration of the royal funerary complexes of kings Unas, Teti and Pepi I. At the very end of his career, probably early in the reign of Pepi I, he was appointed to the position of vizier, an appointment which appears to have been somewhat unexpected, for this title occurs only on the innermost (second) false door (Figure 2, room II) and on the sarcophagus. While his tomb did not suffer any destruction, the tomb chapels of two of his sons (Figure 2, rooms III, IV), lying just to the north, were deliberately smashed to pieces. Considering the socio-political context of the reign of Pepi I, it is possible that the sons of the vizier Qar may have taken part in conspiracies against the ruling king.

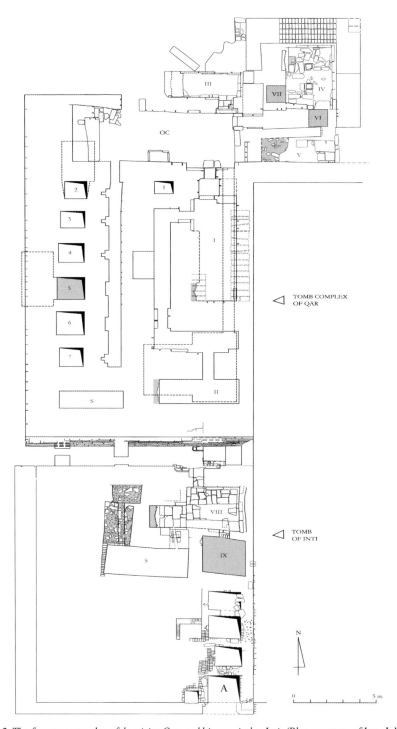

Figure 2. The funerary complex of the vizier Qar and his son, judge Inti. (Plan courtesy of Ing. J. Malátková.)

Malátková.)

Immediately to the south, adjoining the tomb of Qar, lies the mastaba of his oldest son, Inti. Several titles were accorded Inti, including that of judge and official of the pyramid complex of Teti. Likewise, his tomb decoration suffered from destruction but not to the extent of that of his brothers' tombs. The superstructure of Inti's tomb consists of an outer mud brick retaining wall filled with rubble mixed with re-dug bedrock (*tafla*) and sand. The superstructure of the tomb, as well as the partition walls of the shafts, were also built of mud brick. The tomb is separated from the mastaba of Qar, by a narrow corridor oriented to the east-west. The entrance into the corridor is situated on the southwestern corner of the Qar's mastaba (Figure 2). The entrance into the cultic installation is situated in the eastern end of the corridor leading to the small open courtyard (Figure 2, room VIII). In the southwestern corner of this courtyard is a deep niche which acted as a substitute for a funerary chapel. A monolithic limestone false door occupied the entire western wall and the northern and southern walls of the niche bear finely carved representations of Inti, his wife Merut and his favorite dog, called Idjem, who watches a procession of offering bearers.

An interesting feature of the decoration of the northern wall is the oldest preserved love song (Vachala 2003). Two musicians are facing each other; one plays the harp while the other sets time by clapping. Above them, the text of the love song is inscribed, although partly damaged: 'I love you, being smitten with your beauty'.

The architecture of Inti's tomb is unusual in that it includes a row of five burial shafts to the south of the small open courtyard. Generally, the burial shafts are expected to be situated to the west of the related funerary chapel, where the false doors of the shaft owners are placed. The western walls of the burial shafts within the tomb of Inti also bear simple false doors, but only roughly outlined in mud brick. The northernmost shaft belongs to the judge Inti (Figure 2, area IX), and the four other shafts perhaps belonged to Inti's sons, three for whom we have names: Senedjemib, Ankhemtjenenet and Sefkhu. In the small burial chamber of the other shaft (C), an inscribed piece of a wooden coffin bearing the name of Ankhemtjenenet was found. The next two shafts (B and D) were found completely looted.

I will now focus on the preliminary analysis of the archaeological material coming from the last, or southernmost shaft within Inti's tomb (Figure 2, shaft A). The analysis and the evaluation of the material in question form part of my current PhD thesis (Vlčková in preparation).

The archaeological context of shaft A

The shaft and its related burial chamber were excavated during two archaeological seasons in 2000 and 2002, both of which took place in the fall. The shaft itself measures 16 m deep and its internal dimensions measure 2.5 by 2.5 m. With regard to stratigraphy, it is important to note that the southern part of the outer mud brick retaining wall was pulled down in the area of shaft A to the level of the surrounding bedrock, perhaps due to the activity of ancient robbers.

The shaft filling consisted of a sequence of sand layers mixed with re-dug *tafla* and chips of local limestone. Towards the bottom of the shaft the composition of the filling became more homogeneous. There was no clear difference between the composition of the filling of the bottom part of shaft and the filling of the burial chamber, both of which consisted mainly of clean windblown sand.

The shaft and the burial chamber yielded two different groups of archaeological material – finds originating from the stratified filling of the shaft appear to be in a secondary position while finds in the burial chamber, which consisted of parts of the funerary equipment, were

Petra Vlčková

found *in situ*. The former group consists of decorated limestone blocks, the majority of which were found in two different levels of the fill – the first being in the uppermost four meters (measured from the crown of the preserved wall), and the second being in the last five meters measured up from the bottom of the shaft. In turn, these blocks can be divided into two separate groups based on their method of decoration: blocks with painted low relief and blocks bearing engaged statues. Two of the blocks bore the remains of an inscription which included the full name of the tomb owner, Pepi-Meriherishef, with the beautiful name Meri. An abbreviated form of his name, Meriherishef, is also partly preserved.

The fragments of low relief cannot be joined together precisely but it is possible to reconstruct the general scene which originally consisted of a scene of spear fishing in a papyrus thicket (Harpur 1987, 197–203). The blocks are so fragmentary that it is not possible to determine whether the scene originally represented only one figure with a spear (most likely the tomb owner), or two figures oriented face-to-face; one spearing and the other fowling. The scale of tomb owner is slightly larger than life-size. He is represented facing to the right and stands upon a papyrus boat in a striding pose with a spear in his hand. The papyrus thicket was probably situated just in front of the boat. Behind the spearing scene, at least three registers of offering bearers are preserved. Within the filling of the shaft, dozens of small fragments of painted reliefs representing offering bearers and heaps of offerings were found.

Some of the decorated blocks bear fully preserved reliefs and original paint (Figure 3). Other blocks were completely chiseled out, and consequently the relief decoration is only preserved in its

Figure 3. Limestone block with polychrome relief decoration – birds in a papyrus thicket. The mastaba of Inti, shaft A (Excavation No. 39/JJ/2000), late 6th Dynasty. (Photograph courtesy of the Archive of the Czech Institute of Egyptology, Prague.)

Figure 4. Limestone block showing decoration chiseled away but discernable in 'negative form' The block derives from the marshes scene and depicts Nilotic fish under the papyrus boat of the tomb owner. The mastaba of Inti, shaft A (Excavation No. 14/JJ/2000), late 6th Dynasty. (Photograph courtesy of the Archive of the Czech Institute of Egyptology, Prague.)

'negative form' (*e.g.* fish from the marshes scene; Figure 4). Where the relief decoration is preserved, the artistic quality is very good with some finely painted details, as exemplified in the details of the birds in a papyrus thicket, as well as the broad collar and ribbon of the tomb owner.

The second group is represented by large limestone blocks decorated with statues carved in high relief (*i.e.* engaged statues, which are accompanied by representations and inscriptions in sunk relief, Figure 5). Altogether, three large blocks were excavated, with two complete and two fragmentary statues and a corner of another niche with a minimum of five statues attested.

The statues are each of a single standing male figure within its own niche without torus molding or cornice. The figures of the tomb owner are approximately 65 cm tall and fit precisely into the niches, which are approximately 31 cm wide and 9 cm deep. Piers, which are 19 cm wide and inscribed with the abbreviated name of the tomb owner – Meriherishef – and some of his titles, separate the individual niches. The figures stand in a rigid, erect posture with both feet together and both arms hanging down beside the body. The hands form fists and hold a rolled or folded cloth. The figures of the tomb owner wear simple undecorated kilts, broad collars and flaring wigs that cover part of the ear and hang almost to the shoulder. The curls of the wigs are roughly cut. The face is squarish, with muscles only slightly indicated around the mouth. The shoulders are broad and the torso tapers to a slender waist. The arms and legs are tubular in shape with the muscles suggested around the kneecaps.

The original color of the blocks is partially preserved. The surface of each block was originally painted red, and the hieroglyphic signs carved in sunk relief were filled with a greenish

Figure 5. Limestone block with two engaged statues of Pepi-Meriherishef, and a partly preserved autobiographical inscription. The mastaba of Inti, shaft A (Excavation No. 16/JJ/2000), late 6th Dynasty. (Photograph courtesy of the Archive of the Czech Institute of Egyptology, Prague.)

paste that is only partially preserved. On the figures themselves, traces of red color indicating the skin are preserved, especially on the necks and faces. The appearance of the name of Pepi-Meriherishef, with the beautiful name Meri, enabled us to join both groups of decorated blocks, *i.e.* the engaged statues and the relief fragments. On the blocks decorated with the engaged statues of Pepi-Meriherishef, part of the section with his titles has survived. He held both honorific titles, such as *smr-wˁtj*, and *špsj-nswt*, and functional titles, such as *ẖntj-š Mn-nfr-Ppy*. Two of his titles are of particular interest:

1.   *r Nẖn (n) zȝb* 'judge of Nekhen', alternative reading, *zȝb iry Nẖn*, 'juridicial official' and 'mouth of Nekhen' (Jones 2000, no. 2953, 808). Although the precise meaning is elusive, the title probably incorporates both juridicial and administrative duties. All together, there are 25 known holders of this title dating to the Old Kingdom (Callender 2000, table II, 376–380). All but two of them were buried in the Memphite necropolises. This concentration of titles within the Memphite necropolises suggests that there may be a correspondence between occupation, at least for individuals involved in the court administration, and tomb location (see also Y. Shirai, this volume). During the most recent Czech excavations two more holders of the title 'judge of Nekhen' were discovered.

2.   *jmy-ẖt ḥm(w)-nṯr (m) mrt Ppy* 'under-supervisor/assistant inspector of the priests of *mrt*-sanctuary of Pepi' (probably Pepi II). At least nine *mrt*-sanctuaries are known from the Old Kingdom epigraphical evidence, although none are yet attested archaeologically. Traditionally, the sanctuary is thought to have been linked with either the royal mortuary cult or the cult of the goddess Hathor, mistress of the sycamore (Bárta 1983, 101). *Mrt*-sanctuaries associated with the royal cult of Pepi I typically use his throne names – Nefersahor and Meryre. Until now, only one example was known where a priestly title mentioned the *mrt*-sanctuary of Pepi II and explicitly used the name Pepi (Bárta 1983, 101). Thus, the title on the block from shaft A of Inti's tomb seems to represent a second occurrence.

In addition to the titles and name of the tomb owner carved on the piers and a horizontal line in the offering formula above the niches, the blocks decorated with engaged statues have yielded another important textual find. In the lower parts of two blocks, just under the niches, there is fragmentary inscription which forms part of an 'ideal autobiography' of Pepi-Meriherishef. The phrases used in his inscription show close parallels with the so-called 'Saqqara group' of ideal autobiographies (Kloth 2002, 262–274) which consists of 11 autobiographies that use similar phraseology. The most important and the best preserved texts in this group – the biographies of Khentika Ikhekhi, Neferseshemptah, Neferseshemre and Idu – can be dated to the reign of Pepi I or slightly later. As the name of this group suggests, these autobiographies derive from Saqqara (the Teti Pyramid Cemetery and the Unas Cemetery) or had close connections with it (mastaba of Idu from Giza, G 7102; Kanawati 1999, 285). According to Kloth (2002, 273), similarities in usage among the biographical texts suggest that they may have derived from the same master text, possibly housed in a temple or other library.

Thus far, the evidence that has been found from the tomb of Pepi-Meriherishef comes from its decorative program; the tomb proper has not yet been discovered. However, the evidence – based on geographical observations, the preliminary results of an archaeological survey conducted at Abusir South during the 2001 season, and general stratigraphic observations made in shaft A – strongly suggests that the tomb lies in the area to the south of the mastaba of Inti.

General remarks on the engaged statues

Within the general decorative program of a tomb, the arrangement of the blocks with engaged statues varies in how they are integrated with other architectural elements (*e.g.* the false door) and their installation within the overall decorative program of the wall. The composition of a false door with an engaged statue placed in the central niche is well known from this period. Wiebach (1981, 142–144) lists seven examples from the Old Kingdom, the best known of which includes the false doors of Netjernefer (CG 1447, Borchardt 1937, 130–132, fig. 1447) and Iteti (Murray 1905, 19, pl. 19), as well as the tomb of Mereruka from Saqqara (Duell 1938, pl. 147). It is interesting to note that other similarly sculptured monuments are documented as coming from the village of Abusir (*e.g.* the false doors of Netjernefer and Iteti), and there are other related objects from the Saqqara area. These stylistic similarities suggest that a tradition of incorporating engaged statues within architectural elements of the tomb developed in the Abusir-Saqqara area.

The only exception which does not support the attribution of this development to the Abusir-Saqqara area, is the tomb of Idu from Giza (G 7102; Simpson 1976, pl. 29a–b). However, his family appears to have had strong relations with owners of contemporary Saqqara tombs based on iconographic, social and epigraphic evidence (his autobiography is consistent with the 'Saqqara group'). Therefore, it is possible to include Idu's tomb and that of his son, Qar, to this group (Kanawati 1999, 285–286). Furthermore, the daughter of Idu (Simpson 1976, pl. 38), who bears the very rare name, Bendjet, may have been identified with Bendjet, the wife of vizier Inumin (Kanawati 2003, 66–71), whose tomb is located in the Teti Pyramid Cemetery.

The engaged statues of Pepi-Meriherishef

In order for the engaged statues installation – which includes the representation of the seated tomb owner executed in sunk relief and the autobiographical inscription – to be incorporated into a single coherent decorative unit, it is impossible that Pepi-Meriherishef's blocks would have derived from a false door arrangement. The only known examples of the incorporation of an engaged statue into a false door are characterized by a single standing engaged statue in the central niche (Wiebach 1981, 142–144). There is no evidence for the incorporation of both the autobiographical inscription and the seated tomb representation into the decoration of a false door. Therefore, Pepi-Meriherishef's blocks could have only come from the wall decoration of his tomb.

There are at least three parallels for the style, composition and technique used in the decoration blocks of Pepi-Meriherishef: the rock-cut tomb of Irukaptah at Saqqara (De Rachewiltz 1960; McFarlane 2000), the mastaba of Qar at Giza (Simpson 1976, 1–18), and the rock-cut tomb of Kaherptah at Giza (Kendall 1981).

One of the closest iconographic parallels is found in the unfinished tomb of Irukaptah 'the butcher of the king's repast, and royal *wab*-priest' (Figure 6), situated on the southern side of the causeway of Unas (De Rachewiltz 1960; McFarlane 2000). The precise dating of this tomb is a point of debate, varying from the 5th Dynasty to the First Intermediate Period. The tomb has 14 niches cut into three of the four walls, each

Figure 6. Rock-cut statues in the tomb of Irukaptah at Saqqara (north and east walls), late 5th Dynasty. (© Petra Vlčkova.)

containing a single rock-cut statue. The statues represent the same type of engaged statue as found on the blocks of Pepi-Meriherishef, *i.e.* a single standing figure in an individual niche. The original decorative program, which was not fully realized (these statues were left in various stages of manufacture), incorporated five other rock-cut statues into the eastern wall of the chapel. This tomb of Irukaptah also provides an example for the combination of high relief decoration (engaged statues) and painted motifs, including sailing to Abydos and a fowling scene, although painted with less care (McFarlane 2000, pl. 15).

Although the tomb of Irukaptah shows the combination of engaged statues and small-scale painted decoration set alongside each other, the biggest challenge for the investigator regarding Pepi-Meriherishef concerns the understanding of the relationship between the nearly life-size painted low relief blocks and the panels with engaged statues. Thus, the reconstruction of the tomb proves to be a considerable problem.

Another possible reconstruction is suggested by the decoration on the face of a north pillar in the tomb of Kaherptah 'King's acquaintance, judge and he who is in charge of the reversion offerings' (tomb G 7721) at Giza dated to the latter part of the 6th Dynasty (Kendall 1981, 107–108, 111, fig. 4). Here, the rock-cut statue and low relief form a single decorative unit. The niche is located in the lower part of the pillar and contains a single rock-cut statue of the tomb owner. Above it, a representation of a standing man, executed at the same scale as the statue, is carved in low relief. He is accompanied by a small figure of his son and two vertical inscriptions identifying both individuals. However, the combination of both decorative elements (engaged statue and relief) may have been dictated by the size and shape of the pillar upon which they were placed.

Although the tomb of Kaherptah provides evidence for the combination of the engaged statues and low relief in a single decorative unit, the combination of blocks, with engaged statues and life-size decoration executed in low relief (*i.e.* the marshes scene), still presents a considerable stylistic question. The solution may lie in their separate location within the tomb structure. A possible structural parallel can be found in the tombs of Qar and Idu at Giza where fragments of low relief decoration are situated in the superstructure and open courtyard. In his volume on the Giza mastabas, Simpson (1976, 1) suggests the existence of the combination of a visible and functional mastaba superstructure above the subterranean rock-cut chapel. According to Simpson (1976, n. 1), Reisner reported excavating the remains of mud brick walls that could delimit the area of a tomb and thus form its superstructure in the shape of mastaba. I am inclined to follow this suggestion for the reconstruction of the tomb of Pepi-Meriherishef.

The use of separate limestone blocks for the engaged statues could be explained by the poor quality of the bedrock at Abusir. Similarly, the casing of walls of rock-cut chapels, *e.g.* the door jambs of the tomb of Iyenhor (Hassan and Izkander 1975, 60), is a feature that is well documented in the small rock-cut tombs in the Unas Cemetery at Saqqara where the quality of bedrock is also poor.

The problem of the analysis and the evaluation of the decoration of the tomb of Pepi-Meriherishef can be related to a broader socio-cultural transformation within Egyptian culture that began at the very end of the Old Kingdom and continued into the First Intermediate Period. In this period, numerous aspects of court culture underwent a democratization. This transition can be evidenced by the appearance of iconographic features that were previously restricted to high-ranking individuals, such as the representation of the tomb owner gesturing while seated, as seen on the decorated blocks of Pepi-Meriherishef (Figure 7). Proceeding this period, only the highest-ranking officials were represented wearing a shoulder-length wig, sitting on a chair with leonine legs, and gesturing with one arm extending an open hand with upturned palm, while holding either a staff or a scepter in the other hand (Kanawati 1999, 284–289). Altogether, there are seven known occurrences of this type of representation of the tomb owner dating to the Old Kingdom. Four of the tomb owners held the highest administrative title of vizier. The other three officials also belonged to the highest

Figure 7. Detail of the relief representing Pepi-Meriherishef gesturing while seated. The mastaba of Inti, shaft A (Excavation No. 17/JJ/2000), late 6th Dynasty. (Photograph courtesy of the Archive of the Czech Institute of Egyptology, Prague.)

levels of Egyptian administration. However, Pepi-Meriherishef, a private individual of a middle rank and not associated with the court, is represented in the manner of a high ranking court official, with a staff in his hand.

According to the present iconographic evidence, the occurrence of this type of pose, where the tomb owner gestures while seated on a chair, is geographically restricted, occurring mainly at the Teti Pyramid Cemetery at Saqqara. Chronologically, this iconography is restricted to tomb owners who held their positions during the reign of Teti and the first half of the reign of Pepi I. The pose also appears to have been socially restricted, occurring in the tomb of only the highest officials, mostly viziers. Of course, the possibility that Pepi-Meriherishef held the title of a vizier cannot be excluded with certainty since only part of the inscriptional and decorative program of his tomb has been found. However, it is highly unlikely since his surviving titles are those of a middle-class official. Pepi-Meriherishef very probably did not posses those titles held by that group of officials whose political position could potentially lead to the vizierate, such as 'the overseer of the great court', 'the overseer of all king's works', etc.

Conclusion

The archaeological evidence from Abusir South dating to the later part of the Old Kingdom confirms the socio-cultural situation as documented at the North Saqqara necropolis (Kanawati 2003, 25–137). The archaeological excavations at the Abusir-Saqqara cemeteries have revealed similar impacts of social behavior in the sphere of funerary practice. As discussed above, during the first half of the 6th Dynasty acts of *damnatio memoriae* against particular individuals, including the dismantling of whole tombs, was carried out. This phenomenon was part of the vindictive system enforced by Pepi I after he re-seized power and put down the plots against him. This then raises the question: Was Pepi-Meriherishef among the punished dignitaries? We still do not know.

In the course of this analysis of the fragmentary decorated blocks deriving from the tomb of Pepi-Meriherishef, I have attempted to shed more light on various aspects of the development of non-royal tomb architecture and its decorative program at the end of the Old Kingdom. Nevertheless, until the location of tomb of this official is discovered, these conclusions necessarily remain hypothetical.

Nonetheless, the archaeological evidence originating from work at Abusir South offers new perspectives on traditionally held views based on developments attested at Abusir North. On the basis of individual aspects of the archaeological data, *i.e.* the position of tombs, titles of the tomb owners, and the evidence of the Abusir papyrus archives, it is possible to integrate these data with the archaeological material from Abusir North (Daoud 2000; Schäfer 1908, 1–14), and evidence for contemporary royal funerary cults which the tomb owners served. In contrast, the tomb owners buried at Abusir South appear to have been more heavily involved in state administration and more deeply embroiled in the political situation at the royal court. Thus, the evidence from their tombs can be associated with, and permits greater understanding of, the political instability in the first half of the 6th Dynasty as attested in the Saqqara necropolis as a whole.

Czech National Centre of Egyptology, Charles University

Acknowledgements

I am deeply grateful to Prof. Miroslav Verner, the former director of the Czech Institute of Egyptology, and to both deputy field directors, Assist. Prof. Miroslav Bárta and Assist. Prof. Břetislav Vachala, for the opportunity to participate in excavations and to study the archaeological evidence from Abusir. I would also like to thank Ing. Vladimír Brůna, Geoinformatics Laboratory of the University of J. E. Purkyně, Usti for the preparation of the Abusir topographic plan, and Ing. Jolana Malátková for the plan of the funerary complex of Qar and Inti.

References

Bárta, W. 1983, Zur Lokalisierung und Bedeutung der *mrt*-Bauten, *Zeitschrift für ägyptische Sprache und Altertumskunde* 110, 98–104.

Bárta, M. 2001, *Abusir V: The cemeteries at Abusir South*. SetOut, Prague.

Bárta, M. 2002, The Czech Institute's Ten Years of Excavation at Abusir South, *KMT: A Modern Journal of Ancient Egypt* 13.1, 18–28.

Bárta, M. and Callender, V. G. 1996, A Family of Judges at Abusir South: The Czech Institute of Egyptology's 1995 discovery of the tomb of Qar, *KMT: A Modern Journal of Ancient Egypt* 7.2, 32–39.

Borchardt, L. 1937, *Denkmäler des Alten Reiches (ausser den Statuen) im Museum von Kairo Nr. 1295–1808, Teil 1: Catalogue général des antiquités égyptiennes du musée du Caire*. Reichsdruckerei, Berlin.

Callender, V. G. 2000, À propos the Title of *r Nḫn n zȝb*, in M. Bárta and J. Krejčí (eds.), *Abusir and Saqqara in the Year 2000*, 361–380. Academy of Science of the Czech Republic, Oriental Institute, Prague.

Daoud, K. A. 2000, Abusir During the Herakleopolitan Period, in M. Bárta and J. Krejčí (eds.), *Abusir and Saqqara in the Year 2000*, 193–206. Academy of Science of the Czech Republic, Oriental Institute, Prague.

De Rachewiltz, B. 1960, *The Rock Tomb of Irw-kȝ-Ptḥ*. E. J. Brill, Leiden.

Duell, P. 1938, *The Mastaba of Mereruka, Part II*. University of Chicago Press, Chicago.

Harpur, Y. 1987, *Decoration in Egyptian Tombs of the Old Kingdom*. Keegan Paul, London.

Hassan, S. and Iskander, Z. 1975, *Mastabas of Princess Hemet-Ra and Others: Excavations at Saqqara, 1937–1938, 3*. General Organisation for Government Printing Offices, Cairo.

Jones, D. 2000, *An Index of Ancient Egyptian Titles, Epithets and Phrases of the Old Kingdom*. 2 vols. Archaeopress, Oxford.

Kanawati, N. 1999, Some Iconographic Peculiarities in the Teti Cemetery, in Ch. Ziegler (ed.), *L' art de l'Ancien Empire égyptien: Actes du colloque organisé au musée du Louvre par le Service culturel les 3 et 4 avril 1998*, 281–310. La documentation Française, Paris.

Kanawati, N. 2003, *Conspiracies in the Egyptian Palace: Unis to Pepi I*. Routledge, London.

Kendall, T. 1981, An Unusual Rock-cut Tomb at Giza, in W. K. Simpson and W. M. Davis (eds.), *Studies in Ancient Egypt, the Aegean, and the Sudan: Essays in honor of Dows Dunham on the occasion of his 90th birthday, June 1, 1980*, 104–114. Museum of Fine Arts, Boston.

Kloth, N. 2002, *Die (auto-) biographischen Inschriften des ägyptischen Alten Reiches: Untersuchungen zu Phraseologie und Entwicklung Studien zur altägyptischen Kultur*. Helmut Bruske, Hamburg.

McFarlane, A. 2000, *The Tomb of Irukaptah: The Unis Cemetery at Saqqara, 1*. Aris and Phillips, Warminster.

Murray, M. A. 1905, *Saqqara Mastabas, Part I*. B. Quaritch, London.

Posener-Kriéger, P. 1976, *Les Archives du Temple Funéraire de Néferirkarê-Kakaï (les papyrus d'Abousir)*. Institut français d'archéologie orientale, Cairo.

Schäfer, H. 1908, *Priestergräber und andere Grabfunde vom Ende des Alten Reiches bis zur griechischen Zeit vom Totentempel des Ne-user-Rê. Ausgrabungen der Deutschen Orient-Gessellschaft in Abusir 1902–1904, 2*. Buchhandlung Hinrichs, Leipzig.

Simpson, W. K. 1976, *The Mastabas of Qar and Idu G 7101 and G 7102*. Giza *Mastabas, 2*. Department of Egyptian and Ancient Near Eastern Art, Museum of Fine Arts, Boston.

Vachala, B. 2003, Das älteste Liebeslied? in N. Kloth, K. Martin and E. Pardey (eds.), *Es werde niedergelegt als Schriftstück: Festschrift für Hartwig Altenmüller zum 65. Geburtstag*, 429–431. Helmut Buske, Hamburg.

Verner, M. 1993, The Tomb of Kaaper, *Zeitschrift für ägyptische Sprache und Altertumskunde* 120, 84–105.

Verner, M. 1994, The Tomb of Fetekta and a Late 5 – Early Dynasty 6 Cemetery in South Abusir, *Mitteilungen des Deutschen Archäologischen Instituts, Abteilung Kairo* 50, 295–305.

Verner, M. 1996, Excavations at Abusir: Seasons of 1994/95 and 1995/96, *Zeitschrift für ägyptische Sprache und Altertumskunde* 124, 71–85.

Verner, M. 2002, *Abusir: Realm of Osiris*. The American University in Cairo Press, Cairo.

Verner, M. *et al.* 1990, *Unearthing Ancient Egypt 1958–1988: Activities of the Czechoslovak Institute of Egyptology in Egypt*. Charles University Press, Prague.

Vlčková, P. in preparation, *Aspects of Non-royal Funerary Architecture at the End of Old Kingdom in the Memphite Necropolis*. Unpublished PhD thesis, Charles University, Prague.

Wiebach, S. 1981, *Die ägyptische Scheintür: Morphologische Studien zur Entwicklung und Bedeutung der Hauptkultstelle in den Privat-Gräbern des Alten Reiches*. Borg GmbH, Hamburg.

The Festival Calendar at Deir el-Medina

Heidi Wikgren

Introduction

In ancient Egypt processional festivals were important occasions for the general public to participate in the cult of their gods (Assmann 1991, 108–110; *cf.* Spalinger 1998, 245; for Egyptian Festivals see Altenmüller 1977; Bleeker 1967). References in documents pertaining to the community of royal workmen on the west bank of the Nile at Thebes show that the members of the community of tomb builders celebrated many different types of festivals (Helck 1964; Sadek 1987, 169–181; Valbelle 1985, 318-335). The feasts of Amenhotep I have been dealt with by Černý (1927, 182–186), who identified six different feasts of the deceased king. Helck (1968), moreover, traced six feasts associated with various noteworthy events of the king's life. Helck (1964) also compiled a festival calendar of Deir el-Medina naming most of the annual feasts of the community. Unfortunately, he only had a limited number of sources at his disposal, as much of the textual material was still unpublished at the time. Sadek (1987, 171–175) and Valbelle (1985, 332–335) have both collected valuable reference lists of the feasts. However, most of the festivals celebrated in the village only feature once or twice in the various sources, and the references reveal little about the frequency or the length of the festivals. In view of the numerous references it does seem as though the tomb-builders would have feasted approximately once a week (see Sadek 1987, 169–181) and would have celebrated a feast of Amenhotep I seven times a year (Bierbrier 1982, 96–97).

In order to reconstruct an updated yearly festival roster of the workmen's community, I focus on the references to the days of working and inactivity in the work journals dating to the Ramesside Period (see Helck 1964; see also Janssen 1997, 87–98). Unfortunately, the documentation of the activities of the work crew is not complete. Moreover, the work journals are by nature heterogeneous, *i.e.* their objective and therefore their content differ from one text to another. The journals are often discontinuous with an insufficient number of entries to reconstruct one complete year, and many years are missing completely (see Valbelle 1985, 49–55).

The main theme of this paper is to establish a festival calendar of annual feasts celebrated at Deir el-Medina (see Figure 1). In order to fill some of the gaps in the information from the labour accounts listing days of working and inactivity (see Appendix 1 for the documents used), I have also studied entries that do not explicitly state whether the crew was working or free (see Janssen 1997, 87–98), but, nevertheless, could imply either of these. For example, the accounts of the distribution of wicks (*ḥbs*) for lighting the tomb under construction (see Appendix 1) suggest that the crew worked on the days in question (Černy 1973, 48; Donker van Heel and Haring 2003, 56–58; Janssen 1997, 115). Indeed, the days of wick distribution coincide with the working days mentioned in the labour accounts, whereas the days omitted in the wick accounts agree with the days the crew was free (Donker van Heel and Haring 2003, 56–58; Janssen 1997, 115). Furthermore, the absentee accounts listing day by day the absences of individual workmen (see Appendix 1) indicate that the rest of the crew was working on those particular days (Helck 1964, 140; Janssen 1980, 132). In general, the 9th and 10th days of the week were stated to be work-free, or they were omitted from the journals (Helck 1964, 141; Janssen 1980, 132; Janssen 1997, 115). Consequently, other days of the week similarly omitted from the lists may be presumed to have been work-free, particularly if the entries continue after the omission (Janssen 1980, 132–134). However, the days omitted in the lists of absences of individual workmen should not automatically be taken to be work-free (Janssen 1980, 132; *cf.* Helck 1964, 141–155): they might have been days when everyone was at work with nobody being absent.

Although still in progress, the study of the above-mentioned sources reveals that, in addition to the 'weekends', several other days of the year seem to have been annually work-free. Most of these coincide with the dated feasts known from various texts (see Appendix 2). However, there are some differing entries, especially during the reigns of Amenmesse, Seti II and Siptah (*e.g.* O. Ashmolean 167, O. Cairo 25514, O. Cairo 25520), as well as towards the end of the 20th Dynasty (*e.g.* P. Turin 1898 + 1937 + 2094/244, P. Turin 2029 + 2078/162 + 2001 + 2078/161, P. Turin 2071/224 + 1960). The following feasts seem, nonetheless, to have been celebrated regularly during the Ramesside Period: the eponymous festivals, *i.e.* feasts from which the names of the months originated; the feasts of such gods as Sokar and Ptah; the feasts of the divine, deceased Pharaoh Amenhotep I and queen Ahmose Nefertari; and the accession days of Seti I, Ramesses II and Ramesses III. The length of many of the festivals, however, seems to vary somewhat from year to year. The evidence for these annual feasts and for their approximate lengths will be presented below. Firstly, the eponymous feasts will be discussed in general, followed by each individual eponymous festival celebrated at Deir el-Medina in chronological order. Secondly, the other feasts celebrated in honour of various deities will be focused on. Lastly, the celebrations of the accession days of certain kings in the workmen's community will be dealt with.

Eponymous feasts

Most of the eponymous festivals were situated at the beginning of the month and gave name to the preceding month (Spalinger 1995, 30–31; see also Parker 1950, 43–47, 57–60). However, some eponymous feasts, such as the Feast of Thoth, the Opet Festival, and the Beautiful Feast of the Valley, took place on a day other than the first of the month (see Schott 1950: 82–107) and gave name to the month in which the celebrations of the festival in question started. Many references to eponymous feasts are known from Deir el-Medina, and almost certainly the names of these feasts were occasionally used to refer to months (Van Walsem 1982, 217). For example, O. DeM 1265, which has the title, 'A [book] for seeing the beauty in the months of the year', states the names of several months, while other months are identified by the feast celebrated in the month in question (Van Walsem 1982, 215–217), whereas O. BM 29560 lists either the month-names or the eponymous feasts in chronological order (Van Walsem 1982, 215–220). The reason for the phenomenon of celebrating eponymous feasts at Deir el-Medina is not readily apparent and discussion concerning this point must be left for later.

Eponymous feasts: I–IV *ꜣḥt*

The New Year's Festival at the beginning of I *ꜣḥt* was the first big celebration of the year all over Egypt (Germond 1981, 194; Schott 1950, 81–82; see also Alliot 1949, 302–433). The feast gave its name *wpt-rnpt* to the last month of the year, also known as the 'Coming of Horus', *pꜣ-šmt-n-Ḥr*, and the 'Birth of Re-Horakhty', *mswt Rꜥ-Ḥr-ꜣḥty* (later *mswt-Rꜥ*, Greek

Mesore; Parker 1950, 47; *cf.* Spalinger 1995, 26–27). At Deir el-Medina the feast lasted for two or three days (see Appendix 2 for references; Helck 1964, 156), and *wpt-rnpt* seems to have been the designation of both this particular festival and of IV *šmw* (see Appendix 2). In the workmen's community, references to *p3-šmt-n-Ḥr* have so far not been found with a date (see Appendix 2), but the term appears to have been used as a month-name in O. BM 29560 (see Van Walsem 1982, 220). The 'Birth of Re-Horakhty' seems to have been either an alternative name of this feast at Deir el-Medina or the name of the first day of the festival (see Appendix 2; see also Parker 1950, 47). The second alternative is perhaps supported by the *Tagewählkalender*, where the first day of the year is described as the 'Birth of Re-Horakhty' (P. Cairo JE 86637).

Another feast to be celebrated in the first month was the Feast of Thoth, which gave its name to I *3ḥt* (Greek *Thouth*; Parker 1950, 45–46; for Thoth see Bleeker 1973, 106–160; Derchain-Urtel 1981), and which was fixed on the 19th of that month (Schott 1950, 82; Spalinger 1994, 52). Falling on the ninth day of the second week of the month, *i.e.* on a day usually work-free at Deir el-Medina, the feast is not mentioned in the work journals (Spalinger 1994, 52). There are, however, other indications that the feast was celebrated at the village, such as O. DeM 603, where the scribe Qensety writes to ask for some paint and reed pens in order to fill his palette on the day of Thoth (see also Appendix 2).

The Opet Festival was the eponymous feast of II *3ḥt* (Greek *phaophi*; Parker 1950, 45; Van Walsem 1982, 220–221; see also Murnane 1982). The festival was celebrated in Eastern Thebes, and during the reign of Thutmose III the festivities lasted for 11 days, whereas by the end of the reign of Ramesses III the festival had been lengthened to 27 days (Blackman 1925, 250, n. 3). At Deir el-Medina, however, the festival seems to have had little impact on the work schedule of the crew (see Appendix 2; Helck 1964, 157). Nevertheless, according to O. DeM 46 (reign of Ramesses IV), the crew was given a reward (*mkw*) on the occasion of the Opet Festival on III *3ḥt* 11. Furthermore, O. Cairo 25504 (reign of Merneptah) states that the chief of the treasury came to reward the crew on that same day. However, no mention is made of the Opet Festival in this ostracon. There are some additional indications that III *3ḥt* 11 might have been a work-free day at Deir el-Medina (see Appendix 2), and thus it is not unthinkable that the inhabitants joined in the celebrations of the Opet Festival (*cf.* Helck 1964, 156–157).

Most references to a feast of Hathor at Deir el-Medina seem to refer to private feasts (see Sadek 1987, 192–196; for Hathor see Allam 1963; Bleeker 1973, 22–101) with the exception of the communal Feast of Hathor (Greek *Athyr*) celebrated on IV *3ḥt* 1–2 (see Appendix 2). In O. Michaelides 33 the festival is said to occur on IV *3ḥt* 1; moreover, both the first and second day of the month were work-free at Deir el-Medina (see Appendix 2).

Eponymous feasts: I–IV prt

The beginning of I *prt* marked the celebration of the Festival of *Nḥb-k3w*, which seems to have been acknowledged throughout the country since the Middle Kingdom (Schott 1950, 93–94; for the god Nehebkau see Shorter 1935; Zandee 1960, 98–100). The inhabitants of the village are known to have joined in the festival (see Appendix 2; Helck 1964, 157), which celebrated the beginning of a new season and was associated with the feast of the New Year (Gardiner 1915, 124; Graindorge-Héreil 1994, 279), while at the same time being a feast of kingship (Bárta 1982, 389; Gardiner 1915, 124). At Deir el-Medina the Feast of *nḥb-k3w* was generally called *k3-ḥr-k3* (Greek *Choiak*; see Appendix 2). Given that *k3-ḥr-k3* means 'ka upon *ka'* and *nḥb-k3w*, 'uniting the kas', the two names are probably alternative titles for the same festival (Gardiner 1906, 139; *cf.* Shorter 1935, 41). A magical literary text (O. DeM 1059) from Deir el-Medina mentions 'the seven days of *k3y-ḥr-k3*'. Graffito 2087, furthermore, relates how the crew was bringing forth (*ms*) *k3-ḥr-k3* to Meretseger on I *prt* 5. If one assumes

	I *3ḫt* Thouth	II *3ḫt* Phaophi	III *3ḫt* Athyr	IV *3ḫt* Choiak	I *prt* Tybi	II *prt* Mechir
1	New Year			Hathor	*K3-ḥr-k3*	Mut
2	New Year			Hathor	*K3-ḥr-k3*	Mut
3	New Year				*K3-ḥr-k3*	Mut
4					*K3-ḥr-k3?*	Mut
5				Amun?		
6						
7						
8						
9						
10						
11			Opet			
12						
13						
14						
15						
16						
17						
18						
19	Thoth					
20						
21						
22						
23						
24						
25				Sokar		
26				Sokar		
27						
28						
29						
30						Mut

Figure 1. The Festival Calendar of Deir el-Medina. Columns give the name of

that the festival had already started during the preceding weekend (see the Great Festival of Amenhotep I below), I *prt* 5 would have been the seventh day of the feast. However, according to most sources from Deir el-Medina the feast seems to have lasted only until the third or the fourth day of the month (see Appendix 2; *cf.* Helck 1964, 157). Moreover, the fact that Graffito

III *prt* Phamenoth	IV *prt* Pharmuthi	I *šmw* Pakhons	II *šmw* Payni	III *šmw* Epiphi	IV *šmw* Mesore
Mechir	Amenhotep I	Renenutet	(Valley)		Ipip
Mechir	Amenhotep I	Renenutet			Ipip
		Renenutet			
Ptah					
Ptah					
				Amenhotep I	
				Amenhotep I	
			Nefertari?		
			Nefertari		
Amenhotep I					
				Seti I	
		Ramesses III			
				Ramesses II	
Amenhotep I					
Amenhotep I					

the month and rows give the day, with the possible annual festivals indicated.

2087 is situated in the Valley of the Kings might indicate that the crew had been working on the fifth day despite the observance of the rituals related in this graffito. Thus, at Deir el-Medina the Festival of *k3-ḥr-k3* seems to have lasted for six days at the most.

Certain ostraca found at Deir el-Medina occasionally mention the Feast of *ḥnw Mwt*, 'Sailing of Mut' (see Appendix 2; Černý 1943, 175; Geßler-Löhr 1983, 416–419; Van Walsem 1982, 224; for goddess Mut see Te Velde 1988). The only dated reference to the feast occurs in P. Turin 2008 + 2016, where the feast is said to have taken place on I *prt* 30. Since *ḥnw Mwt* follows *k3-ḥr-k3* in O. BM 29560, and the first days of II *prt* seem to have been work-free (see Appendix 2), I suggest that at Deir el-Medina the 'Sailing of Mut' was celebrated on II *prt* 1–4 (see also Helck 1964, 157), possibly already starting at the end of the previous month (Gardiner 1955, 11–12; see the Great Festival of Amenhotep I below). This feast is probably the same as the 'Sailing of Bastet' which, according to a stela of Thutmose III from the temple of Mut of Isheru at Karnak, took place on I *prt* 29 (Altenmüller 1977, 176; Schott 1950, 95; Te Velde 1988, 400). After all, one of the most frequent epithets of the goddess at Deir el-Medina was 'Mut of Isheru' (Noberasco 1981, tavola [12] Caratteristiche delle Divinità Maggiore) who, during the Ramesside Period, took the role of the Eye of Re during the Festival of *ḥnw Mwt* (Geßler-Löhr 1983, 417–418; Te Velde 1988, 400). In O. DeM 1265, I *prt* is called *t3-ˁ3bt* (Greek *Tybi*), as the month was generally known (Černý 1943, 179–180; Parker 1950, 45–46), but at Deir el-Medina the principal name of this month, or at least of the eponymous feast, seems to have been the 'Sailing of Mut' (Černý 1943, 175–176).

There are, as far as I am aware, no explicitly dated references either from Deir el-Medina or elsewhere to the Feast of *mḥyr* (*cf.* Valbelle 1985, 320). The month of *Mechir* is mentioned in O. DeM 1265, and in O. BM 29560 *pn-mḥyr* is listed after the 'Sailing of Mut' (see also Appendix 2). One would, therefore, expect to find the eponymous feast *Mechir* at the beginning of III *prt*, and indeed, there are some indications of the first two days of the aforementioned month being work-free (see Appendix 2; see also Feast of Ptah in chapter on *Feasts of various deities*). The feast *mḥy*, mentioned in O. Berlin 10637, is likely to be a variant writing for *mḥyr* (Valbelle 1985, 320).

According to O. Cairo 25234, the Great Festival of Amenhotep I (Greek *Phamenoth*), the alleged founder of the community, started on III *prt* 29. The text describes how the crew rejoiced for four days 'in front of' (*m-b3ḥ.f*) the deceased king, drinking with their wives and children (for Amenhotep I see Černý 1927; Schmitz 1978). The fact that the festival occurred during this period is confirmed by the work journals where inactivity (*wsf*) is reported on these same four days (see Appendix 2). This feast is probably not the same as the one celebrated on III *prt* 21 in honour of Amenhotep I (O. Cairo 25559; that day seems to have been the anniversary of the death of the king; see chapter on *Feasts of various deities*; *cf.* Helck 1964, 158).

Eponymous feasts: I–IV *šmw*

The feast of the snake and nurse goddess Renenutet occurred at the beginning of I *šmw* (see Appendix 2; Helck 1964, 158; Schott 1950, 103; for Renenutet see Broekhuis 1971; Derchain 1972; Wildung 1972), and the previous month was known as *pn-rnnwtt* (Greek *Pharmuthi*; Parker 1950, 45–46). The 'Feast of Renenutet' which occurred on IV *prt* 1, as mentioned in O. DeM 35, is thus most likely a reference to the month-name (Van Walsem 1982, 237, n. 49). Elsewhere in Egypt, I *šmw* 1 was often a harvest feast in honour of the birth of Nepri, the personification of grain, who is occasionally shown being suckled by Renenutet (Leibovitch 1953, 73–74; see also O. Ashmolean 49). However, the Festival Calendar in the Late Period temple at Esna states that the feast of I *šmw* 1 is called the 'Feast of Renenutet' (Sauneron 1962, 21). Furthermore, a hymn for 'Revealing the face' in the same temple mentions that Khnum gives birth to Renenutet in the first (month) of summer (Sauneron 1962, 159).

O. DeM 1265 from Deir el-Medina states that IV *prt* is the month 'one [says] all gods were born in it' (Van Walsem 1982, 233, n. 13). Unfortunately, the text is too damaged to provide much additional information. The birth of Renenutet is, however, mentioned in the section dealing with IV *prt*. Another ambiguous reference to gods, birth and a month occurs in O. Qurna 633. Burkard (1999, 10) translates the passage in question (lines 3–4) as 'ihre Götter gebären in diesem Monat' (*i.e.* their gods are giving birth this month), but the passage might be understood as a reference to IV *prt* and be translated as 'their gods are born in this month' (for *ms* 'be born' determined with a woman giving birth, see Černý 1939, 68, 7). O. Cairo 25535 mentions, moreover, the 'Birth of Meretseger' as taking place sometime towards the end of IV *prt* but before I *šmw* 4. The 'Birth of Meretseger' may have been an alternative name for the Feast of Renenutet since the two goddesses were often associated with each other (Bruyère 1930, 140; Sadek 1987, 119). Alternatively, 'Birth of Meretseger' may have been the name of one of the days of the festival (see the 'Birth of Re-Horakhty' in chapter on *Eponymous feasts: I–IV ʒḥt*).

The 'Beautiful Feast of the Valley', *pn-int*, (Greek *Payni*; see Foucart 1930; Naguib 1991; Schott 1952) gave its name to II *šmw* (Parker 1950, 45–46). The feast commenced with the new moon (Helck 1964, 159; Schott 1950, 107) making it difficult to determine precisely when the festival was celebrated (see Appendix 2). For example, in O. Turin 57034 (reign of Ramesses III) Amun is said to have crossed the river on I *šmw* 12, *i.e.* on the fifth day of a period of six consecutive work-free days. O. Cairo 25538 mentions, however, that in the sixth regnal year of Seti II, Amun crossed the river (back) to Thebes on II *šmw* 25. Furthermore, in O. Cairo 25515, from the same regnal year, II *šmw* 19–26 are said to be work-free. Moreover, according to O. Ashmolean 11, dated to the 20th Dynasty, Amun was supposed to cross on II *šmw* 25, but the procession never took place. In this text, the days before and after the event seem to have been workdays. The length of the 'Beautiful Feast of the Valley' at Deir el-Medina is thus impossible to determine.

Ipip (Greek *Epiphi*) is another name of the hippopotamus goddess Ipet, also called Ipy (Černý 1958, 207), whose feast during the New Kingdom was celebrated at Thebes on III *šmw* 28 until IV *šmw* 2 under the name of *ipt-ḥmt.s* (Gardiner 1955, 12). P. Turin 1898 + 1937 + 2094/244 states that IV *šmw* 2 was work-free at Deir el-Medina because of the Feast of *ipip* and that IV *šmw* 1 was work-free as well (see also Helck 1964, 159). O. DeM 209 gives additional support to this as the crew is said to be free at a feast (*wsf m ḥb*) on both these days (see also Appendix 2).

Feasts of various deities

In addition to the eponymous festivals, other feasts were celebrated regularly at Deir el-Medina. On IV *ʒḥt* 25–26 the inhabitants of Deir el-Medina joined in the celebrations for the god Sokar (*cf.* Helck 1964, 157; see Bleeker 1967, 51–90; Graindorge-Héreil 1994; Janssen 1997, 127–128). According to the Medinet Habu Festival Calendar, the 25th day was called the Feast of the Goddesses and the 26th was the Sokar feast proper (Schott 1950, 91). Only the

Feast of Sokar on IV *ꜣḫt* 26 is mentioned in P. Greg (provenance Deir el-Medina), but both the 25th and the 26th seem to have been work-free at the village (see Appendix 2). During the New Kingdom the Feast of Sokar was an important part of the Osirian Choiak festivities which took place on IV *ꜣḫt* 21–30 (Gaballa and Kitchen 1969, 36; Graindorge-Héreil 1994, 60–62), but at Deir el-Medina the feast seems to have been celebrated in its own right. I have discovered no mention of the other feast days of this cycle (Gaballa and Kitchen 1969, 36–74) in the material found at the village.

On III *prt* 4–5, right after the eponymous Feast of *Mechir*, the Great Feast of Ptah seems to have taken place at Deir el-Medina (see Appendix 2; *cf.* Helck 1964, 158; *cf.* Valbelle 1985, 324; for Ptah see Sandman Holmberg 1946). O. DeM 401 (second year of Ramesses IV) illustrates how the feast was celebrated during two days by offering to Ptah in the Valley of the Kings in front of the royal tomb under construction. As opposed to O. DeM 401, P. Turin 1898 + 1937 + 2094/244 (third year of Ramesses X) mentions a Feast of Ptah occurring on the first day of the month. This difference in dates suggests that the festival calendar of Deir el-Medina might have changed by the end of the Ramesside Period and the two feasts at the beginning of the month, *i.e.* *mḥyr* and the Feast of Ptah, had merged (Valbelle 1985, 324). It is also possible that certain problems mentioned in the Turin Papyrus, such as irregularities with the payment of wages and the subsequent strikes, led to changes in the festival calendar. Helck (1964, 158) believed that the whole beginning of the month was dedicated to a feast of Ptah. This might be supported by the fact that at Medinet Habu the Feast of Amun 'in his feast of the lifting of the sky' was celebrated from II *prt* 29 to III *prt* 1 (Schott 1950, 96–97). This feast is a Theban variant of the Memphite Feast of Ptah (Altenmüller 1977, 177). Thus, in Thebes a feast of Ptah was celebrated at the turn of the month. Moreover, no hints on the purpose of the Feast of Mechir have been found, the name itself probably having something to do with a type of basket of the same name (Černý 1958, 206). Therefore, the two feasts, Mechir and the Great Feast of Ptah, could even be the same festival. For now, although with reservations, I feel compelled to see here two separate feasts.

On the 21st day of the same month, III *prt*, a feast of Amenhotep I appears to have been celebrated (Sadek 1979; Schmitz 1978, 22–26; *cf.* Helck 1964, 158). III *prt* 21 was the accession day of Thutmose I, the successor of Amenhotep I (Sethe 1906, 79–81). Thus, it must also have been the anniversary of the death of the village patron (Sadek 1979, 52). Unfortunately, the little surviving evidence we have for the activities of that day at Deir el-Medina is contradictory: O. Cairo 25559, from the first year of a Ramesside king, mentions a procession of the statue of the divine king to the Valley of the Kings and the distribution of curd from the storehouse on this day. However, according to O. DeM 760, the crew was working in an unspecified year on this same day (see Appendix 2).

Another feast day for Amenhotep I seems to have been celebrated on III *šmw* 12–13 (Helck 1968, 72; Schmitz 1978, 27–29; *cf.* Helck 1964, 159). III *šmw* 11 appears to have been a working day (see Appendix 2) despite the fact that P. Turin 1949 + 1946 reports the 'Appearance (*ḥꜥ*) of Amenhotep I' on this day. However, no working is reported on III *šmw* 12–13 (see Appendix 2). Furthermore, O. BM 5637 recounts a theft from a private storehouse on III *šmw* 13 while the owner was at his father's chapel celebrating the 'Appearance of Amenhotep I'.

On II *šmw* 15 the 'Sailing of Nefertari' took place (see Appendix 2; Helck 1964, 158–159). According to P. Turin 1898 + 1937 + 2094/244, the celebrations had already started on II *šmw* 14, although that day was less frequently work-free (see Appendix 2). The queen in question, Ahmose Nefertari (see Gitton 1975), was worshipped at the village together with her son Amenhotep I (Gitton 1975, 5).

IV *ȝḥt* 5 also seems to have been a work-free day at Deir el-Medina (see Appendix 2). According to Helck (1964, 157), this day might have been celebrated as a feast of Amun mentioned on IV *ȝḥt* 13(?) in Thutmose III's Festival Calendar at Karnak. The documentation originating from Deir el-Medina, as far as I am aware, gives no explicit reason for this day to have been work-free.

Accession days of Seti I, Ramesses II and Ramesses III

Throughout the Ramesside Period the accession day of Seti I was celebrated on III *šmw* 24 (see Appendix 2; Helck 1964, 159; Helck 1990, 207–208). In O. Ashmolean 11 this feast was called 'Sailing' (*ẖn*), not 'Appearance' (*ḫꜥ*), as was done with the other kings' accessions days (see below). Thus, it seems that the mention in O. Cairo 25503 of a work-free day due to the 'Sailing' of a king sometime after the 20th day of III *šmw* refers to the accession day of Seti I on the 24th, and not to the accession day of Ramesses II on the 27th day of the same month (*cf.* Helck 1990, 206). Even without the reference in O. Cairo 25503, there is ample evidence for the celebration of the accession of Ramesses II, at least at Deir el-Medina, on III *šmw* 27 (see Appendix 2; Helck 1964, 159; Helck 1990, 206–207).

As far as I know, the earliest dated reference at Deir el-Medina to the celebration of the accession of Ramesses III on I *šmw* 26 (Helck 1990, 206) comes from the 31st regnal year of the king (see Appendix 2). In year 25 of Ramesses III, the day seems to have been a workday as lamps were distributed according to O. Turin 57033. After the death of the king, the 'Appearance (*ḫꜥ*) of Ramesses III' was mentioned as occurring on I *šmw* 26 as late as the third year of Ramesses X (P. Turin 1898 + 1937 + 2094/244).

Conclusion

In sum, the royal workmen and their families living at Deir el-Medina celebrated many annual festivals. Most of these lasted more than one day as can be seen from the work-free days mentioned explicitly and implicitly in the journals. Many of the eponymous festivals occurred on the first few days of the month and thus, also at the beginning of the week. In the cases of the Great Feast of Amenhotep I and the 'Sailing of Mut', the festivities seem to have started already during the preceding 'weekend'. Since the evidence for these annual feasts comes largely from the labour, lamp and absentee accounts, where the weekends are usually work-free and often omitted, it is impossible to establish whether other feasts started on the weekend as well. Nevertheless, this possibility should, in my opinion, not be ruled out. In fact, most of the dated references to feasts originate from these same accounts dealing with the work in the royal tombs. Here it seems natural that only feast days taking place on workdays should be noted down.

In addition to the feasts discussed above, several other feasts and work-free days are referred to in texts found at Deir el-Medina (see Sadek 1987, 169–181; Valbelle 1985, 318–335). For instance, there are some festivals (see Appendix 2) which seem to have been celebrated only occasionally. Moreover, the epagomenal days at the end of the year appear to have been work-free (see Appendix 2), although it is not certain whether they were considered feast-days (Helck 1964, 159). There also seems to be several other days that might have been work-free, but for which the evidence is as yet inconclusive. All these references will have to be dealt with at a later point.

Unfortunately, it is not possible within the constraints of this paper to deal with the social, historical and cultural relevance of these annual feasts. The significance of the eponymous feasts must also be discussed later. I do hope, nevertheless, that this reconstruction of the festival calendar at Deir el-Medina will serve as a reference tool for anyone who needs information on the feasts, their frequency, and their length in the workmen's community. I am confident that, when all the material referring to the rituals, offerings, and chapels, as well as to the separate incidents on the known feast days has been thoroughly studied and compared with the research on festivals elsewhere in Egypt, the study will produce valuable information on the feasts celebrated at Deir el-Medina.

University of Helsinki

Acknowledgements

I would like to express my gratitude to Dr. Jaana Toivari-Viitala for reading the manuscript and for the corrections and useful suggestions she made. I would also like to thank the CRE 2003 Organising Committee for opening the symposium to graduate students from outside the United Kingdom. This study was supported by the Academy of Finland.

References

Allam, S. 1963, *Beiträge zum Hathorkult (bis zum Ende des Mittleren Reiches)*. Hessling, Berlin.
Alliot, M. 1949, *Le culte d'Horus à Edfou au temps de Ptolémées, I*. Institut français d'archéologie orientale, Cairo.
Altenmüller, H. 1977, Feste, in W. Helck and W. Westendorf (eds.), *Lexikon der Ägyptologie, II*, cols. 171–191. Otto Harrassowitz, Wiesbaden.
Assmann, J. 1991, Das ägyptische Prozessionsfest, in J. Assmann (ed.), *Das Fest und das Heilige: Religiöse Kontrapunkte zur Alltagswelt*, 105–122. Mohn, Gütersloh.
Bakir, A. El-M. 1966, *The Cairo Calendar No. 86637*. General Organisation for Goverment Printing Office, Cairo.
Bárta, W. 1982, Nehebkau (-fest), in W. Helck and W. Westendorf (eds.), *Lexikon der Ägyptologie, IV*, cols. 388–390. Otto Harrassowitz, Wiesbaden.
Bierbrier, M. 1982, *The Tomb-builders of the Pharaohs*. British Museum Publications, London.
Blackman, A. M. 1925, Oracles in Ancient Egypt, I, *Journal of Egyptian Archaeology* 11, 249–255.
Blackman, A. M. 1926, Oracles in Ancient Egypt, II, *Journal of Egyptian Archaeology* 12, 176–185.
Bleeker, C. J. 1967, *Egyptian Festivals: Enactments of Religious Renewal*. E. J. Brill, Leiden.
Bleeker, C. J. 1973, *Hathor and Thoth: Two key figures of the ancient Egyptian religion*. E. J. Brill, Leiden.
Broekhuis, J. 1971, *De godin Renenwetet*. Van Gorcum, Assen.
Bruyère, B. 1930, *Mert Seger à Deir el Médineh*. Institut français d'archéologie orientale, Cairo.
Burkard, G. 1999, "Die Götter gebären in diesem Monat": Ostrakon Qurna 633, *Göttinger Miszellen* 169, 5–15.
Černý, J. 1927, Le culte d'Amenophis Ier chez les ouvriers de la nécropole thébaine, *Bulletin de l'Institut français d'archéologie orientale* 27, 159–203.

Černý, J. 1935, *Catalogue général des antiquités égyptiennes du Musée du Caire Nos. 25501–25832.* Institut français d'archéologie orientale, Cairo.

Černý, J. 1935–1970, *Catalogue des ostraca hiératiques non littéraires de Deir el-Médineh, I–V, VII.* Institut français d'archéologie orientale, Cairo.

Černý, J. 1936, Datum des Todes Ramses' III. und der Thronbesteigung Ramses' IV, *Zeitschrift für Ägyptische Sprache und Altertumskunde* 72, 109–118.

Černý, J. 1939, *Late Ramesside Letters.* Fondation Égyptologique Reine Élisabeth, Brussels.

Černý, J. 1943, The Origin of the Name of the Month Tybi, *Annales du Service des Antiquités de l'Égypte* 43, 173–181.

Černý, J. 1958, Some Coptic Etymologies III, *Bulletin de l'Institut français d'archéologie orientale du Caire* 57, 203-213.

Černý, J. 1973, *The Valley of the Kings: Fragments d'un manuscrit inachevé.* Institut français d'archéologie orientale, Cairo.

Černý, J. 1978, *Papyrus hiératiques de Deir el-Médineh, I.* Institut français d'archéologie orientale, Cairo.

Černý, J. and Gardiner, A. H. 1957, *Hieratic Ostraca, I.* Griffith Institute, Oxford.

Černý, J. and Sadek, A. A. 1970, *Graffiti de la montagne thébaine, III, 2.* Centre de documentation et d'études sur l'ancienne Égypte, Cairo.

Daressy, G. 1901, *Catalogue général des antiquités égyptiennes du Musée du Caire Nos. 25001–25385.* Institut français d'archéologie orientale, Cairo.

Derchain, P. 1972, Review of J. Broekhuis, De godin Renenwetet, Van Gorcum, Assen, 1971, *Chronique d'Égypte* 47, 134–138.

Derchain-Urtel, M.-T. 1981, *Thot à travers ses épithètes dans les scènen d'offrandes des temples d'époque gréco-romaine.* Fondation Égyptologique Reine Élisabeth, Brussels.

Donker van Heel, K. and Haring, B. J. J. 2003, *Writing in a Workmen's Village: Scribal practice in Ramesside Deir el-Medina.* Nederlands Instituut voor het Nabije Oosten, Leiden.

Erman, A. (ed.), 1911, *Hieratische Papyrus aus den Königlichen Museen zu Berlin, III.* Hinrichs, Leipzig.

Foucart, M. G. 1930, *La Belle Fête de la Vallée.* Institut français d'archéologie orientale, Cairo.

Gaballa, G. A. and Kitchen, K. A. 1969, The Festival of Sokar, *Orientalia* 38, 1–76.

Gardiner, A. H. 1906, Mesore as the First Month of the Egyptian Year, *Zeitschrift für Ägyptische Sprache and Altertumskunde* 43, 136–144.

Gardiner, A. H. 1915, Review of Frazer, J. G., The Golden Bough: Adonis, Attis, Osiris: Studies in the history of oriental religion (3rd edition, revised and enlarged). London, Macmillan and Co. Ltd., 1914, *Journal of Egyptian Archaeology* 2, 121–126.

Gardiner, A. 1955, The Problem of the Month-Names, *Revue d'Égyptologie* 10, 9–31.

Germond, P. 1981, *Sekhmet et la protection du monde.* Éditions de Belles-Lettres, Geneva.

Geßler-Löhr, B. 1983, *Die heiligen Seen ägyptischer Tempel: Ein Beitrag zur Deutung sakraler Baukunst im alten Ägypten.* Gerstenberg, Hildesheim.

Gitton, M. 1975, *L'épouse du dieu Ahmes Néfertary: Documents sur sa vie et son culte posthume.* Les Belles Lettres, Paris.

Goedicke, H. and Wente, E. F. 1962, *Ostraca Michaelides.* Otto Harrassowitz, Wiesbaden.

Graindorge-Héreil, C. 1994, *Le Dieu Sokar à Thèbes au Nouvel Empire.* Otto Harrassowitz, Wiesbaden.

Grandet, P. 2000, *Catalogue des ostraca hiératiques non littéraires de Deîr el-Médînéh, VIII.* Institut français d'archéologie orientale, Cairo.

Helck, W. 1964, Feiertage und Arbeitstage in der Ramessidenzeit, *Journal of the Economic and Social History of the Orient* 7, 136–166.

Helck, W. 1968, Zur Chronologie Amenophis' I, in W. Helck (ed.), *Festschrift für Siegfried Schott zu seinem 70. Geburtstag am 20. August 1967*, 71–72. Otto Harrassowitz, Wiebaden.

Helck, W. 1990, Drei Ramessidische Daten, *Studien zur Altägyptischen Kultur* 17, 205–214.

Helck, W. 2002, *Die datierten und datierbaren Ostraka, Papyri und Graffiti von Deir el-Medineh.* Otto Harrassowitz, Wiesbaden.

Janssen, J. J. 1980, Absence from Work by the Necropolis Workmen of Thebes, *Studien zur Altägyptischen Kultur* 8, 127–152.

Janssen, J. J. 1997, *Village Varia: Ten studies on the history and administration of Deir el-Medina*. Nederlands Instituut voor het Nabije Oosten, Leiden.

Kitchen, K. A. 1975–1990, *Ramesside Inscriptions: Historical and Biographical, I–VIII*. Blackwell, Oxford.

Koenig, Y. 1997, *Les ostraca hiératiques inédits de la Bibliothèque Nationale et Universitaire de Strasbourg*. Institut français d'archéologie orientale, Cairo.

Leibovitch, J. 1953, Gods of Agriculture and Welfare in Ancient Egypt, *Journal of Near Eastern Studies* 12, 73–113.

López, J. 1978, *Ostraca ieratici N. 57001–57092*. Instituto Editoriale Cisalpino – Goliardica, Milan.

Murnane, W. J. 1982, Opetfest, in W. Helck and W. Westendorf (eds.), *Lexikon der Ägyptologie, IV*, cols. 574–579. Otto Harrassowitz, Wiesbaden.

Muszynski, M. 1977, P. Turin Cat. 2070/154, *Oriens Antiquus: Rivista del Centro per le Antichità e la Storia dell'Arte del Vicino Oriente* 16, 183–200.

Naguib, S.-A. 1991, The Beautiful Feast of the Valley, in R. Skarsten, E. J. Kleppe and R. B. Finnestad (eds.), *Understanding and History in Arts and Sciences*, 21–32. Solum, Oslo.

Noberasco, G. 1981, Gli dei a Deir el Medina (Studi su Deir el Medina, 2), *Oriens Antiquus: Rivista del Centro per le Antichità e la Storia dell'Arte del Vicino Oriente* 20, 259–275.

Parker, R. A. 1950, *The Calendars of Ancient Egypt*. University of Chicago, Chicago.

Pleyte, W. and Rossi, F. 1869–1876, *Papyrus de Turin, I–II*. E. J. Brill, Leiden.

Posener, G. 1938–1980, *Catalogue des ostraca hiératiques littéraires de Deir el-Médineh, I–III*. Institut français d'archéologie orientale, Cairo.

Sadek, A. I. 1979, Glimpses of Popular Religion in New Kingdom Egypt, I: Mourning for Amenophis I at Deir el-Medina, *Göttinger Miszellen* 36, 51–56.

Sadek, A. I. 1987, *Popular Religion in Egypt During the New Kingdom*. Gerstenberg, Hildesheim.

Sandman Holmberg, M. 1946, *The God Ptah*. Gleerup, Lund.

Sauneron, S. 1959, *Catalogue des ostraca hiératiques non littéraires de Deir el-Médineh, [VI]*. Institut français d'archéologie orientale, Cairo.

Sauneron, S. 1962, *Les fêtes religieuses d'Esna aux dernier siècles du paganisme*. Institut français d'archéologie orientale, Cairo.

Schmitz, F.-J. 1978, *Amenophis I: Versuch einer Darstellung der Regierungszeit eines ägyptischen Herrschers der frühen 18. Dynastie*. Gerstenberg, Hildesheim.

Schott, S. 1950, *Altägyptische Festdaten*. Akademie der Wissenschaften und der Literatur in Mainz, Wiesbaden.

Schott, S. 1952, *Das schöne Fest vom Wüstentale: Festbräuche einer Totenstadt*. Akademie der Wissenschaften und der Literatur in Mainz, Wiesbaden.

Sethe, K. 1906, *Urkunden der 18. Dynastie (Urkunden IV), I*. Hinrichs, Leipzig.

Shorter, A. W. 1935, The God Nehebkau, *Journal of Egyptian Archaeology* 21, 41–48.

Spalinger, A. J. 1994, Thoth and the Calendars, in A. J. Spalinger (ed), *Revolutions in Time: Studies in ancient Egyptian calendrics*, 45–60. Van Siclen Books, San Antonio.

Spalinger, A. 1995, Notes on the Ancient Egyptian Calendars, *Orientalia* 64, 17–32.

Spalinger, A. 1998, The Limitations of Formal Ancient Egyptian Religion, *Journal of Near Eastern Studies* 57, 240–260.

Te Velde, H. 1988, Mut, the Eye of Re, in S. Schoske (ed.), *Akten des vierten Internationalen Ägyptologen Kongresses München 1985, 3*, 395–403. Buske, Hamburg.

Valbelle, D. 1985, *"Les ouvriers de la tombe": Deir el-Médineh à l'époque ramesside*. Institut français d'archéologie orientale, Cairo.

Van Walsem, R. 1982, Month-Names and Feasts at Deir el-Medîna, in R. J. Demarée and J. J. Janssen (eds.), *Gleanings from Deir el-Medîna*, 215–244. Nederlands Instituut voor het Nabije Oosten, Leiden.

Wildung, D. 1972, Review of J. Broekhuis, De godin Renenwetet. Van Gorcum, Assen, 1971, *Bibliotheca Orientalis* 29, 291–293.

Zandee, J. 1960, *Death as an Enemy According to Ancient Egyptian Conceptions*. E. J. Brill, Leiden.

Appendix 1: Documents used for determining which days were annually work-free

Documents listing days of working and inactivity

O. Ashmolean 11	O. IFAO 383
O. Cairo 25509	O. Petrie 24
O. Cairo 25515	O. Turin 57007
O. Cairo 25529	O. Turin 57028
O. Cairo 25609	O. Turin 57038
O. Cairo 25647	O. Turin 57047
O. DeM 209	P. Greg
O. DeM 339	P. Turin 1898 + 1937 + 2094/244
O. DeM 340	P. Turin 2029 + 2078/162 + 2001 + 2078/161
O. DeM 427	P. Turin 2070/154
O. DeM 760	P. Turin 2071/224 + 1960

Accounts of wick distribution

O. Cairo 25248	O. Strasbourg H 136
O. Cairo 25266	O. Turin 57031
O. Cairo 25516	O. Turin 57032
O. Cairo 25539	O. Turin 57033
O. Cairo 25542	O. Turin 57034
O. Cairo 25543	O. Turin 57043
O. Cairo JE 72454	O. Turin 57044

Accounts of the absences of individual workmen

O. Ashmolean 167	O. Cairo 25520
O. BM 5634	O. Cairo 25783
O. Cairo 25514	O. DeM 594
O. Cairo 25519	O. Varille 6

Appendix 2: Documents used for determining the annual date and length of the festivals

New Year's festival on I *ꜣḥt* 1–3

wpt-rnpt mentioned on I *ꜣḥt* 1–3 O. DeM 209
wpt-rnpt without date O. Berlin 10655 (month-name) P. DeM 2
mswt Rꜥ-Ḥr-ꜣḥty on I *ꜣḥt* 1 P. Turin 1884 P. Turin 1999 + 2009
pꜣ-šmt-Ḥr without date O. BM 29560 (month-name?) P. DeM 2
I *ꜣḥt* 1–3 work-free O. Ashmolean 11 (I *ꜣḥt* 1–2!)

O. Cairo 25266
O. Cairo 25515
O. Cairo 25539
O. DeM 427
O. Turin 57032

Working on I *ꜣḫt* 1
P. Turin 2029 + 2078/162 + 2001 + 2078/161

Working on I *ꜣḫt* 3
O. Ashmolean 11

Feast of Thoth on I *ꜣḫt* 19

Mentioned without date
O. DeM 57 (month-name)
O. DeM 653 (month-name)
O. DeM 1265 (month-name)
O. IFAO 1088

'Day of Thoth'
O. DeM 603

Opet Festival on III *ꜣḫt* 11?

Reward on III *ꜣḫt* 11
O. DeM 46 (on the occasion of Opet Festival)
O. Cairo 25504

III *ꜣḫt* 11 work-free
O. Cairo 25248
O. Cairo 25515

Working on III *ꜣḫt* 11
O. Varille 6

Feast of Hathor on IV *ꜣḫt* 1–2

Mentioned on IV *ꜣḫt* 1
O. Michaelides 33

Mentioned without date
O. BM 29560 (month-name?)
O. DeM 1265 (month-name)
O. Liverpool 13625
O. Michaelides 48

IV *ꜣḫt* 1–2 work-free
O. Cairo 25515
O. Cairo JE 72454
O. Michaelides 33
O. Strasbourg H 136
O. Turin 57038
O. Turin 57047

Working on IV *ꜣḫt* 2
O. Cairo 25520

Festival of *kꜣ-ḥr-kꜣ* on I *prt* 1–3

kꜣ-ḥr-kꜣ on I *prt* 2
P. Berlin 12635

wpw on I *prt* 1

O. Ashmolean 70
k3-ḥr-k3 mentioned without date
O. Berlin 12406
O. BM 29560 (month-name?)
O. DeM 1059
O. DeM 1265 (month-name)
O. IFAO 1088
I *prt* 1–3 work-free
O. Cairo 25542
I *prt* 1–4 work-free
O. Cairo 25515
O. Turin 57043
Working on I *prt* 1–4
O. Cairo 25514

Feast of Mut on I *prt* 30 – II *prt* 4

'Sailing of Mut' mentioned without date
O. BM 29560 (month-name?)
O. DeM 297
O. IFAO 290
O. IFAO 293
O. IFAO 380
O. IFAO 1088
'Sailing of Mut' mentioned on I *prt* 30
P. Turin 2008+2016
II *prt* 1–3 work-free
O. Cairo 25515
O. Cairo 25516
II *prt* 1–4 work-free
O. Cairo 25543
O. Turin 57007
O. Turin 57028
O. Turin 57031

Feast of *Mechir* on III *prt* 1–2

Mentioned without date
O. BM 29560 (month-name?)
O. DeM 1265 (month-name?)
O. IFAO 344
O. Michaelides 12
III *prt* 1–3 work-free
O. Cairo 25542
Working on III *prt* 3
O. IFAO 383
P. Turin 1898 + 1937 + 2094/244
Feast of *mḥy*
O. Berlin 10637

Great Festival of Amenhotep I on III *prt* 29 – IV *prt* 2

Mentioned on III *prt* 29 – IV *prt* 2
O. Cairo 25234

Mentioned without date
O. Berlin 12406
O. BM 29560 (month-name?)
O. DeM 297
O. DeM 1265 (month-name)
O. Louvre E 3263 (month-name?)
IV *prt* 1–2 work-free
O. Cairo 25509
O. Cairo 25515
P. Turin 1898 + 1937 + 2094/244

Feast of Renenutet on I *šmw* 1–3

Mentioned (without date)
O. DeM 35 (month-name)
O. IFAO 1088
I *šmw* 1–3 work-free
O. Cairo 25509
Ascending to work on I *šmw* 3
P. Turin 1898 + 1937 + 2094/244
'Birth of Meretseger' before I *šmw* 4
O. Cairo 25535

Beautiful Feast of the Valley (new moon)

Mentioned without date
O. Cairo 25598 (II *šmw*)
O. Cairo 25644?
O. DeM 127
'Crossing to the west by Amun-Re' on II *šmw* 1
O. Cairo 25265
'The Crossing' on II *šmw* 12
O. Turin 57034 (I *šmw* 8–13 work-free)
'The Crossing of Amun' on II *šmw* 25
O. Ashmolean 11 (working before and after)
O. Cairo 25538 '… (back) to Thebes'
'Eve of the Crossing' on II *šmw* 28
O. Turin 57044

Feast of *Ipip* on IV *šmw* 1–2

Mentioned on IV *šmw* 2
P. Turin 1898 + 1937 + 2094/244
Feast mentioned without date
O. IFAO 1088
IV *šmw* 1–2 'free at a feast'
O. DeM 209
IV *šmw* 1–2 work-free
O. Cairo 25515
O. Cairo 25529
O. Cairo 25609
P. Turin 1898 + 1937 + 2094/244

Feast of Sokar on IV *ꜣḫt* 25–26

Mentioned on IV *ꜣḫt* 26 P. Greg
IV *ꜣḫt* 25–26 work-free O. Cairo 25515 O. Cairo JE 72454 O. DeM 339 (IV *ꜣḫt* 25) O. DeM 340
Working on IV *ꜣḫt* 25–26 P. Turin 2071/224 + 1960

Great Feast of Ptah on III *prt* 4–5

Mentioned on III *prt* 4–5 O. DeM 401
Mentioned on III *prt* 1(–2) P. Turin 1898 + 1937 + 2094/244
Mentioned without date O. DeM 230
III *prt* 4–5 work-free O. Cairo 25542
Working on III *prt* 4–5 O. DeM 594 (Neferhotep off work on III *prt* 5) P. Turin 1989 + (III *prt* 4)

Feast of Amenhotep I on III *prt* 21

'The ascend of Amenhotep I' on III *prt* 21 O. Cairo 25559
Working on III *prt* 21 O. DeM 760

Feast of Amenhotep I on III *šmw* 12–13

'Appearance of Amenhotep I' on III *šmw* 11 P. Turin 1898 + 1937 + 2094/244
'Appearance of Amenhotep I' on III *šmw* 13 O. BM 5637
III *šmw* 11 work-free P. Turin 1949 + 1946
Working on III *šmw* 11 O. Cairo 25515 O. Cairo 25529 O. Cairo 25783
III *šmw* 12 work-free O. Cairo 25529 P. Turin 1898 + 1937 + 2094/244 P. Turin 1949 + 1946
III *šmw* 13 work-free O. Cairo 25529 P. Turin 1898 + 1937 + 2094/244

Feast of Nefertari on II *šmw* (14–)15

'Sailing of Nefertari' mentioned on II *šmw* 15 O. Ashmolean 11

O. DeM 38
II *šmw* 15 work-free O. Cairo 25529 O. Cairo 25647 O. Turin 57033 O. Turin 57034 O. Turin 57044
Working on II *šmw* 15 O. BM 5634
'Sailing of Nefertari' mentioned on II *šmw* 14 P. Turin 1898 + 1937 + 2094/244
II *šmw* 14 work-free O. Cairo 25529 O. Cairo 25647 O. Turin 57044
Working on II *šmw* 14 O. Ashmolean 11 O. BM 5634 O. Cairo 25783

Feast (of Amun?) on IV *ꜣḫt* 5

IV *ꜣḫt* 5 work-free O. Cairo 25515 O. Cairo JE 72454 O. Michaelides 33 O. Strasbourg H 136 O. Turin 57038 O. Turin 57047
Working on IV *ꜣḫt* 5 O. Cairo 25520

Accession of Seti I on III *šmw* 24

'Sailing of Seti I' on III *šmw* 24 O. Ashmolean 11 O. Cairo 25503
III *šmw* 24 work-free O. Cairo 25515 O. Cairo 25529 O. DeM 427 P. Turin 1898 + 1937 + 2094/244
Working on III *šmw* 24 O. Ashmolean 167

Accession of Ramesses II on III *šmw* 27

'Appearance of Ramesses II' on III *šmw* 27 O. Cairo 25533 P. Turin 1898 + 1937 + 2094/244
III *šmw* 27 work-free O. Cairo 25515 O. Cairo 25529 O. DeM 427

P. Turin 1898 + 1937 + 2094/244

Accession of Ramesses III on I *šmw* 26
'Appearance of Ramesses III' on I *šmw* 26 O. DeM 55 (Ramesses III year 31) P. Turin 1898 + 1937 + 2094/244 (Ramesses X year 3)
I *šmw* 26 work-free O. DeM 153 (Ramesses III year 32)
Working on I *šmw* 26 O. Turin 57033 (Ramesses III year 25)

Epagomenal days
Work-free O. Ashmolean 11 O. Cairo 25266 O. Cairo 25515 O. Cairo 25529 O. Cairo 25539 O. DeM 209 O. DeM 427
Working on days 1–4 P. Turin 2070/154
Working on day 4 O. Petrie 24

Other dated feasts mentioned in the texts from Deir el-Medina
Feast of Ptah on II *ȝḫt* 6 O. Turin 57032
Feast of Ptah on II *ȝḫt* 16 O. DeM 45
Appearance of Amenhotep I on II *prt* 29? P. Turin 1906 + 2047/132 + 1939
Sailing on III *prt* 19 P. Turin 1898 + 1937 + 2094/244
'*sšš*' of Amenhotep I on III *prt* 25 (or 15) P. Turin 2006 + 1961
Feast on IV *prt* 19 O. IFAO 1262
Feast on I *šmw* 18 O. Cairo 25815a

Appendix 3: Documents

Graffito 2087	Černý and Sadek 1970, pl. 67

O. Ashmolean	
11	Černý and Gardiner 1957, pl. 25, 2
49	Černý and Gardiner 1957, pl. 7, 1

70	Černý and Gardiner 1957, pl. 48, 1
167	Kitchen 1975–1990 VII, 242–243

O. Berlin	
10637	Erman 1911, pl. 33
10655	Erman 1911, pl. 37
12406	Unpublished; see Van Walsem 1982, 222

O. BM	
5634	Černý and Gardiner 1957, pls. 83–84
5637	Blackman 1926, pl. 42
29560 (= 5639a)	Černý and Gardiner 1957, pl. 85, 1

O. Cairo (CG)	Daressy 1901
25234	pl. 46 (see also Černý 1927, 181–182)
25248	pl. 52
25265	p. 68 (see also Černý 1927, 186, n. 1)
25266	pl. 55 (see Helck 2002, 384–385)

O. Cairo (CG)	Černý 1935
25503	pl. 1
25504	pl. 2
25509	pls. 4–5
25514	pl. 7
25515	pls. 8–9
25516	pp. 13*–14*
25519	pl. 13
25520	pl. 14
25529	pl. 19 (see p. 29* for the verso)
25533	pl. 21
25535	pl. 22
25538	pl. 23
25539	pl. 24
25542	pp. 37*–38*
25543	pl. 25 (see p. 40* for the verso)
25559	pl. 29
25598	pl. 50
25609	pl. 53
25644	pl. 63
25647	pl. 63
25783	pl. 104
25815a	pl. 113

O. Cairo JE 72454	Unpublished; see Helck 2002, 146–161

O. DeM	Černý 1935–1970
35	I, pls. 35–35A
38	I, pls. 18–19
45	I, pls. 34–35A

46	I, pls. 36–38, 36A
55	I, pls. 45–45A
57	I, pls. 45–45A
127	II, pl. 8
153	II, pls. 28, 30
209	III, pls. 7–8
230	III, pl. 18
297	IV, pl. 16
339	IV, pl. 33
340	V, pl. 1
401	V, pl. 16
427	V, pl. 22
653	VII, pl. 13

O. DeM	Sauneron 1959
594	[VI] pls. 22–22a
603	[VI] pls. 25–25a

| O. DeM 760 | Grandet 2000, 161 |

O. DeM	Posener 1938–1980
1059	I, pls. 32–32a
1265	II, pls. 71–73, 73a

O. IFAO (=DeM inv. no.)	
290	Unpublished; see Van Walsem 1982, 224
293	Unpublished; see Van Walsem 1982, 224
344	Unpublished; see Van Walsem 1982, 222
380	Unpublished; see Van Walsem 1982, 224
383	Unpublished; see Helck 2002, 393
1088	Unpublished; see Van Walsem 1982, 221–224, 227, 242
1262	Unpublished; see Helck 2002, 393

O. Michaelides	Goedicke and Wente 1962
12	pl. 64
33	pls. 67–68; see also Kitchen 1975–1990 V, 612–613
48	pls. 71–72

| O. Louvre E 3263 | Černý and Gardiner 1957, pl. 65, 2 |

| O. Petrie 24 | Černý and Gardiner 1957, pl. 21, 3 |

| O. Qurna 633 | Burkard 1999 |

| O. Strasbourg H 136 | Koenig 1997, pl. 127 |

O. Turin (N)	López 1978
57007	pls. 8–8a
57028	pls. 17–18a

57031	pls. 20–20a
57032	pls. 21–21a
57033	pls. 22–22a
57034	pls. 23–23a
57038	pls. 25–25a
57043	pls. 27–27a
57044	pls. 28–28a
57047	pls. 30–30a

| O. Varille 6 | Unpublished; see Helck 2002, 257–258 |

| P. Berlin 12635 | Unpublished; see Van Walsem 1982, 220 |

| P. Cairo JE 86637 | Bakir 1966 |

| P. DeM 2 | Černý 1978, pl. 17 |

| P. Greg | Kitchen 1975–1990 V, 437–448 |

P. Turin (Cat.)	
1884	Kitchen 1975–1990 VI, 644–650
1898 + 1937 + 2094/244	Kitchen 1975–1990 VI, 687–699
1906 + 2047/132 + 1939	Kitchen 1975–1990 VI, 624–630
1949 + 1946	Černý 1936, 110–111
1999 + 2009	Kitchen 1975–1990 VI, 560–566
2006 + 1961	Pleyte and Rossi 1869–1876, pls. 98–101
2008 + 2016	Pleyte and Rossi 1968–1876, pls. 68–69
2029 + 2078/162 + 2001 + 2078/161	Kitchen 1975–1990 VI, 566–598
2070/154	Muszynski 1977
2071/224 + 1960	Kitchen 1975–1990 VI, 637–638, 641–644